ALL-GHOULS SCHOOL™

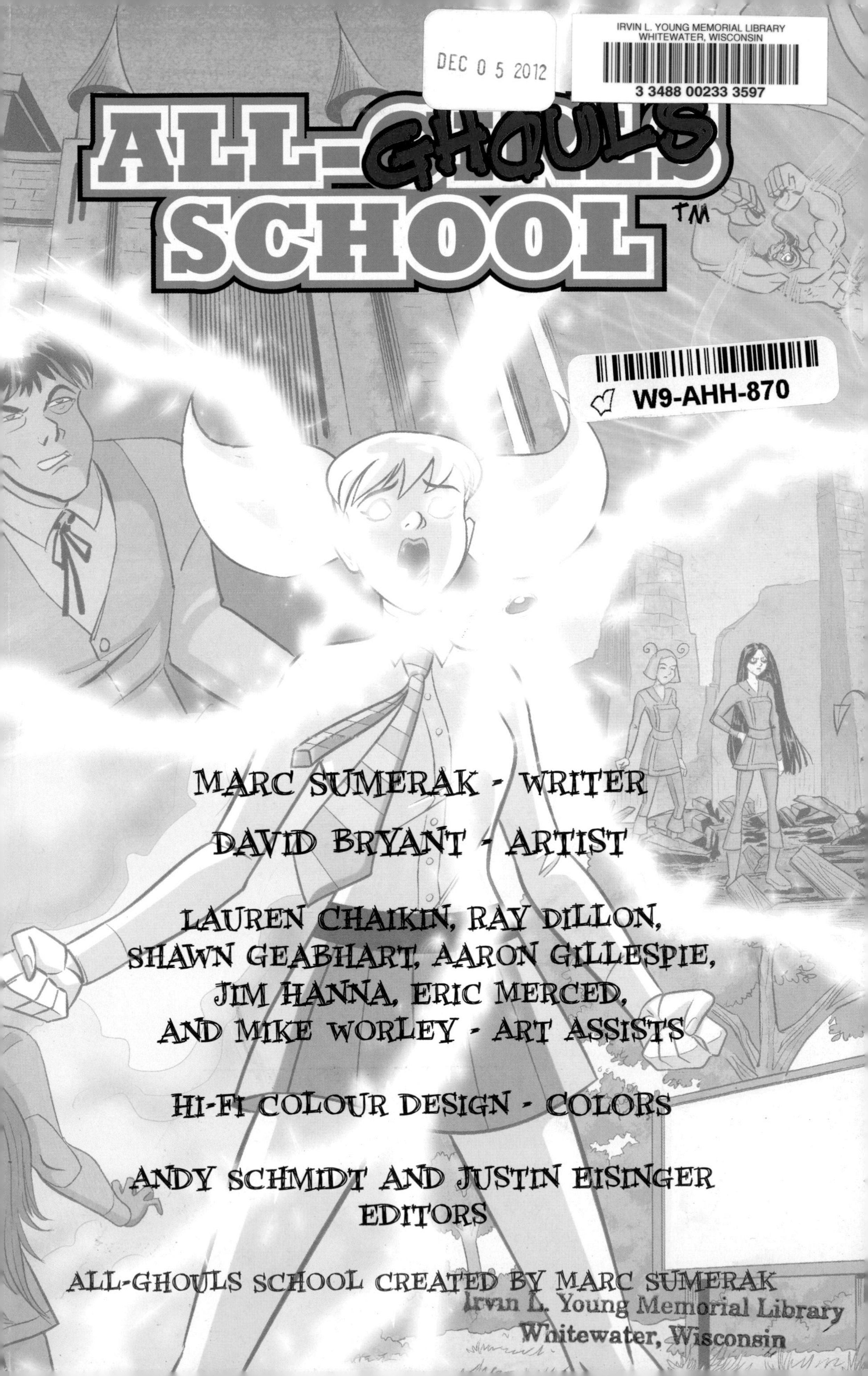

MARC SUMERAK - WRITER

DAVID BRYANT - ARTIST

LAUREN CHAIKIN, RAY DILLON,
SHAWN GEABHART, AARON GILLESPIE,
JIM HANNA, ERIC MERCED,
AND MIKE WORLEY - ART ASSISTS

HI-FI COLOUR DESIGN - COLORS

ANDY SCHMIDT AND JUSTIN EISINGER
EDITORS

ALL-GHOULS SCHOOL CREATED BY MARC SUMERAK

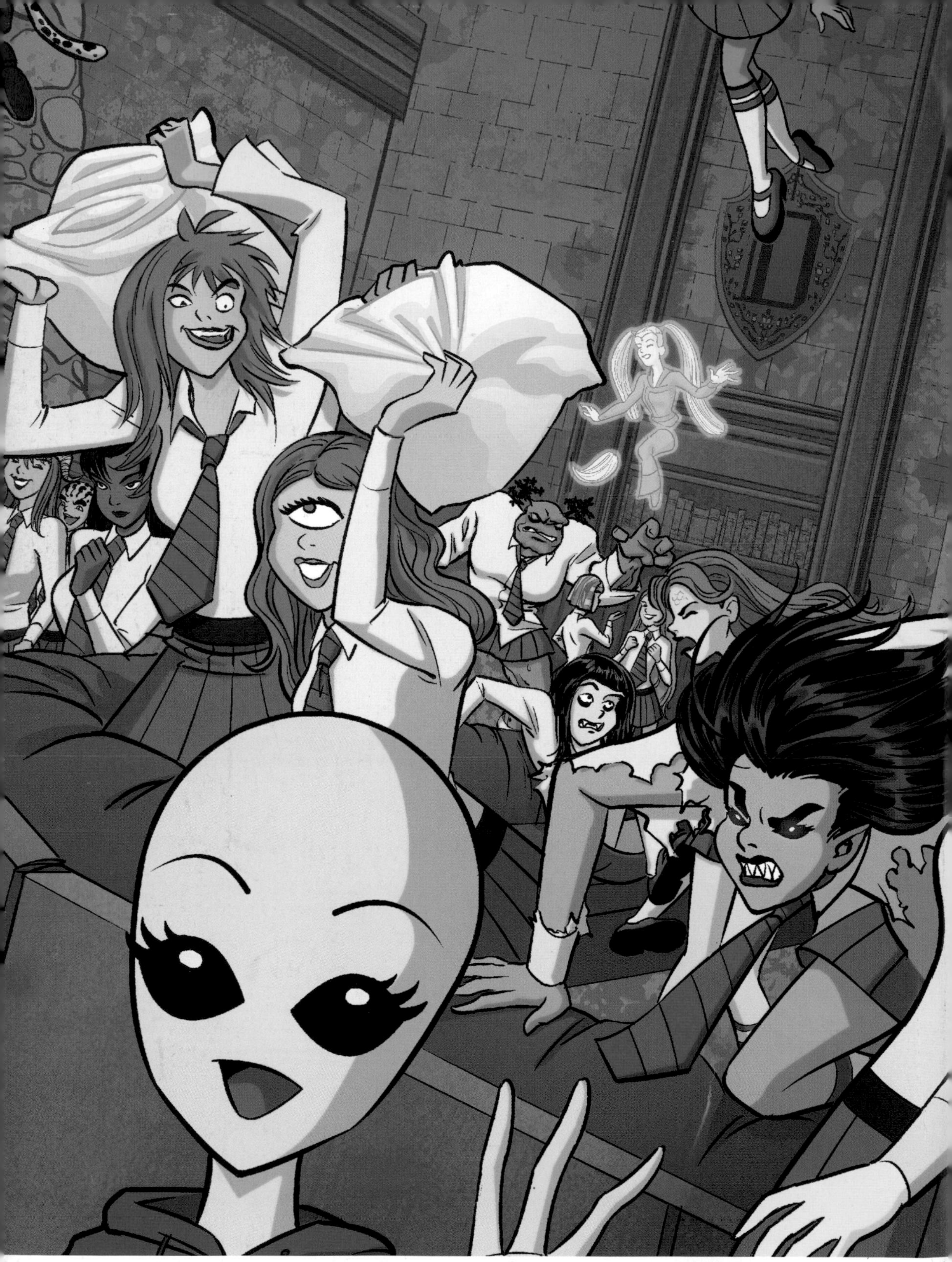

ISBN: 978-1-60010-992-8

14 13 12 11 1 2 3 4

IDW®

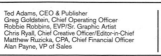

Ted Adams, CEO & Publisher
Greg Goldstein, Chief Operating Officer
Robbie Robbins, EVP/Sr. Graphic Artist
Chris Ryall, Chief Creative Officer/Editor-in-Chief
Matthew Ruzicka, CPA, Chief Financial Officer
Alan Payne, VP of Sales

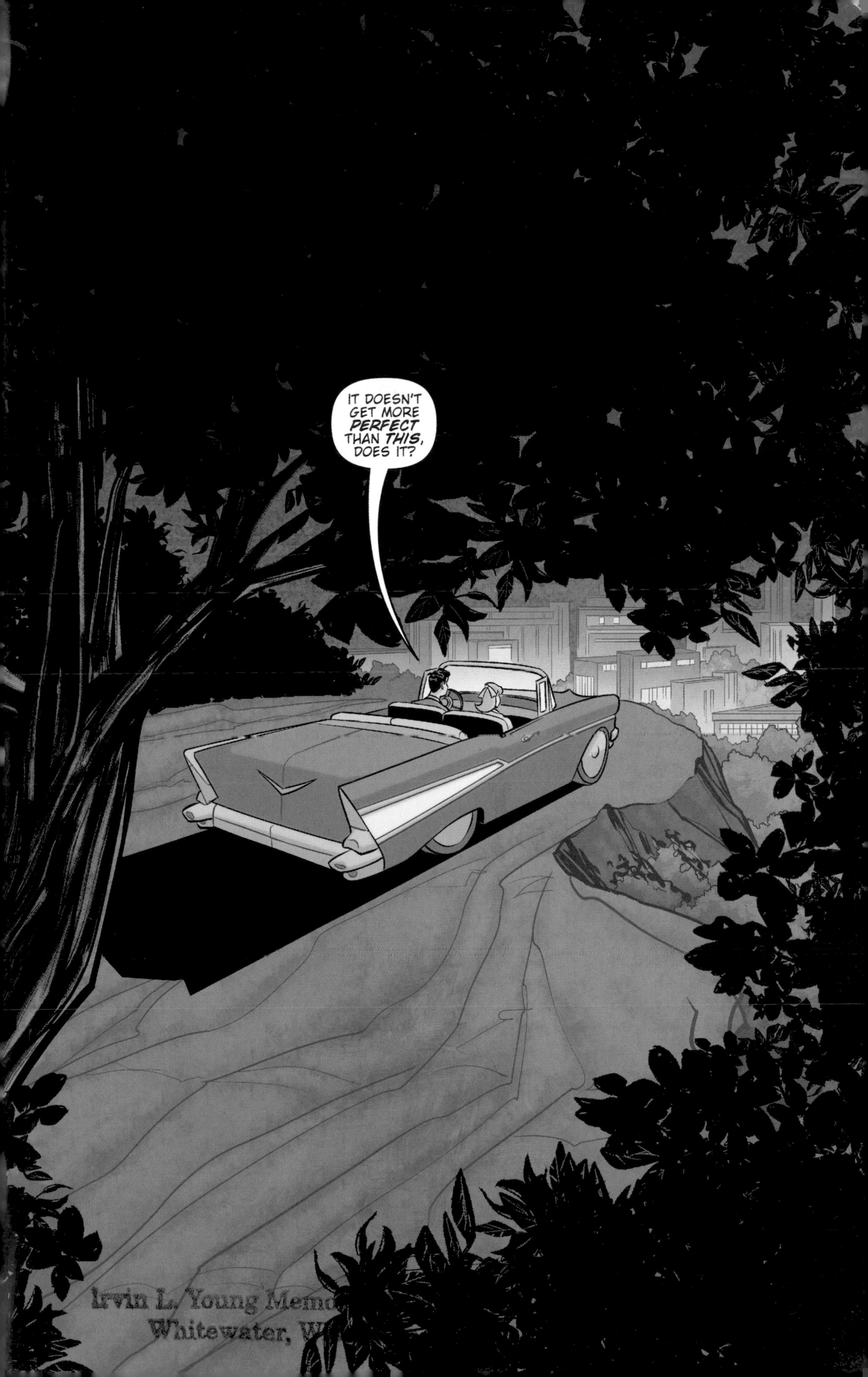
IT DOESN'T GET MORE *PERFECT* THAN *THIS*, DOES IT?

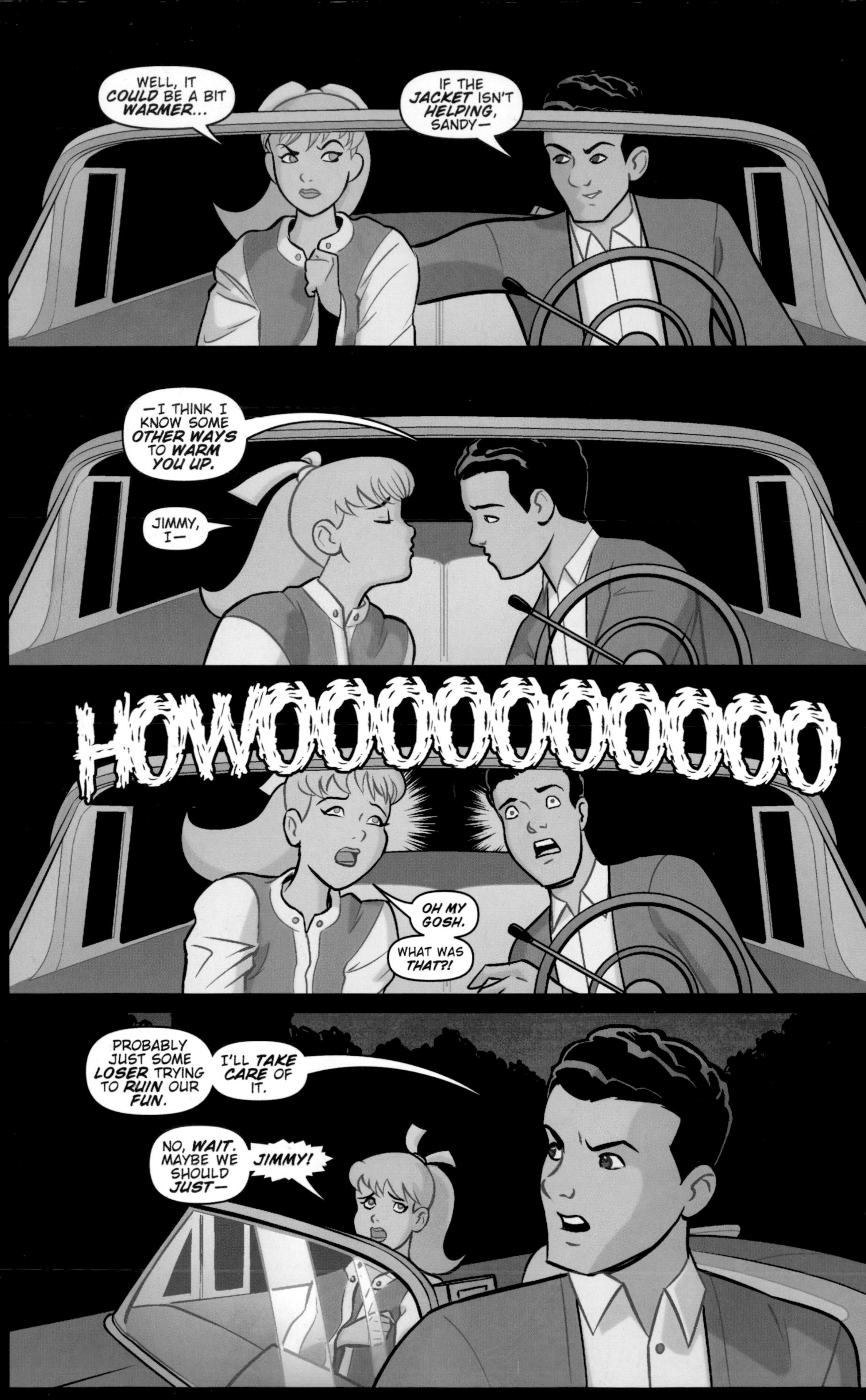
WELL, IT COULD BE A BIT WARMER...
IF THE JACKET ISN'T HELPING, SANDY—
—I THINK I KNOW SOME OTHER WAYS TO WARM YOU UP.
JIMMY, I—
HOWOOOOOOOOOO
OH MY GOSH.
WHAT WAS THAT?!
PROBABLY JUST SOME LOSER TRYING TO RUIN OUR FUN.
I'LL TAKE CARE OF IT.
NO, WAIT. MAYBE WE SHOULD JUST—
JIMMY!

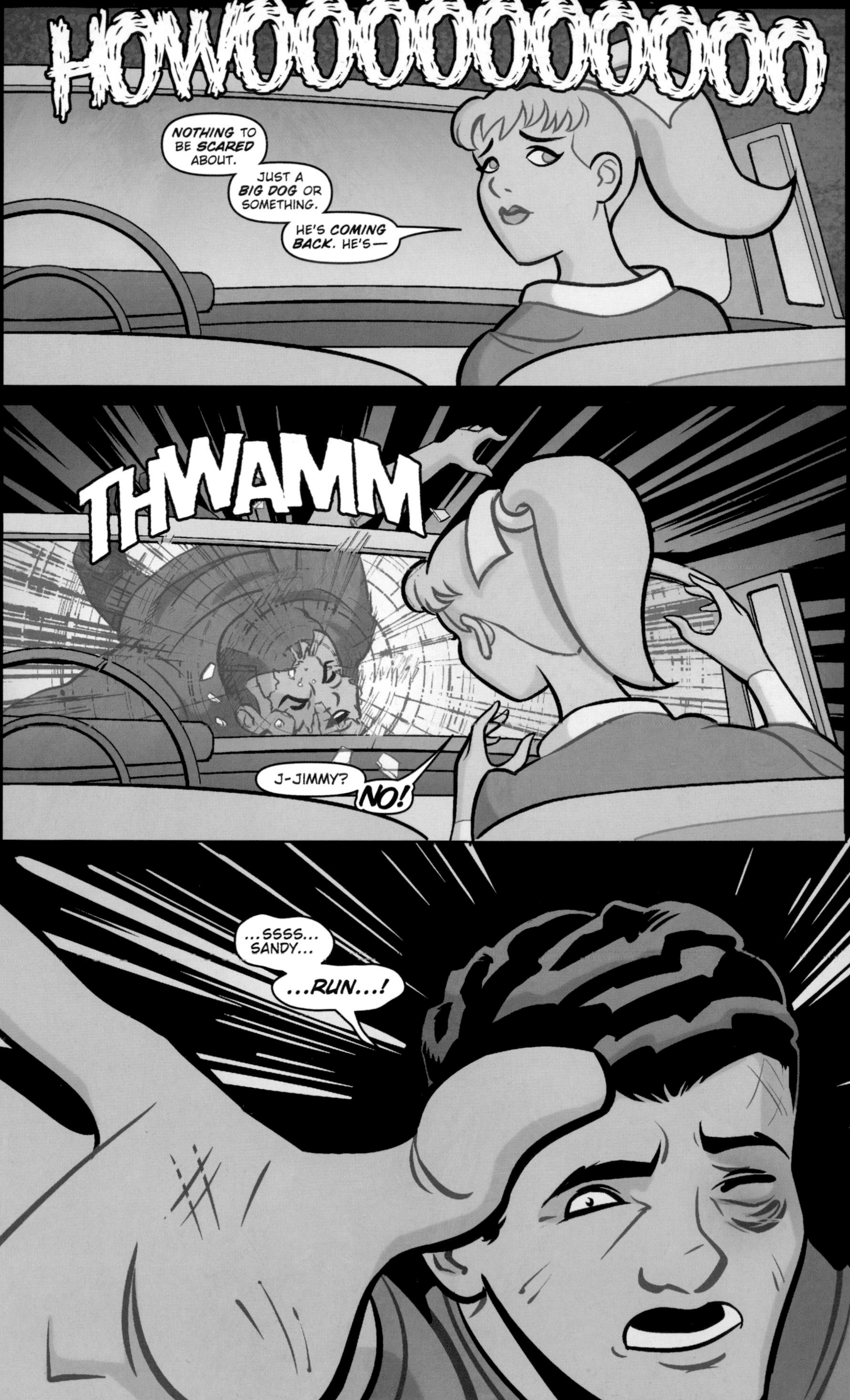
HOWOOOOOOOOOO
NOTHING TO BE SCARED ABOUT.
JUST A BIG DOG OR SOMETHING.
HE'S COMING BACK. HE'S—
THWAMM
J-JIMMY?
NO!
...SSSS... SANDY...
...RUN...!

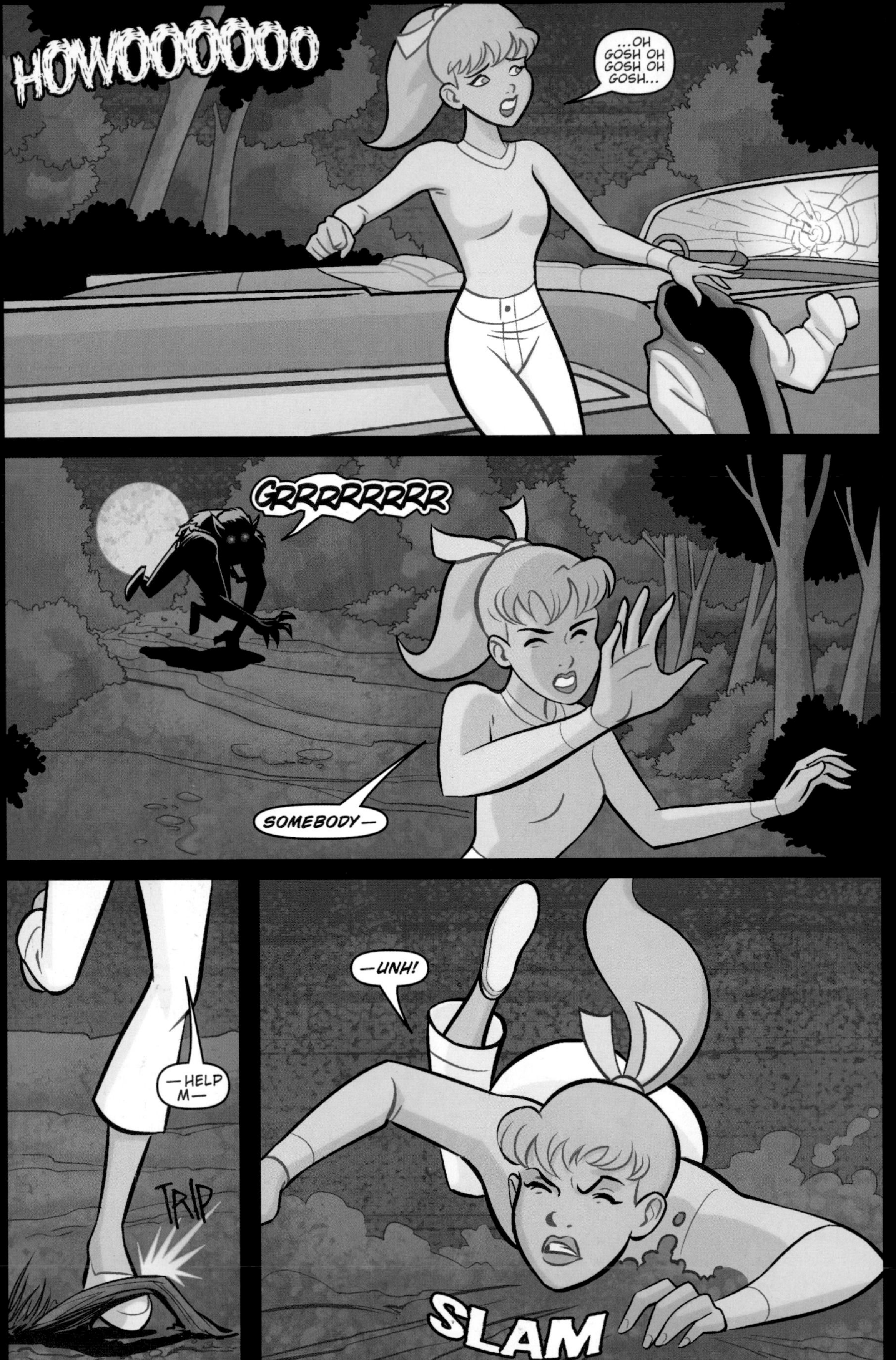
HOWOOOOOOO
...OH GOSH OH GOSH OH GOSH...
GRRRRRRRR
SOMEBODY—
—HELP M—
TRIP
—UNH!
SLAM

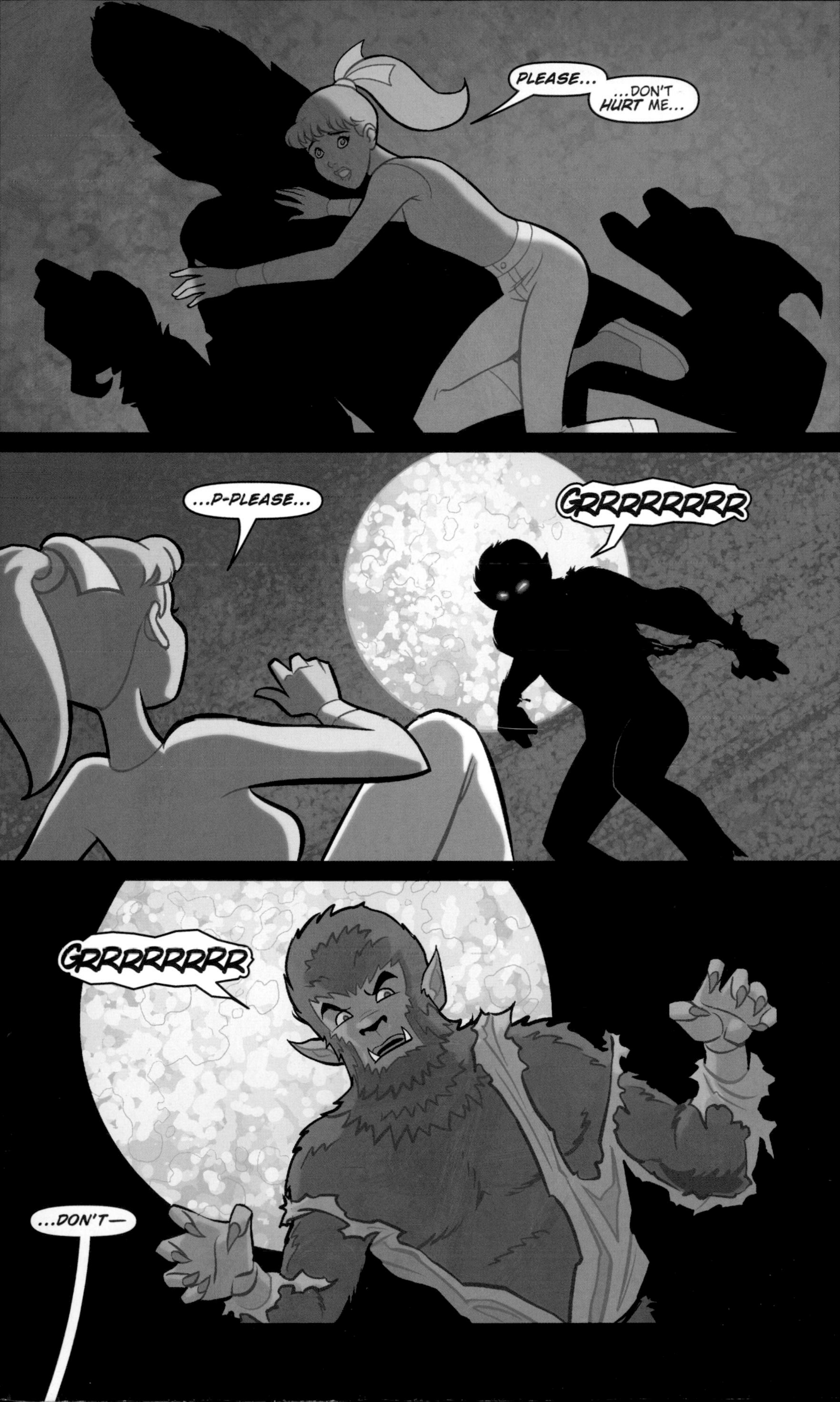
PLEASE...
...DON'T HURT ME...
...P-PLEASE...
GRRRRRRRR
GRRRRRRRR
...DON'T—

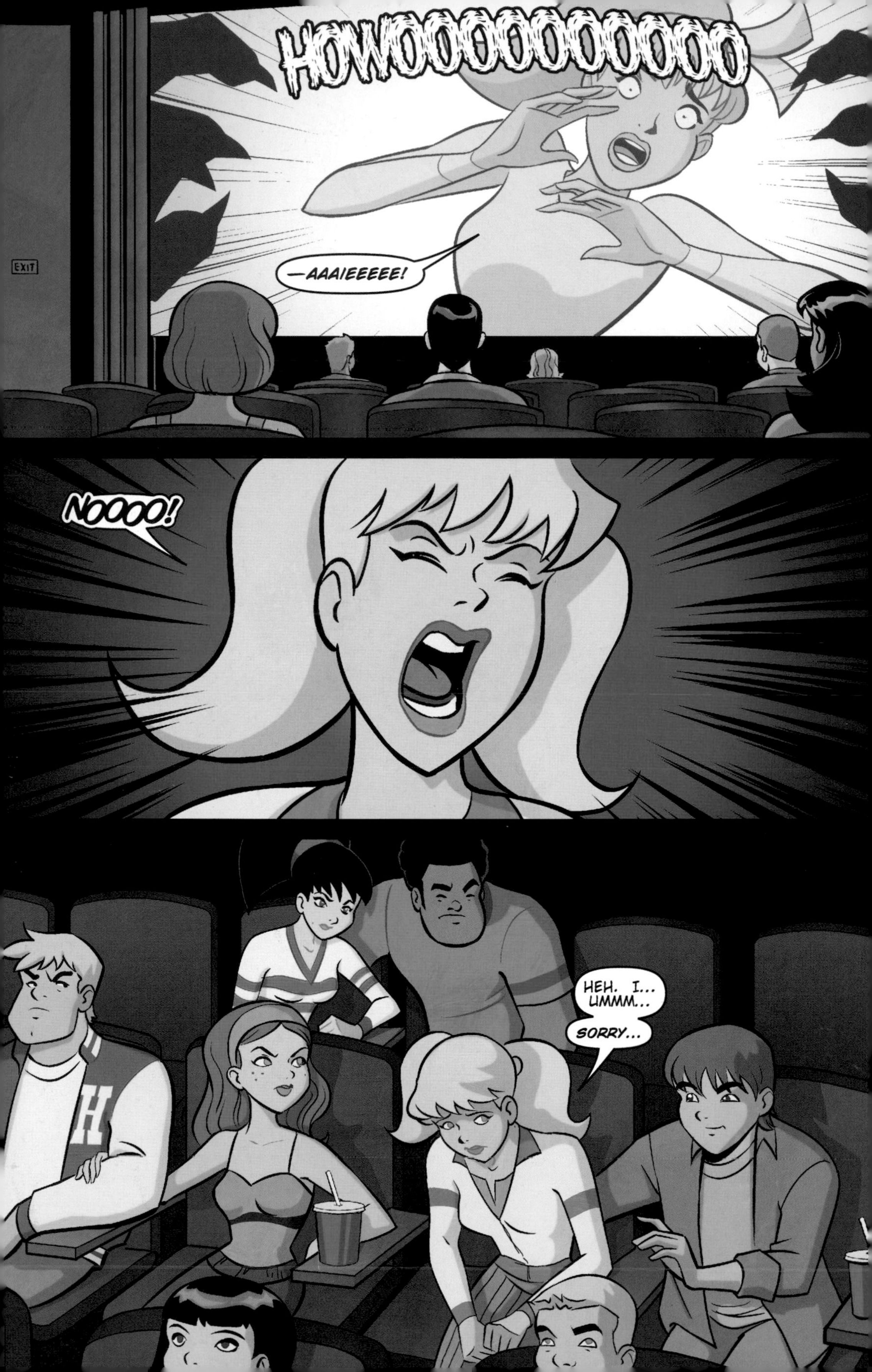
HOWOOOOOOOOOO
EXIT
—AAAIEEEEE!
NOOOO!
HEH. I... UMMM...
SORRY...

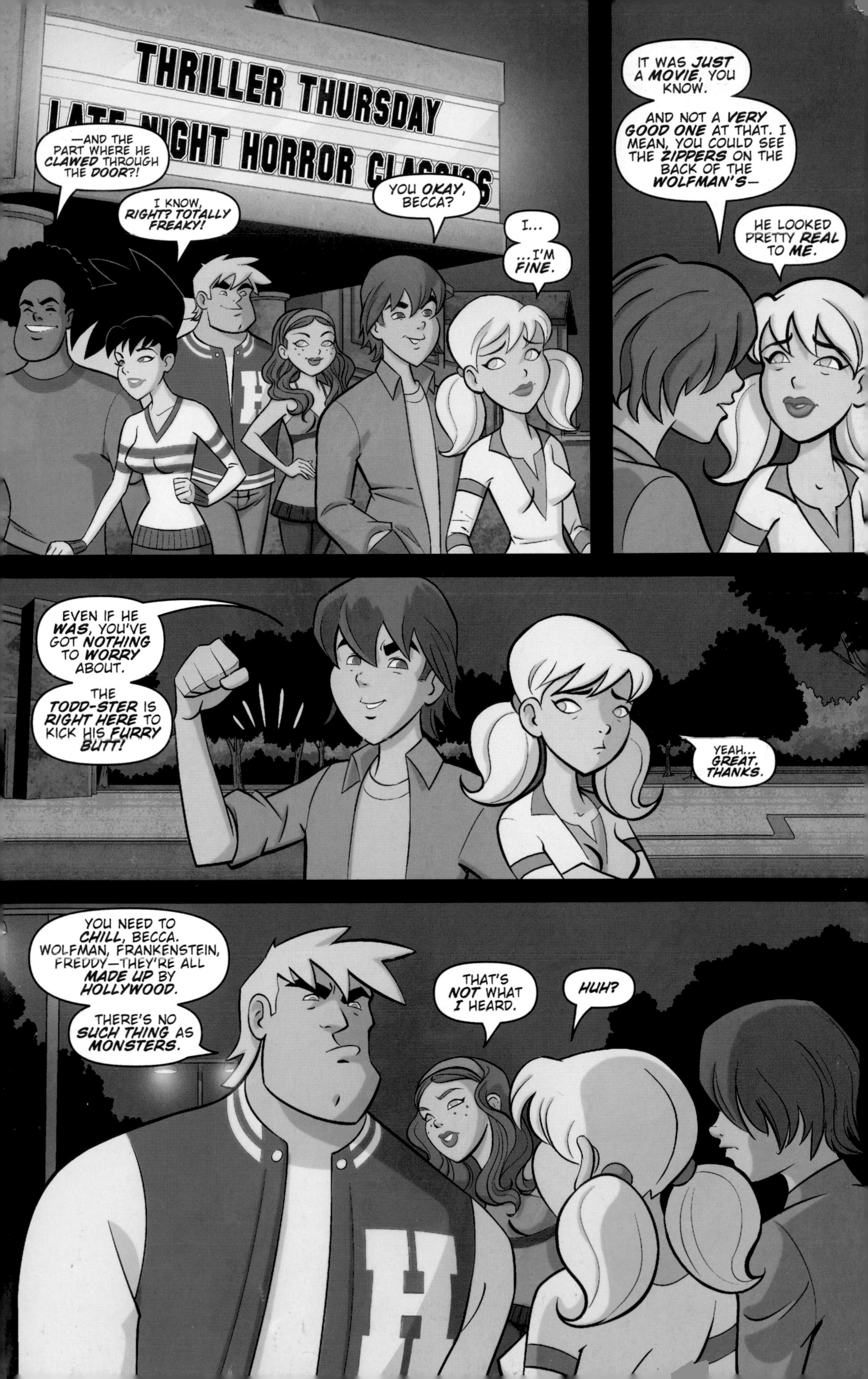
THRILLER THURSDAY
LATE NIGHT HORROR CLASSICS
—AND THE PART WHERE HE CLAWED THROUGH THE DOOR?!
I KNOW, RIGHT? TOTALLY FREAKY!
YOU OKAY, BECCA?
I...
...I'M FINE.
IT WAS JUST A MOVIE, YOU KNOW.
AND NOT A VERY GOOD ONE AT THAT. I MEAN, YOU COULD SEE THE ZIPPERS ON THE BACK OF THE WOLFMAN'S—
HE LOOKED PRETTY REAL TO ME.
EVEN IF HE WAS, YOU'VE GOT NOTHING TO WORRY ABOUT.
THE TODD-STER IS RIGHT HERE TO KICK HIS FURRY BUTT!
YEAH... GREAT. THANKS.
YOU NEED TO CHILL, BECCA. WOLFMAN, FRANKENSTEIN, FREDDY—THEY'RE ALL MADE UP BY HOLLYWOOD.
THERE'S NO SUCH THING AS MONSTERS.
THAT'S NOT WHAT I HEARD.
HUH?

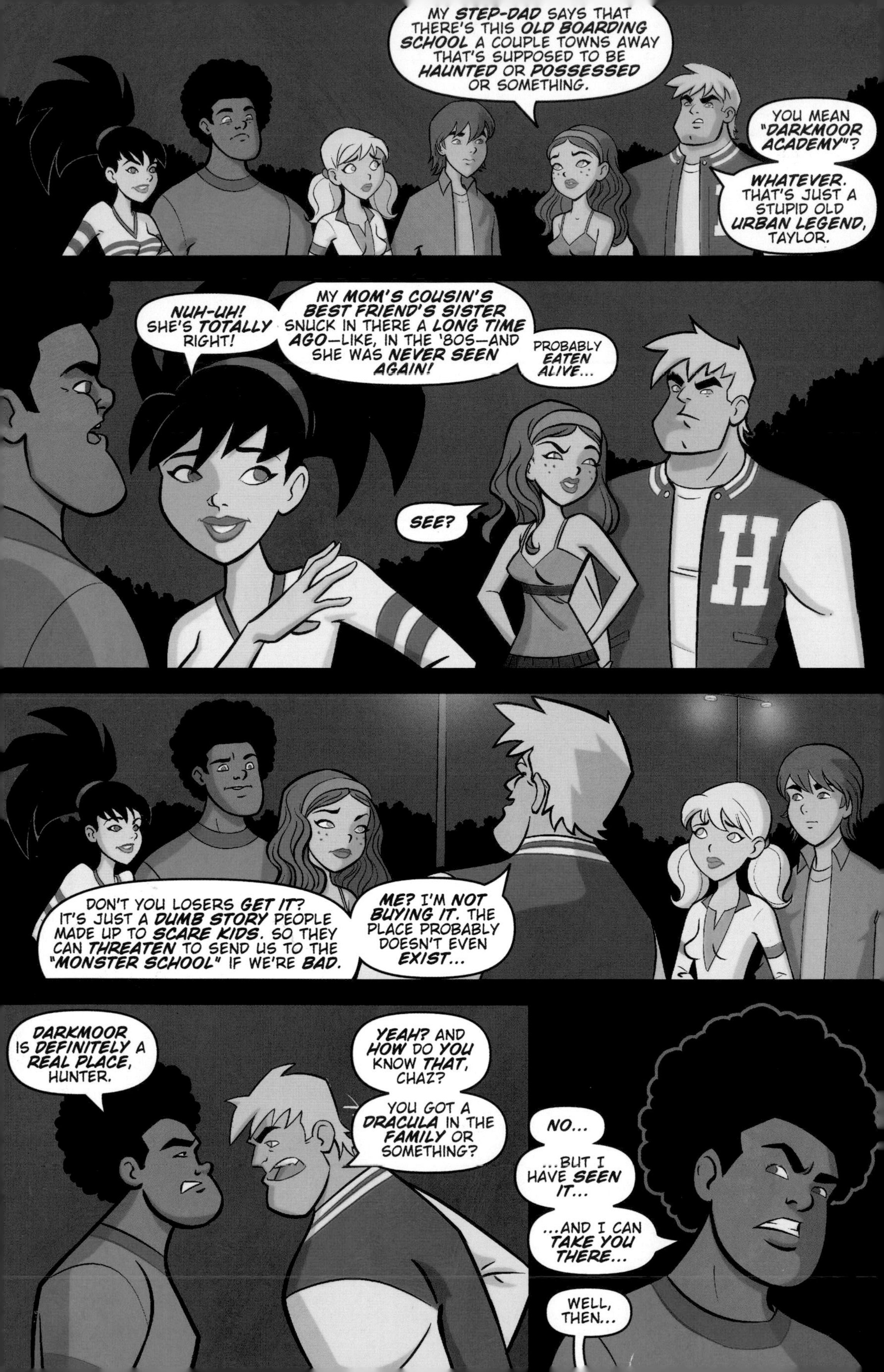

MY STEP-DAD SAYS THAT THERE'S THIS OLD BOARDING SCHOOL A COUPLE TOWNS AWAY THAT'S SUPPOSED TO BE HAUNTED OR POSSESSED OR SOMETHING.
YOU MEAN "DARKMOOR ACADEMY"?
WHATEVER. THAT'S JUST A STUPID OLD URBAN LEGEND, TAYLOR.
NUH-UH! SHE'S TOTALLY RIGHT!
MY MOM'S COUSIN'S BEST FRIEND'S SISTER SNUCK IN THERE A LONG TIME AGO—LIKE, IN THE '80S—AND SHE WAS NEVER SEEN AGAIN!
PROBABLY EATEN ALIVE...
SEE?
DON'T YOU LOSERS GET IT? IT'S JUST A DUMB STORY PEOPLE MADE UP TO SCARE KIDS. SO THEY CAN THREATEN TO SEND US TO THE "MONSTER SCHOOL" IF WE'RE BAD.
ME? I'M NOT BUYING IT. THE PLACE PROBABLY DOESN'T EVEN EXIST...
DARKMOOR IS DEFINITELY A REAL PLACE, HUNTER.
YEAH? AND HOW DO YOU KNOW THAT, CHAZ?
YOU GOT A DRACULA IN THE FAMILY OR SOMETHING?
NO...
...BUT I HAVE SEEN IT...
...AND I CAN TAKE YOU THERE...
WELL, THEN...

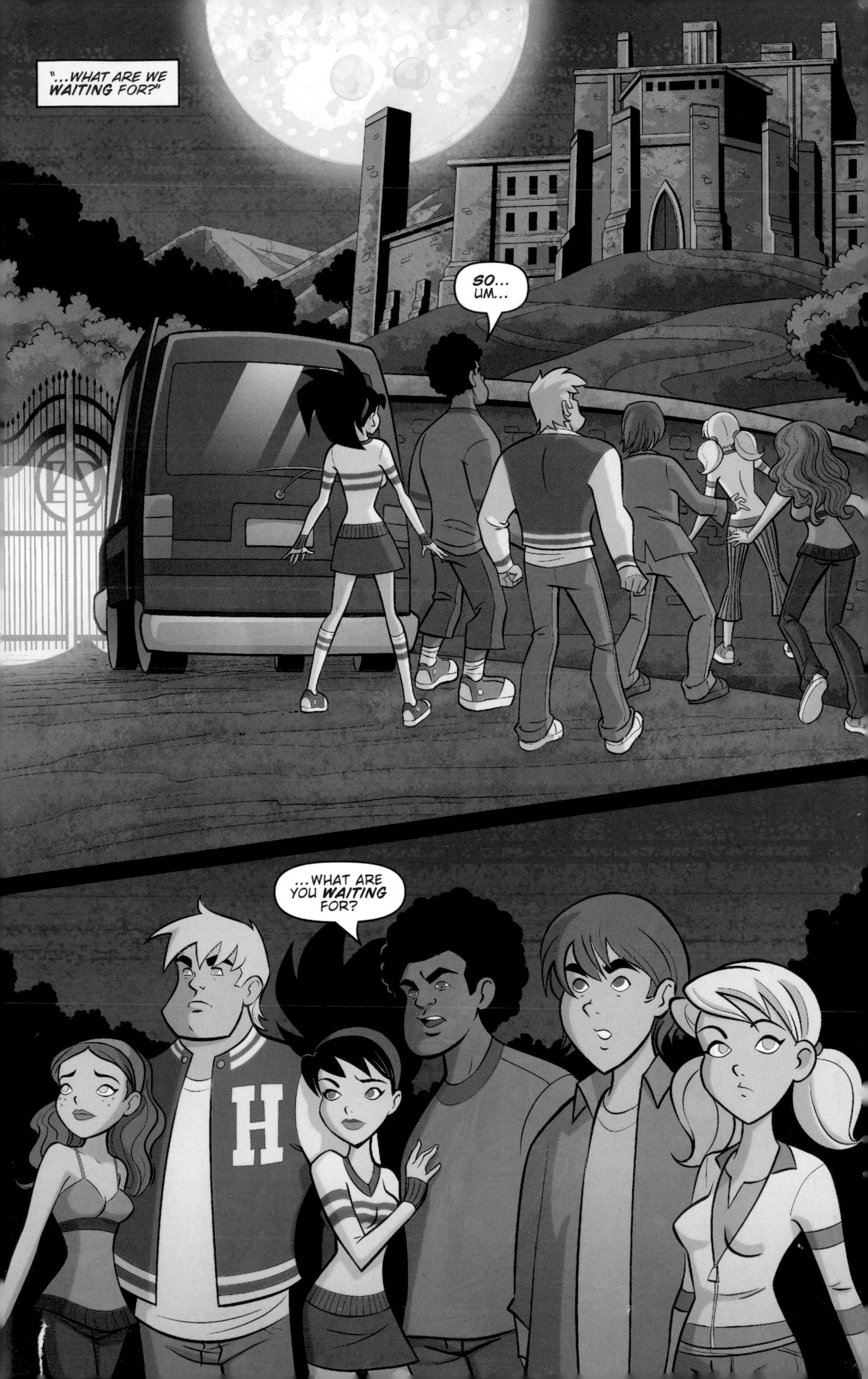
"...WHAT ARE WE WAITING FOR?"
SO... UM...
...WHAT ARE YOU WAITING FOR?

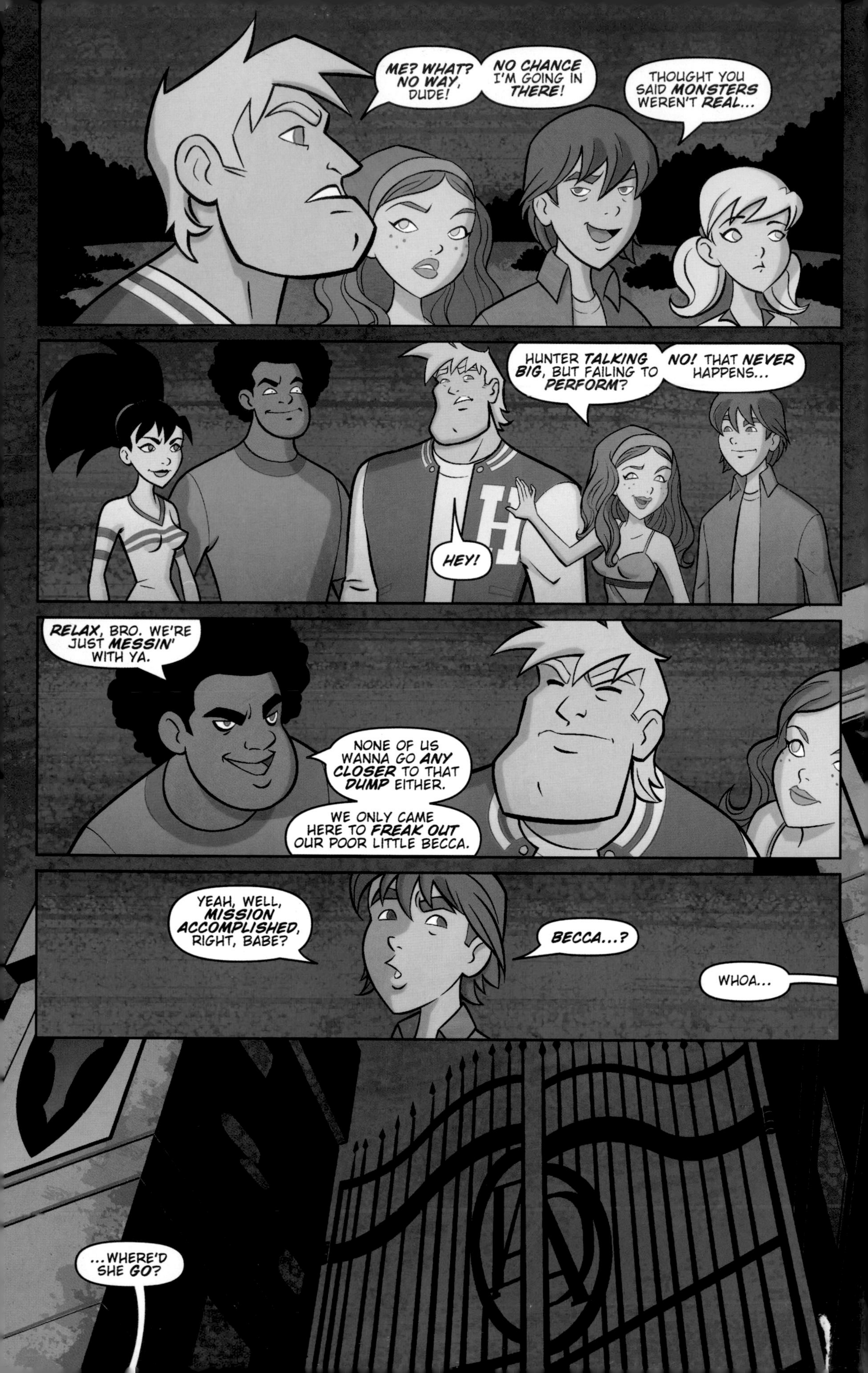
ME? WHAT? NO WAY, DUDE!
NO CHANCE I'M GOING IN THERE!
THOUGHT YOU SAID MONSTERS WEREN'T REAL...
HUNTER TALKING BIG, BUT FAILING TO PERFORM?
NO! THAT NEVER HAPPENS...
HEY!
RELAX, BRO. WE'RE JUST MESSIN' WITH YA.
NONE OF US WANNA GO ANY CLOSER TO THAT DUMP EITHER.
WE ONLY CAME HERE TO FREAK OUT OUR POOR LITTLE BECCA.
YEAH, WELL, MISSION ACCOMPLISHED, RIGHT, BABE?
BECCA...?
WHOA...
...WHERE'D SHE GO?

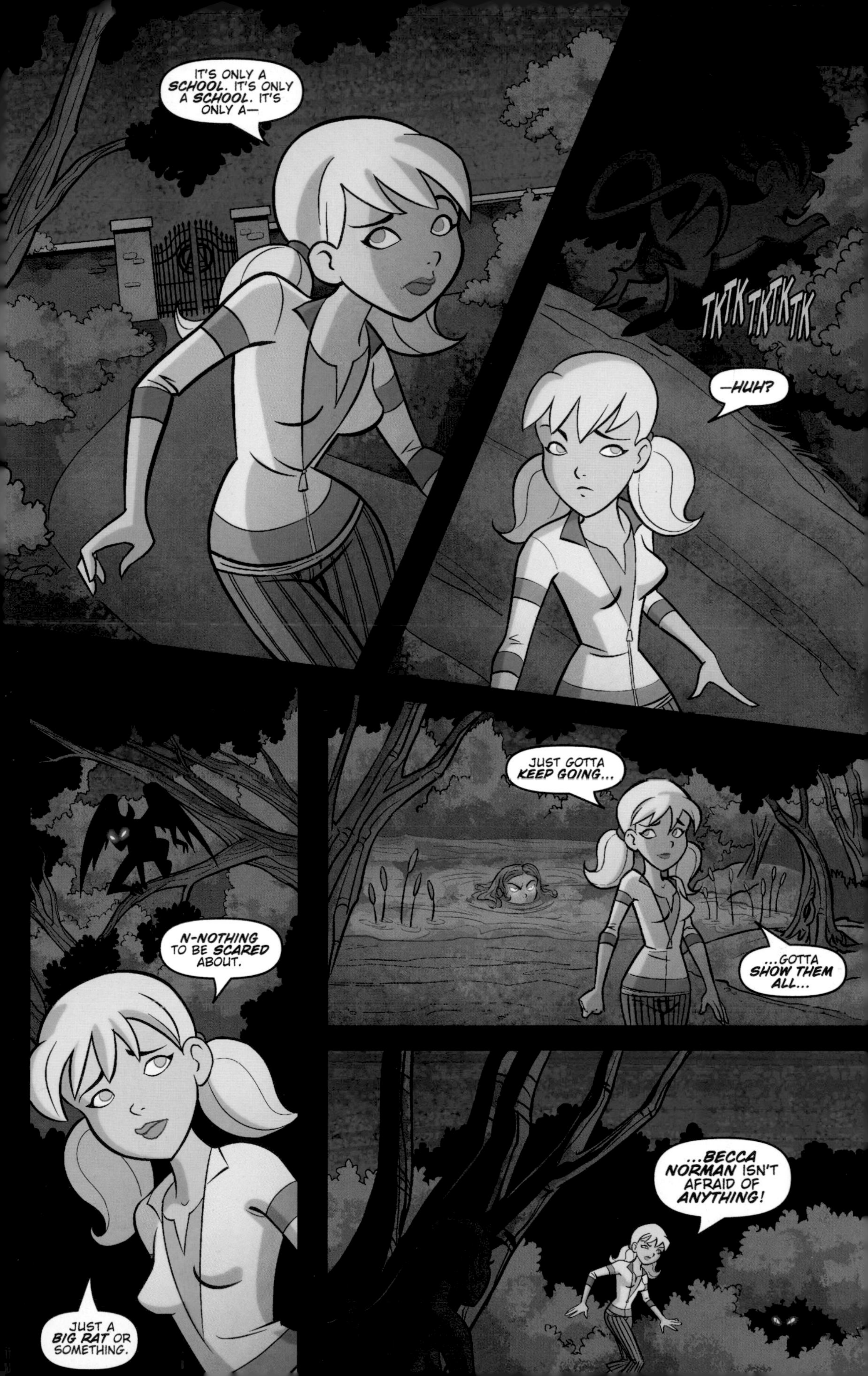
IT'S ONLY A SCHOOL. IT'S ONLY A SCHOOL. IT'S ONLY A—
TKTK TKTKTK
—HUH?
N-NOTHING TO BE SCARED ABOUT.
JUST A BIG RAT OR SOMETHING.
JUST GOTTA KEEP GOING...
...GOTTA SHOW THEM ALL...
...BECCA NORMAN ISN'T AFRAID OF ANYTHING!

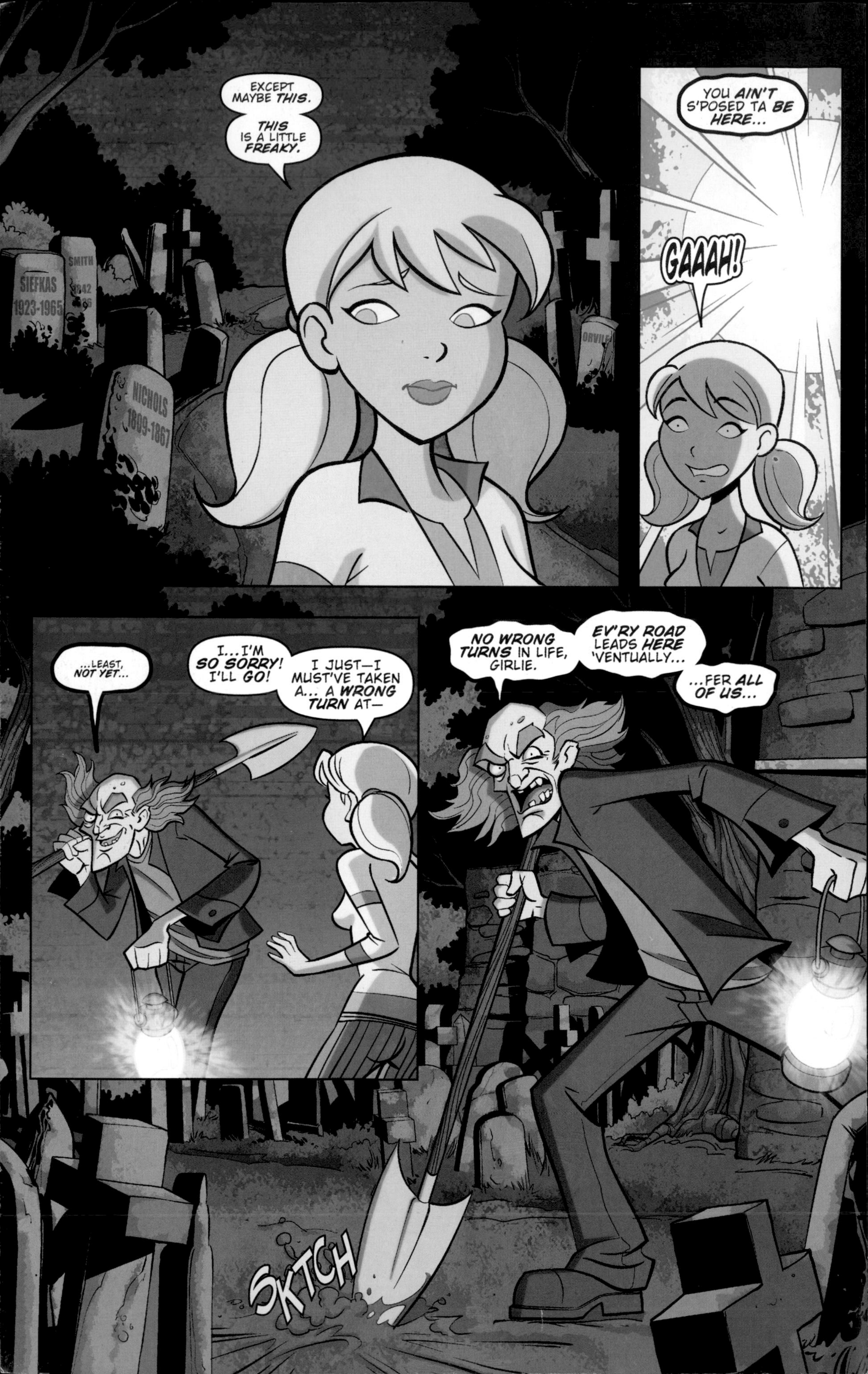
EXCEPT MAYBE THIS.
THIS IS A LITTLE FREAKY.
SIEFKAS 1923-1965
SMITH
NICHOLS 1809-1867
YOU AIN'T S'POSED TA BE HERE...
GAAAH!
...LEAST, NOT YET...
I... I'M SO SORRY! I'LL GO!
I JUST—I MUST'VE TAKEN A... A WRONG TURN AT—
NO WRONG TURNS IN LIFE, GIRLIE.
EV'RY ROAD LEADS HERE 'VENTUALLY...
...FER ALL OF US...
SKTCH

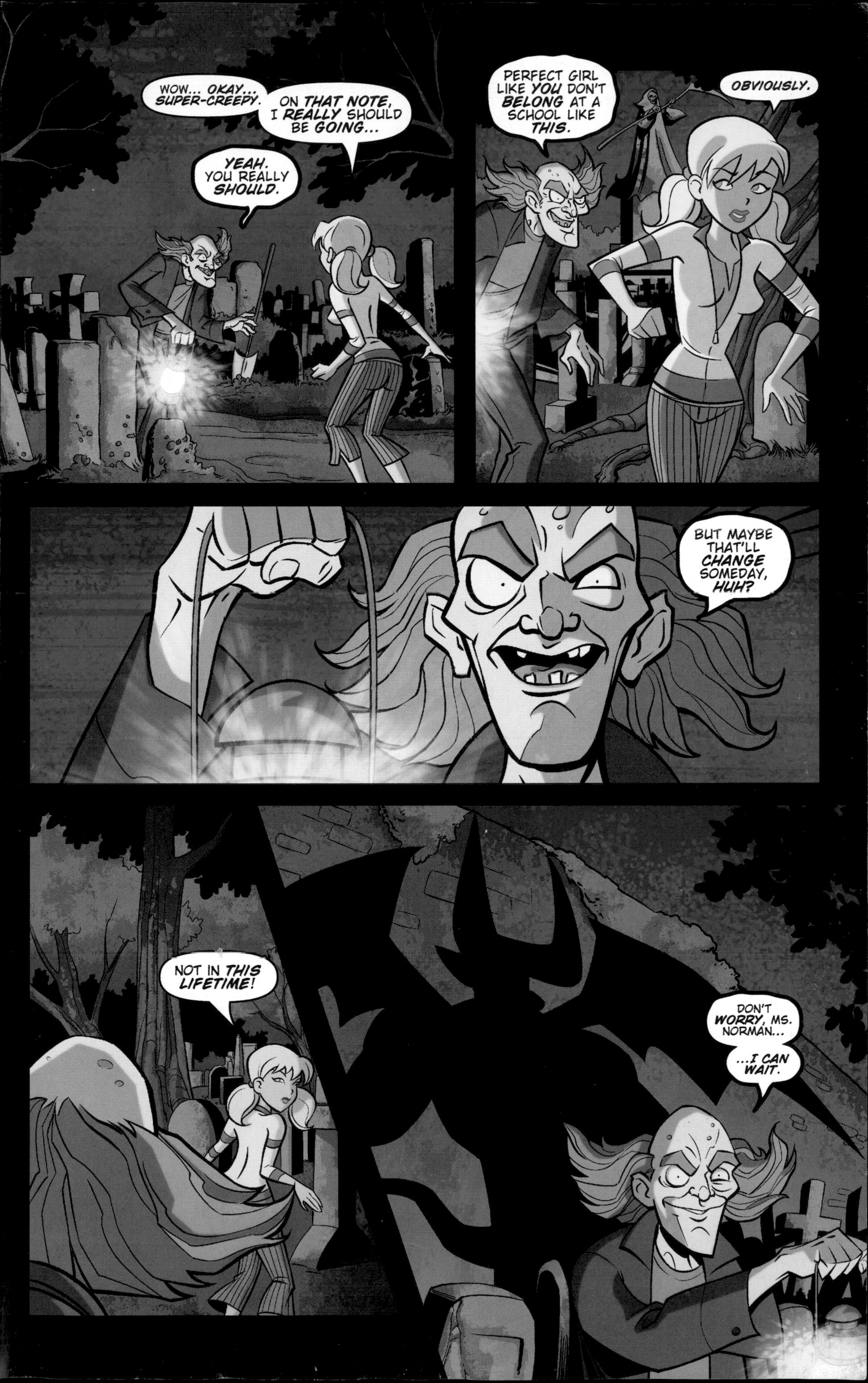
WOW... OKAY... SUPER-CREEPY.
ON THAT NOTE, I REALLY SHOULD BE GOING...
YEAH. YOU REALLY SHOULD.
PERFECT GIRL LIKE YOU DON'T BELONG AT A SCHOOL LIKE THIS.
OBVIOUSLY.
BUT MAYBE THAT'LL CHANGE SOMEDAY, HUH?
NOT IN THIS LIFETIME!
DON'T WORRY, MS. NORMAN...
...I CAN WAIT.

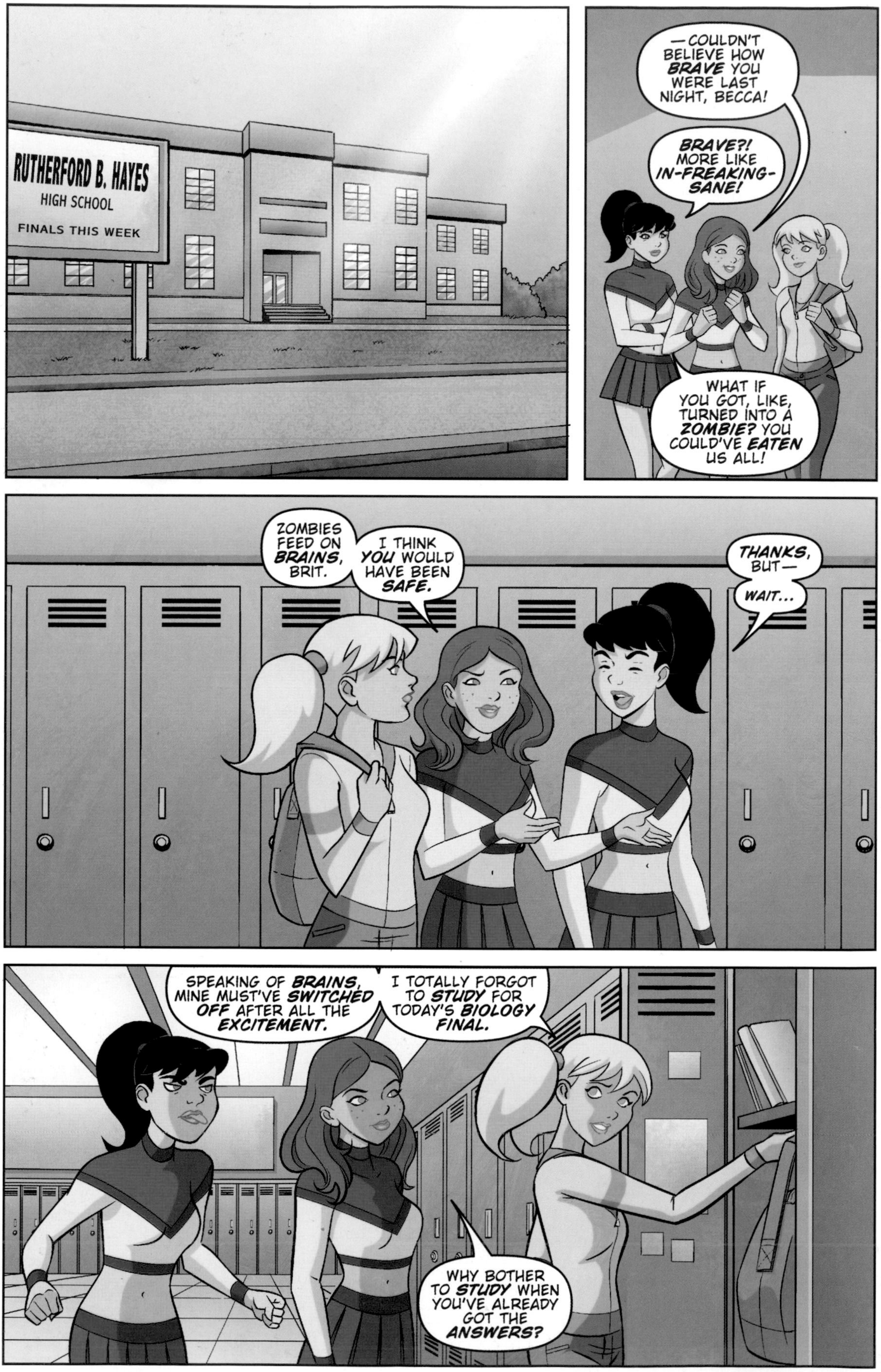
RUTHERFORD B. HAYES
HIGH SCHOOL
FINALS THIS WEEK
—COULDN'T BELIEVE HOW BRAVE YOU WERE LAST NIGHT, BECCA!
BRAVE?! MORE LIKE IN-FREAKING-SANE!
WHAT IF YOU GOT, LIKE, TURNED INTO A ZOMBIE? YOU COULD'VE EATEN US ALL!
ZOMBIES FEED ON BRAINS, BRIT.
I THINK YOU WOULD HAVE BEEN SAFE.
THANKS, BUT—
WAIT...
SPEAKING OF BRAINS, MINE MUST'VE SWITCHED OFF AFTER ALL THE EXCITEMENT.
I TOTALLY FORGOT TO STUDY FOR TODAY'S BIOLOGY FINAL.
WHY BOTHER TO STUDY WHEN YOU'VE ALREADY GOT THE ANSWERS?

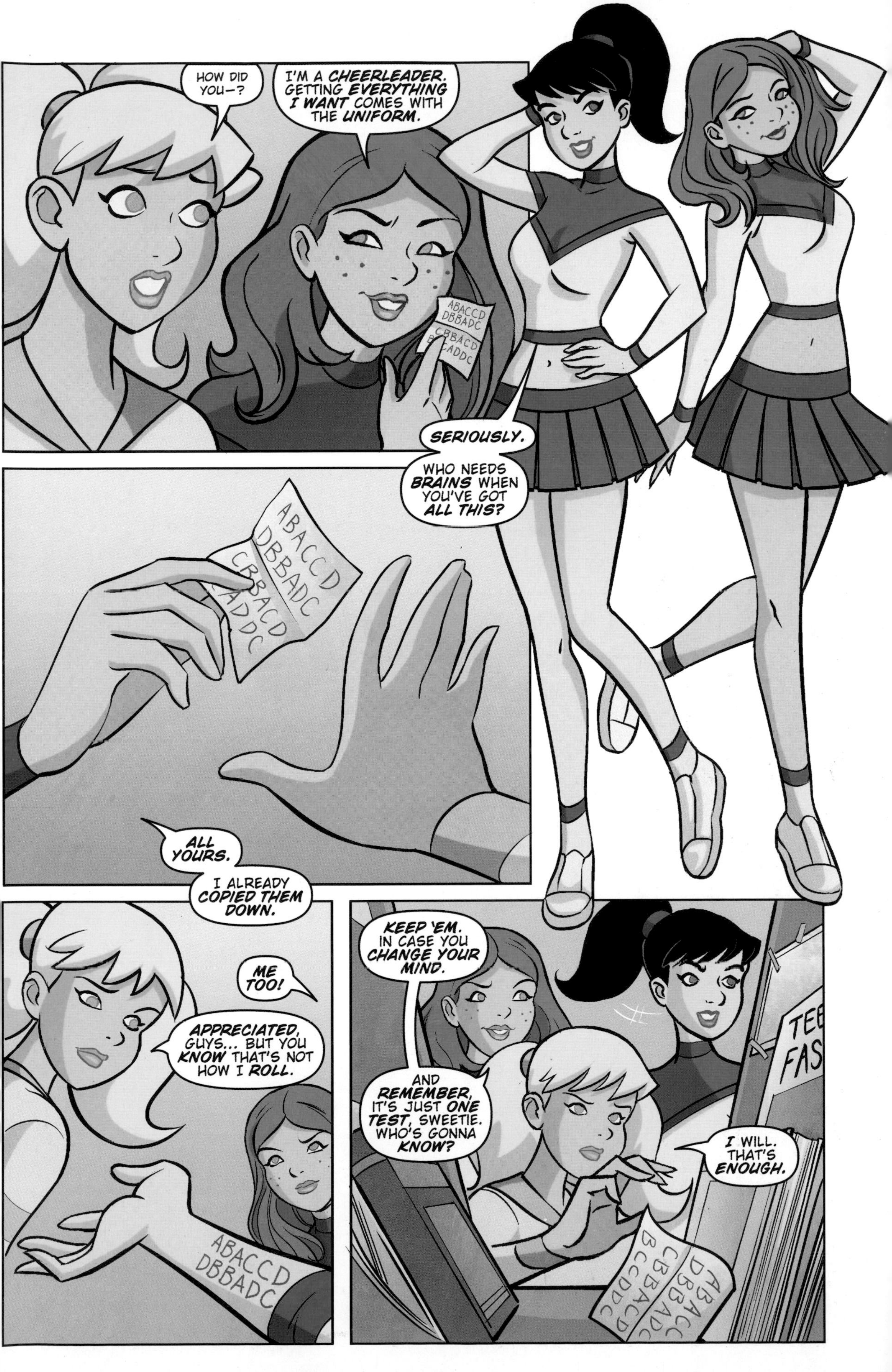
HOW DID YOU–?
I'M A CHEERLEADER. GETTING EVERYTHING I WANT COMES WITH THE UNIFORM.
ABACCD DBBADC CBBACD BCADDC
SERIOUSLY.
WHO NEEDS BRAINS WHEN YOU'VE GOT ALL THIS?
ABACCD DBBADC CBBACD BCADDC
ALL YOURS.
I ALREADY COPIED THEM DOWN.
ME TOO!
APPRECIATED, GUYS... BUT YOU KNOW THAT'S NOT HOW I ROLL.
ABACCD DBBADC
KEEP 'EM. IN CASE YOU CHANGE YOUR MIND.
AND REMEMBER, IT'S JUST ONE TEST, SWEETIE. WHO'S GONNA KNOW?
I WILL. THAT'S ENOUGH.
ABACC DBBADC CBBACD BCCDDC

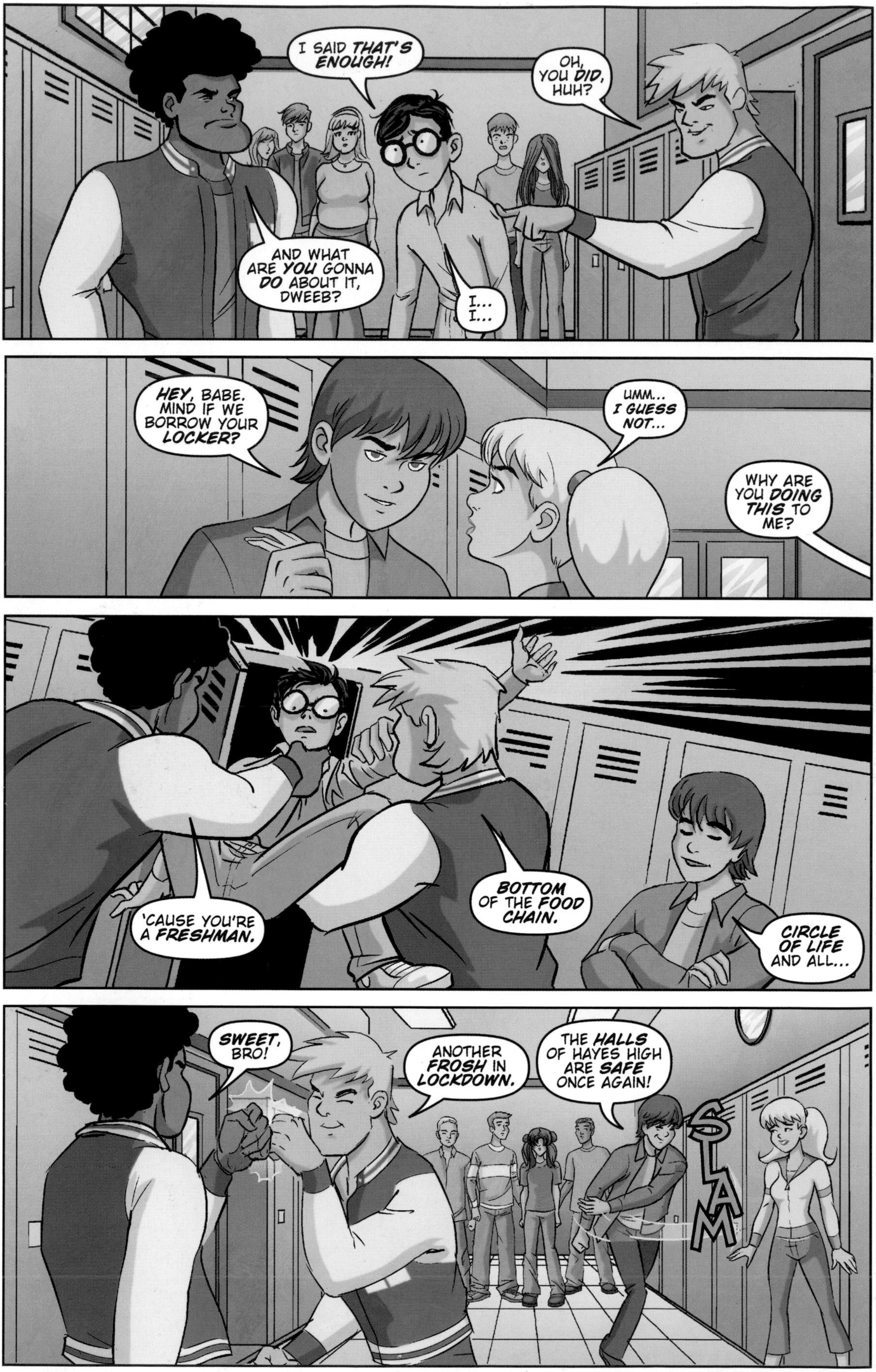
I SAID THAT'S ENOUGH!
OH, YOU DID, HUH?
AND WHAT ARE YOU GONNA DO ABOUT IT, DWEEB?
I... I...
HEY, BABE. MIND IF WE BORROW YOUR LOCKER?
UMM... I GUESS NOT...
WHY ARE YOU DOING THIS TO ME?
'CAUSE YOU'RE A FRESHMAN.
BOTTOM OF THE FOOD CHAIN.
CIRCLE OF LIFE AND ALL...
SWEET, BRO!
ANOTHER FROSH IN LOCKDOWN.
THE HALLS OF HAYES HIGH ARE SAFE ONCE AGAIN!
SLAM

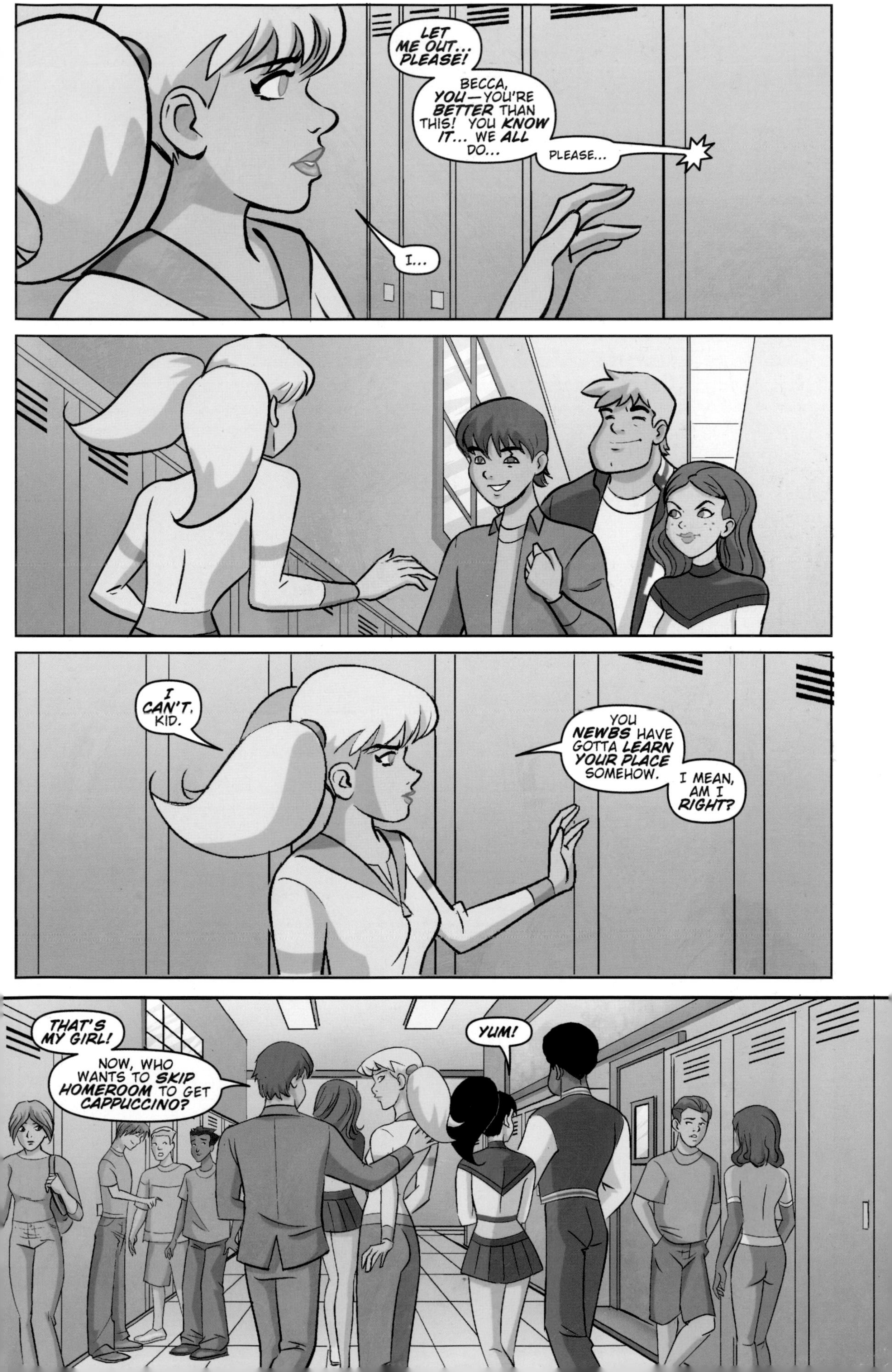
LET ME OUT... PLEASE!
BECCA, YOU—YOU'RE BETTER THAN THIS! YOU KNOW IT... WE ALL DO...
PLEASE...
I...
I CAN'T, KID.
YOU NEWBS HAVE GOTTA LEARN YOUR PLACE SOMEHOW.
I MEAN, AM I RIGHT?
THAT'S MY GIRL!
NOW, WHO WANTS TO SKIP HOMEROOM TO GET CAPPUCCINO?
YUM!

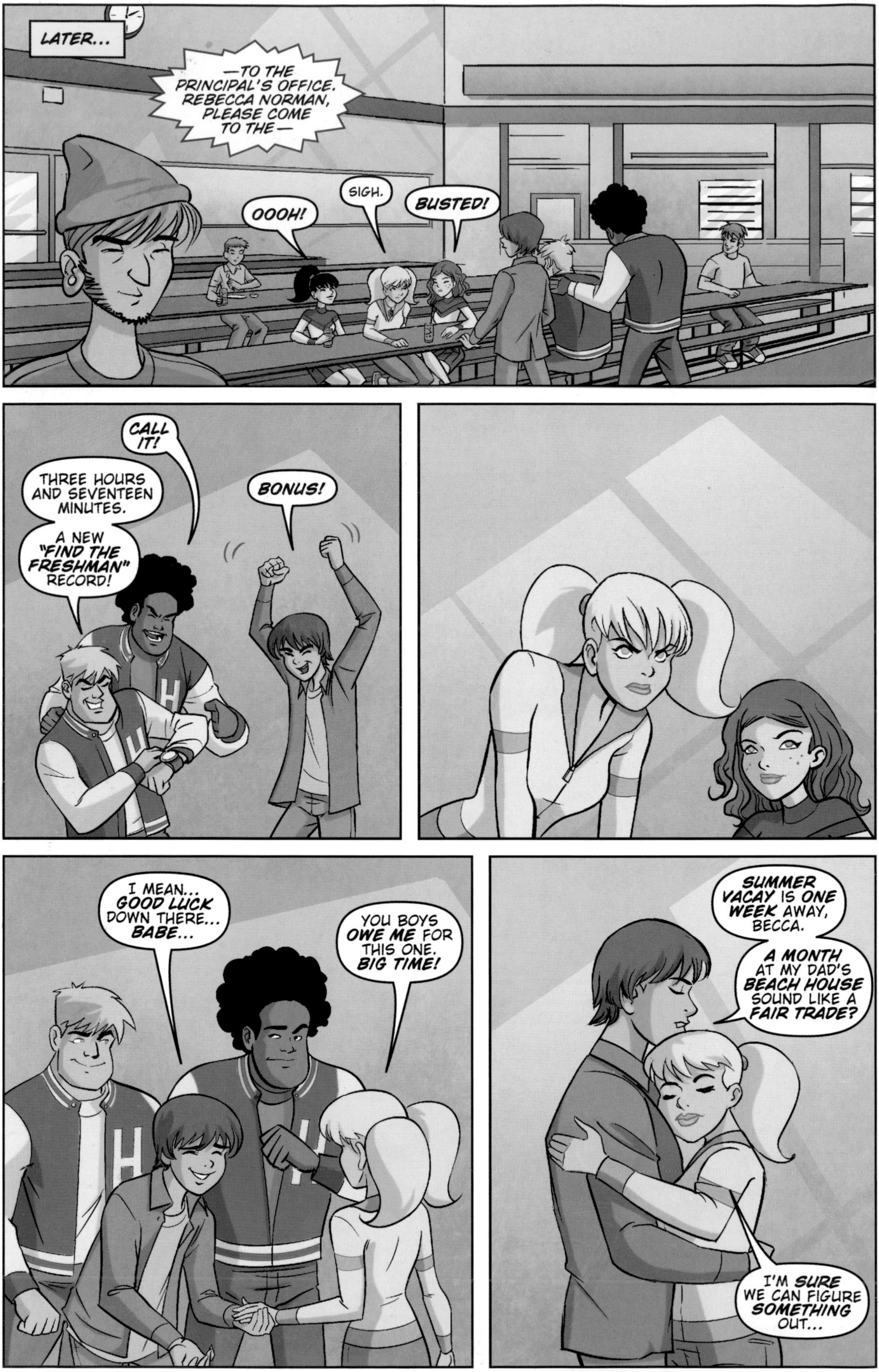
LATER...
—TO THE PRINCIPAL'S OFFICE. REBECCA NORMAN, PLEASE COME TO THE—
OOOH!
SIGH.
BUSTED!
CALL IT!
THREE HOURS AND SEVENTEEN MINUTES.
A NEW "FIND THE FRESHMAN" RECORD!
BONUS!
I MEAN... GOOD LUCK DOWN THERE... BABE...
YOU BOYS OWE ME FOR THIS ONE. BIG TIME!
SUMMER VACAY IS ONE WEEK AWAY, BECCA.
A MONTH AT MY DAD'S BEACH HOUSE SOUND LIKE A FAIR TRADE?
I'M SURE WE CAN FIGURE SOMETHING OUT...

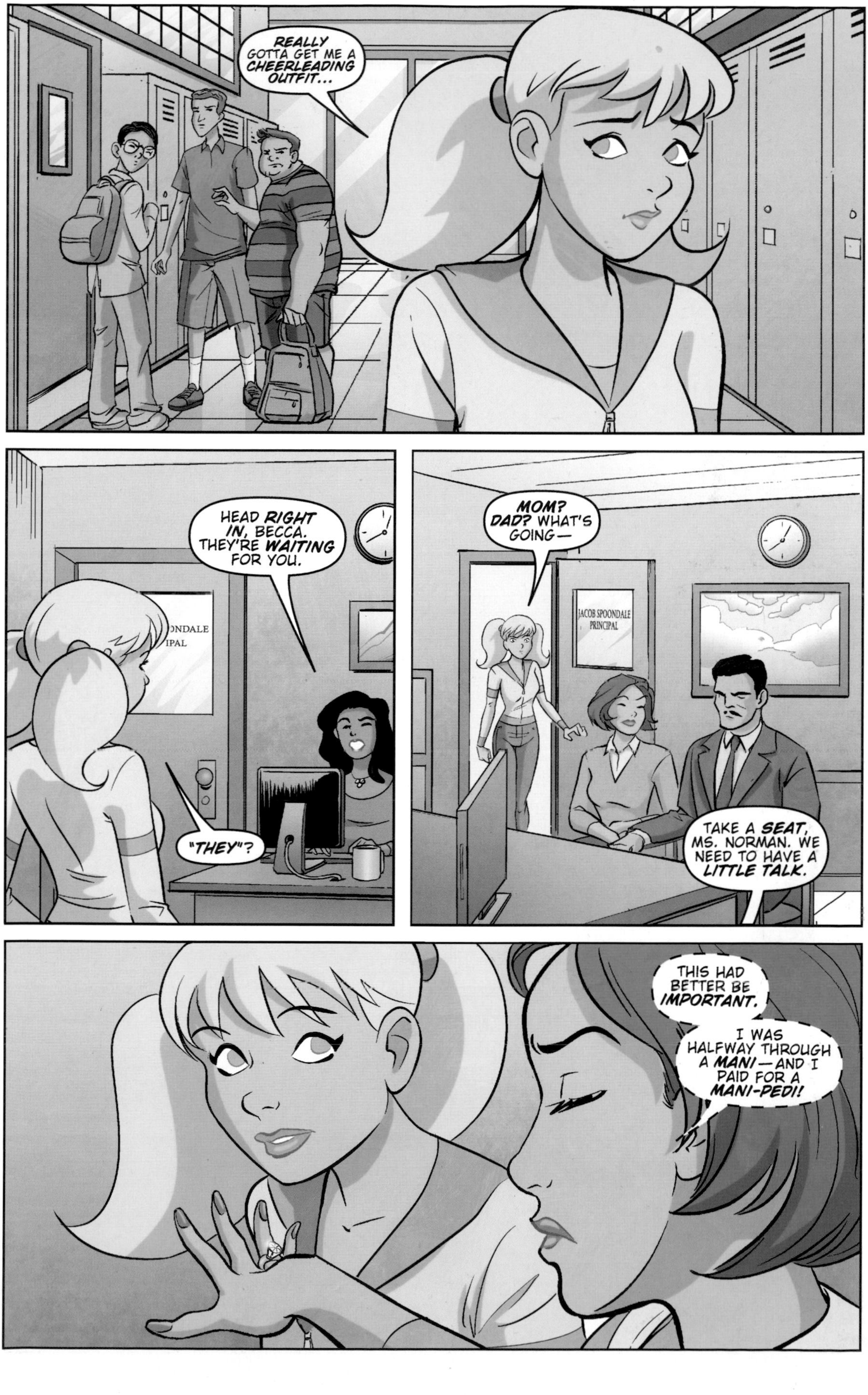

REALLY GOTTA GET ME A CHEERLEADING OUTFIT...
HEAD RIGHT IN, BECCA. THEY'RE WAITING FOR YOU.
"THEY"?
MOM? DAD? WHAT'S GOING—
JACOB SPOONDALE PRINCIPAL
TAKE A SEAT, MS. NORMAN. WE NEED TO HAVE A LITTLE TALK.
THIS HAD BETTER BE IMPORTANT.
I WAS HALFWAY THROUGH A MANI—AND I PAID FOR A MANI-PEDI!

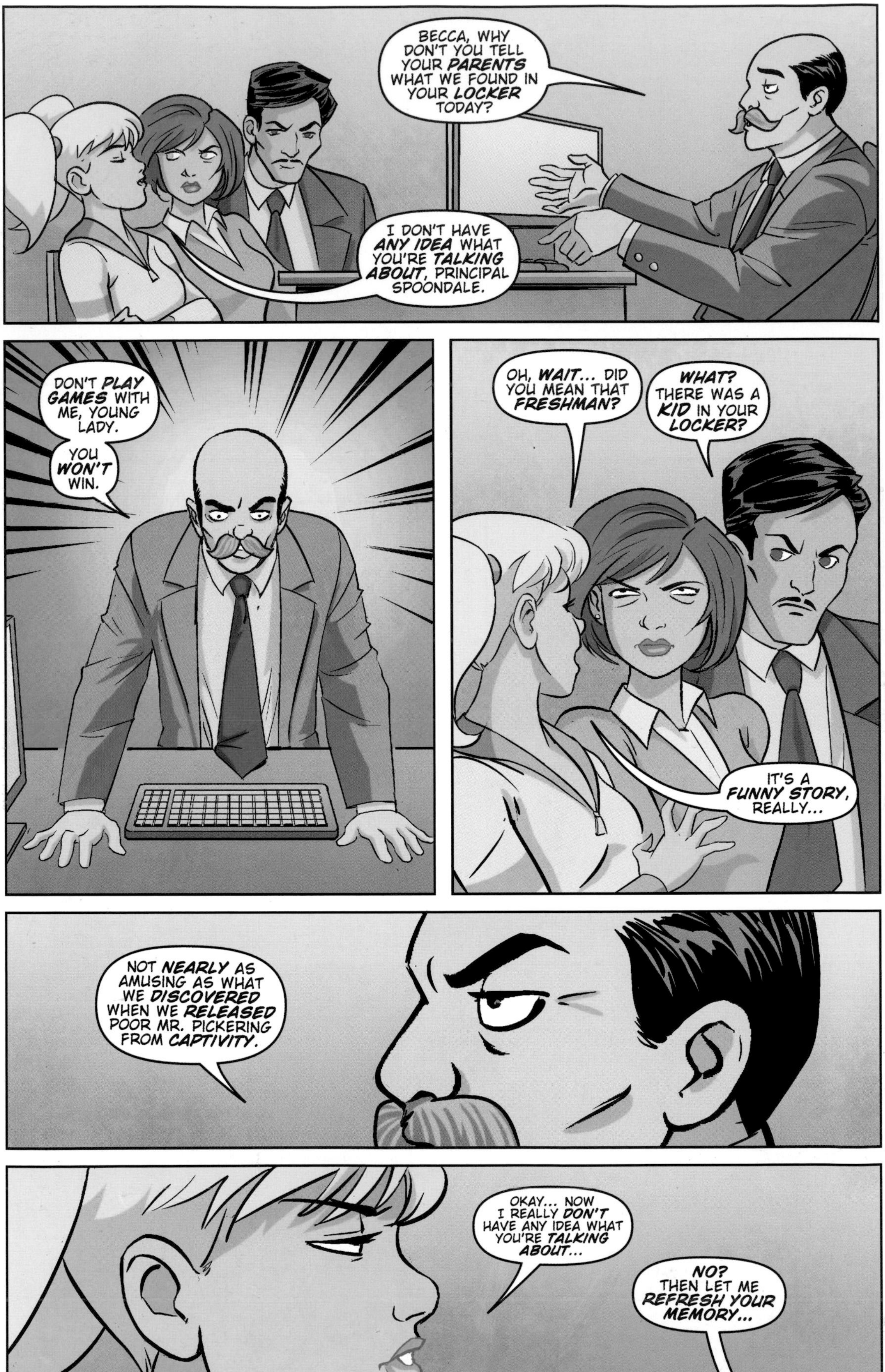
BECCA, WHY DON'T YOU TELL YOUR PARENTS WHAT WE FOUND IN YOUR LOCKER TODAY?
I DON'T HAVE ANY IDEA WHAT YOU'RE TALKING ABOUT, PRINCIPAL SPOONDALE.
DON'T PLAY GAMES WITH ME, YOUNG LADY.
YOU WON'T WIN.
OH, WAIT... DID YOU MEAN THAT FRESHMAN?
WHAT? THERE WAS A KID IN YOUR LOCKER?
IT'S A FUNNY STORY, REALLY...
NOT NEARLY AS AMUSING AS WHAT WE DISCOVERED WHEN WE RELEASED POOR MR. PICKERING FROM CAPTIVITY.
OKAY... NOW I REALLY DON'T HAVE ANY IDEA WHAT YOU'RE TALKING ABOUT...
NO? THEN LET ME REFRESH YOUR MEMORY...

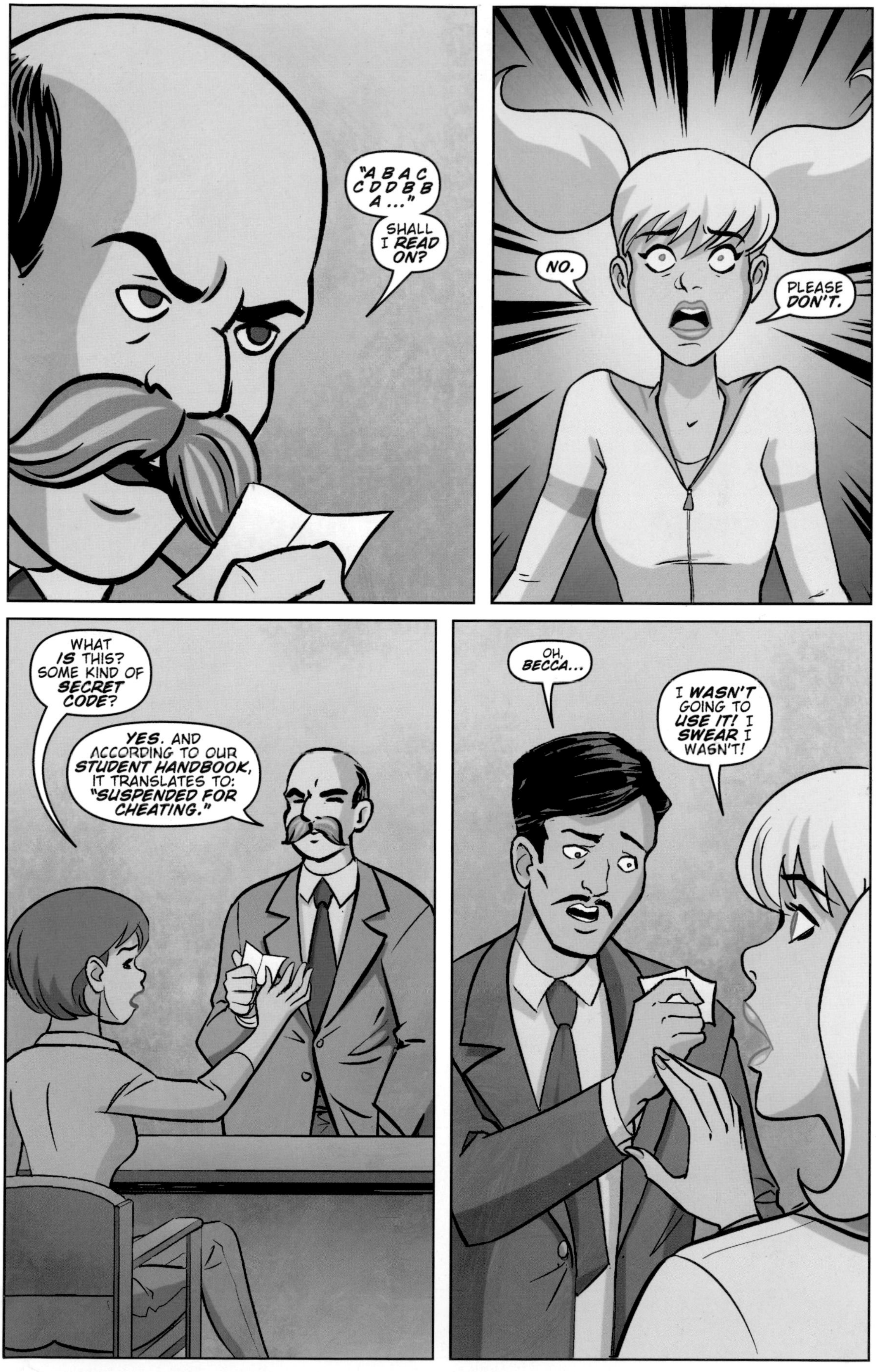
"A B A C C D D B B A..."
SHALL I READ ON?
NO.
PLEASE DON'T.
WHAT IS THIS? SOME KIND OF SECRET CODE?
YES. AND ACCORDING TO OUR STUDENT HANDBOOK, IT TRANSLATES TO: "SUSPENDED FOR CHEATING."
OH, BECCA...
I WASN'T GOING TO USE IT! I SWEAR I WASN'T!

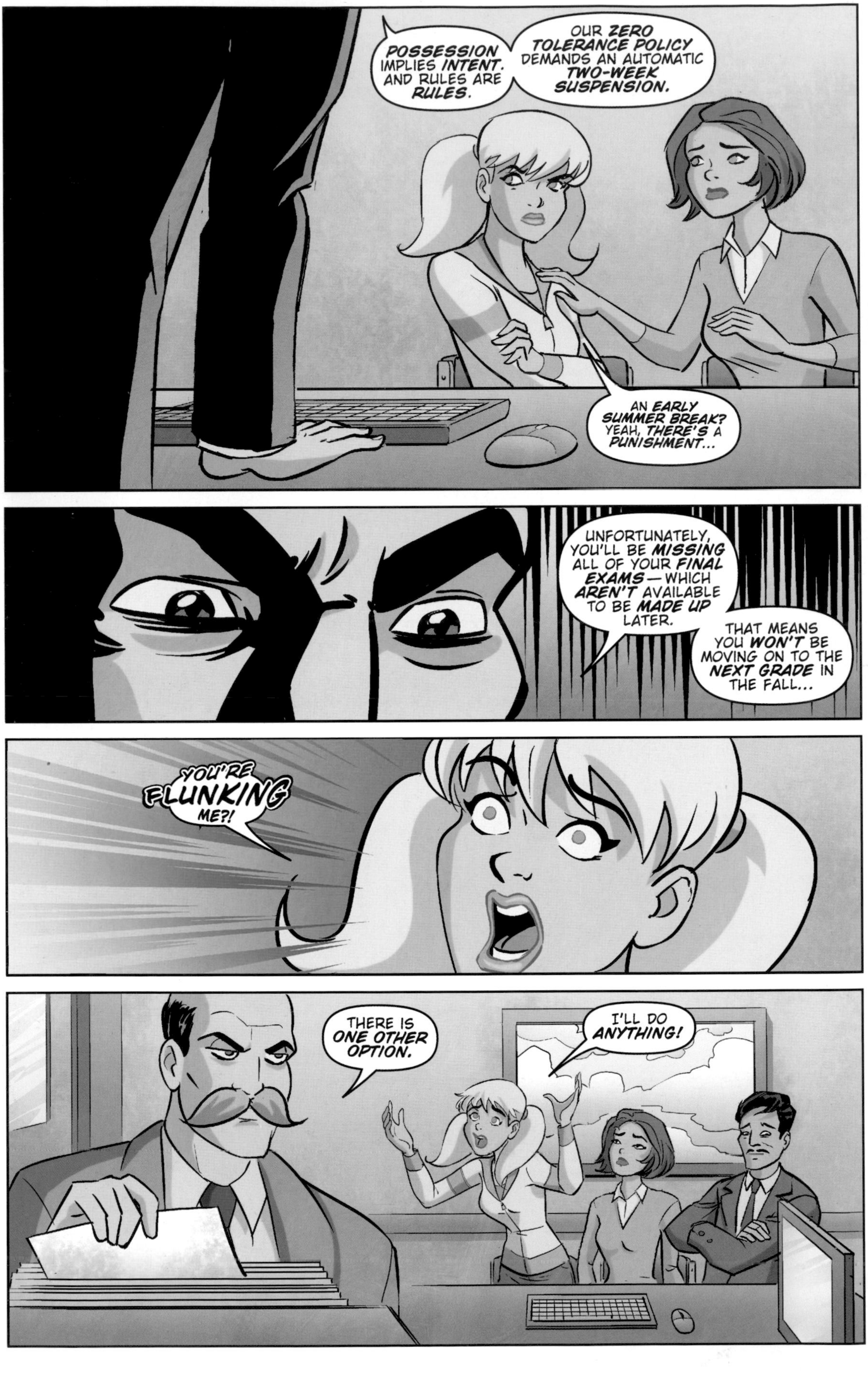
POSSESSION IMPLIES INTENT. AND RULES ARE RULES.
OUR ZERO TOLERANCE POLICY DEMANDS AN AUTOMATIC TWO-WEEK SUSPENSION.
AN EARLY SUMMER BREAK? YEAH, THERE'S A PUNISHMENT...
UNFORTUNATELY, YOU'LL BE MISSING ALL OF YOUR FINAL EXAMS—WHICH AREN'T AVAILABLE TO BE MADE UP LATER.
THAT MEANS YOU WON'T BE MOVING ON TO THE NEXT GRADE IN THE FALL...
YOU'RE FLUNKING ME?!
THERE IS ONE OTHER OPTION.
I'LL DO ANYTHING!

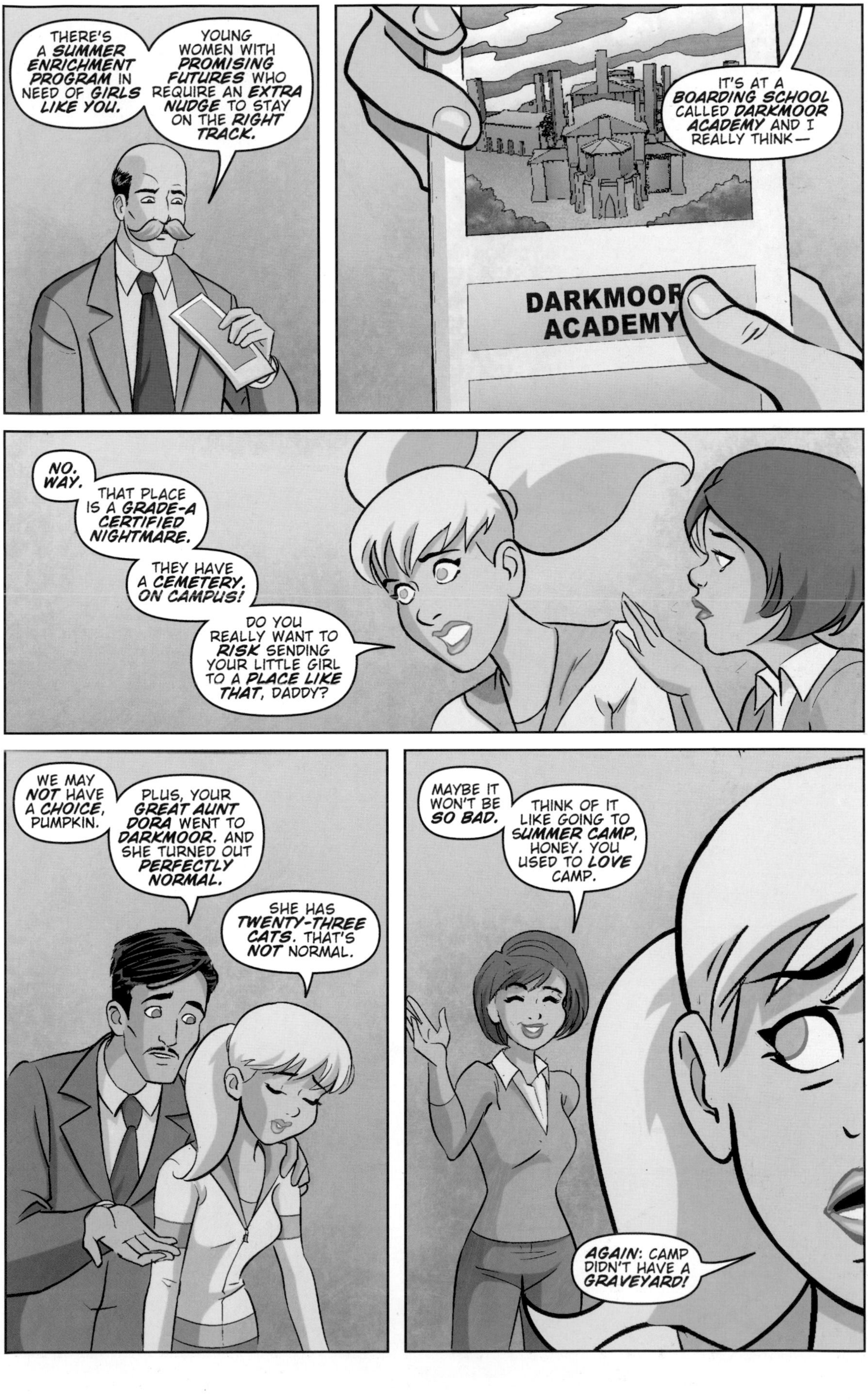

THERE'S A **SUMMER ENRICHMENT PROGRAM** IN NEED OF **GIRLS LIKE YOU.**
YOUNG WOMEN WITH **PROMISING FUTURES** WHO REQUIRE AN **EXTRA NUDGE** TO STAY ON THE **RIGHT TRACK.**
IT'S AT A **BOARDING SCHOOL** CALLED **DARKMOOR ACADEMY** AND I REALLY THINK—
DARKMOOR ACADEMY
NO. WAY.
THAT PLACE IS A **GRADE-A CERTIFIED NIGHTMARE.**
THEY HAVE A **CEMETERY. ON CAMPUS!**
DO YOU REALLY WANT TO **RISK** SENDING YOUR LITTLE GIRL TO A **PLACE LIKE THAT**, DADDY?
WE MAY **NOT** HAVE A **CHOICE**, PUMPKIN.
PLUS, YOUR **GREAT AUNT DORA** WENT TO **DARKMOOR**. AND SHE TURNED OUT **PERFECTLY NORMAL.**
SHE HAS **TWENTY-THREE CATS**. THAT'S **NOT** NORMAL.
MAYBE IT WON'T BE **SO BAD.**
THINK OF IT LIKE GOING TO **SUMMER CAMP**, HONEY. YOU USED TO **LOVE** CAMP.
AGAIN: CAMP DIDN'T HAVE A **GRAVEYARD!**

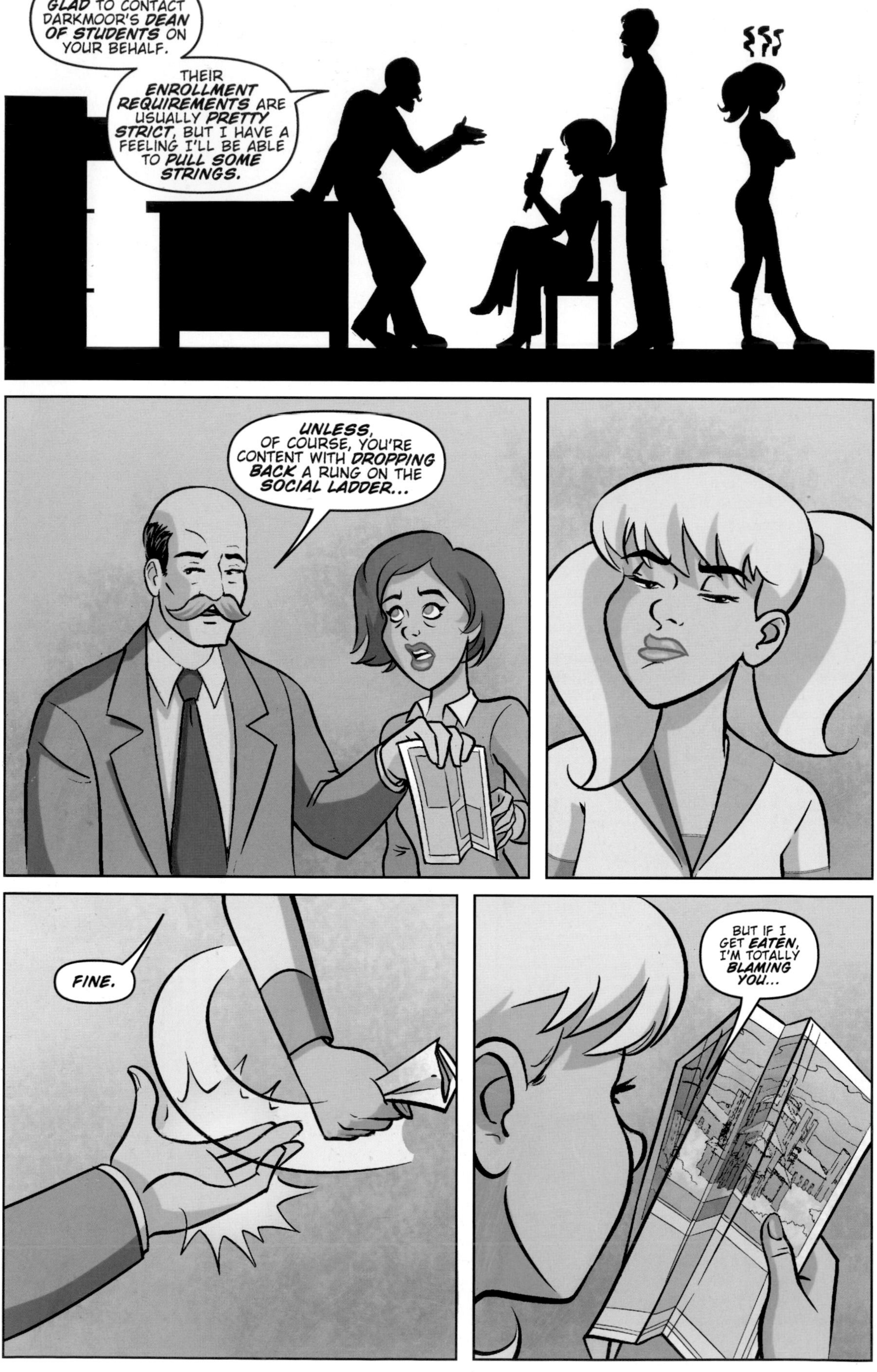
I WOULD BE GLAD TO CONTACT DARKMOOR'S DEAN OF STUDENTS ON YOUR BEHALF.
THEIR ENROLLMENT REQUIREMENTS ARE USUALLY PRETTY STRICT, BUT I HAVE A FEELING I'LL BE ABLE TO PULL SOME STRINGS.
UNLESS, OF COURSE, YOU'RE CONTENT WITH DROPPING BACK A RUNG ON THE SOCIAL LADDER...
FINE.
BUT IF I GET EATEN, I'M TOTALLY BLAMING YOU...

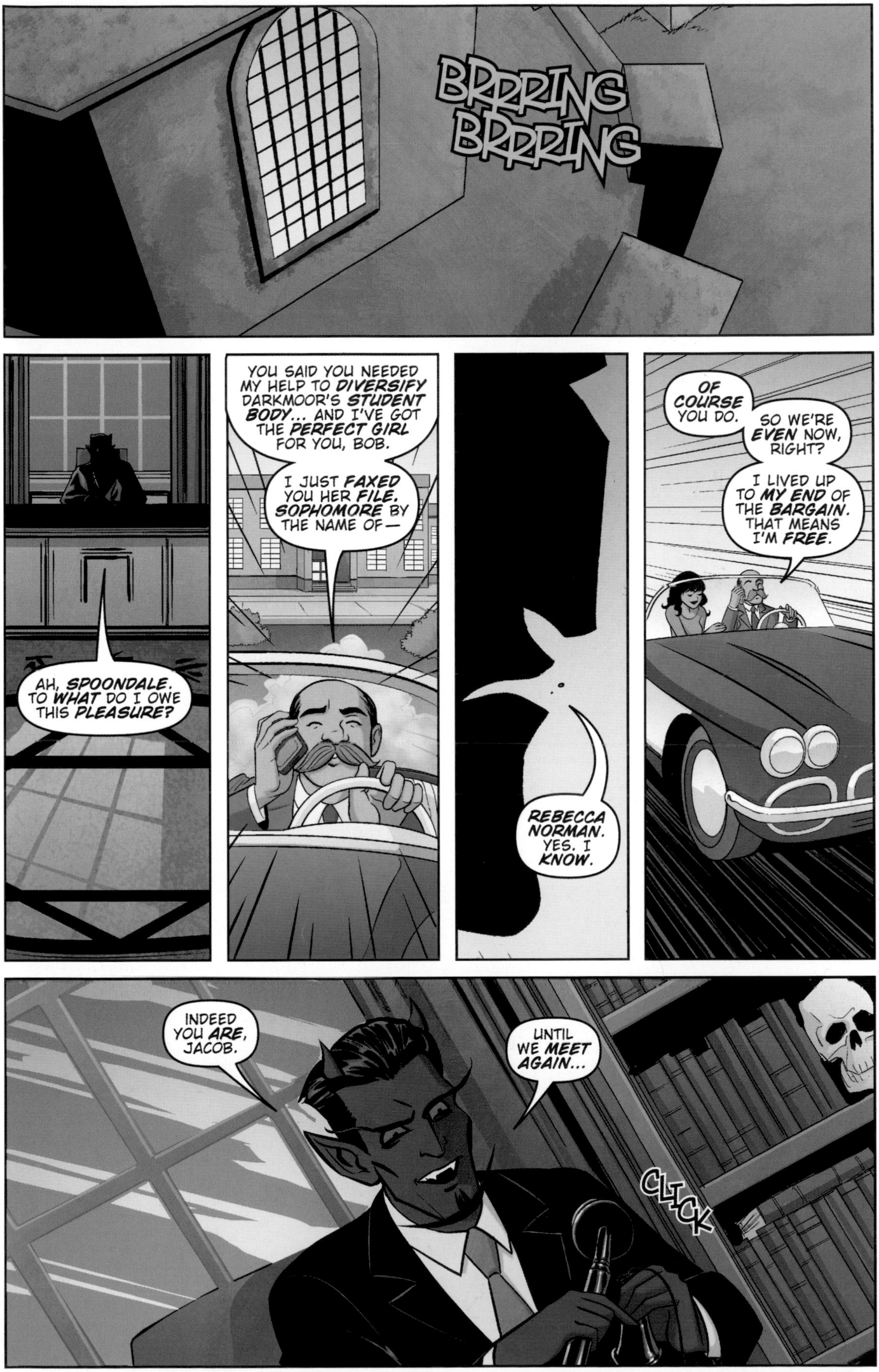
BRRRING
BRRRING
AH, SPOONDALE. TO WHAT DO I OWE THIS PLEASURE?
YOU SAID YOU NEEDED MY HELP TO DIVERSIFY DARKMOOR'S STUDENT BODY... AND I'VE GOT THE PERFECT GIRL FOR YOU, BOB.
I JUST FAXED YOU HER FILE. SOPHOMORE BY THE NAME OF—
REBECCA NORMAN. YES. I KNOW.
OF COURSE YOU DO.
SO WE'RE EVEN NOW, RIGHT?
I LIVED UP TO MY END OF THE BARGAIN. THAT MEANS I'M FREE.
INDEED YOU ARE, JACOB.
UNTIL WE MEET AGAIN...
CLICK

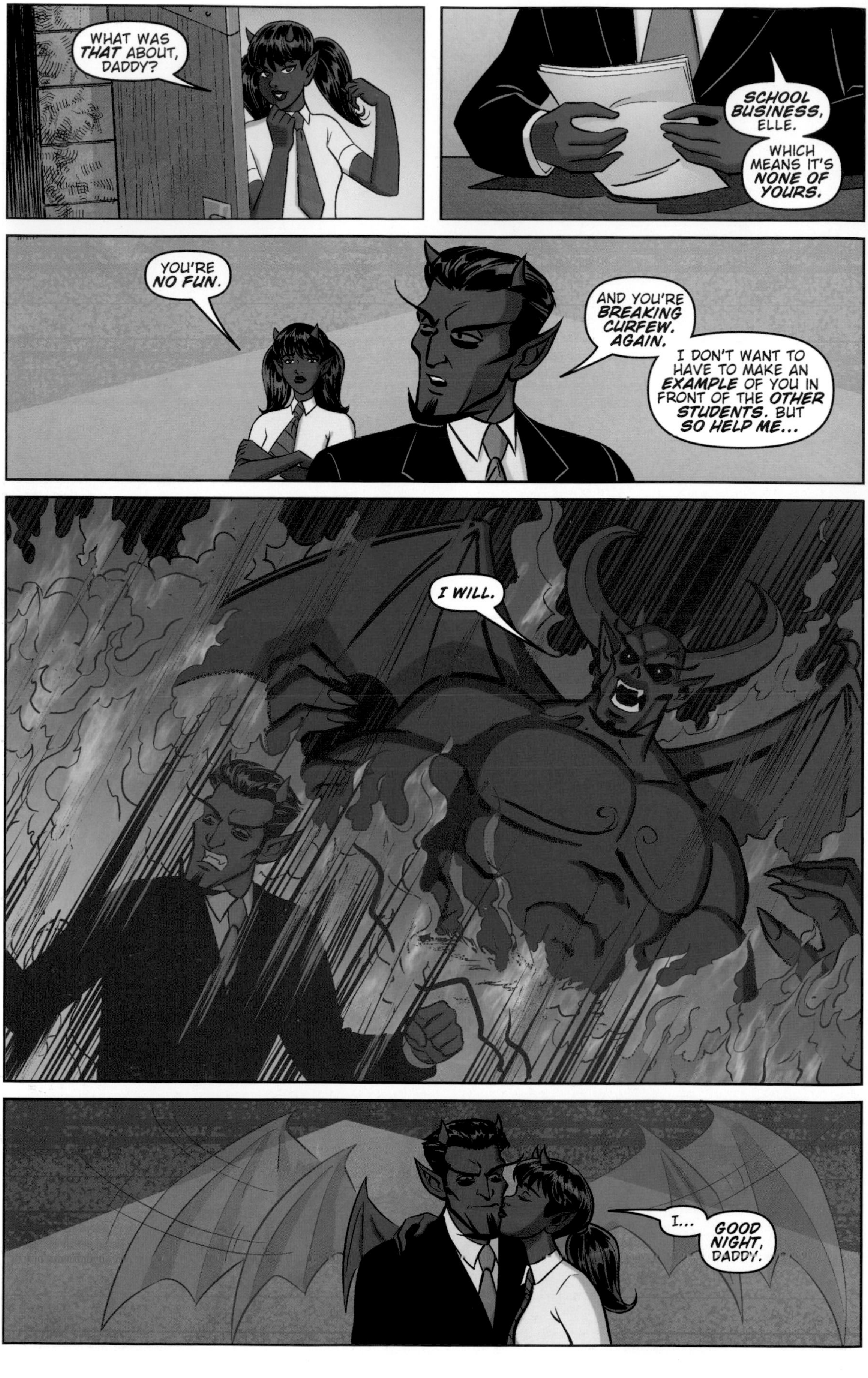
WHAT WAS THAT ABOUT, DADDY?
SCHOOL BUSINESS, ELLE.
WHICH MEANS IT'S NONE OF YOURS.
YOU'RE NO FUN.
AND YOU'RE BREAKING CURFEW. AGAIN.
I DON'T WANT TO HAVE TO MAKE AN EXAMPLE OF YOU IN FRONT OF THE OTHER STUDENTS. BUT SO HELP ME...
I WILL.
I... GOOD NIGHT, DADDY.

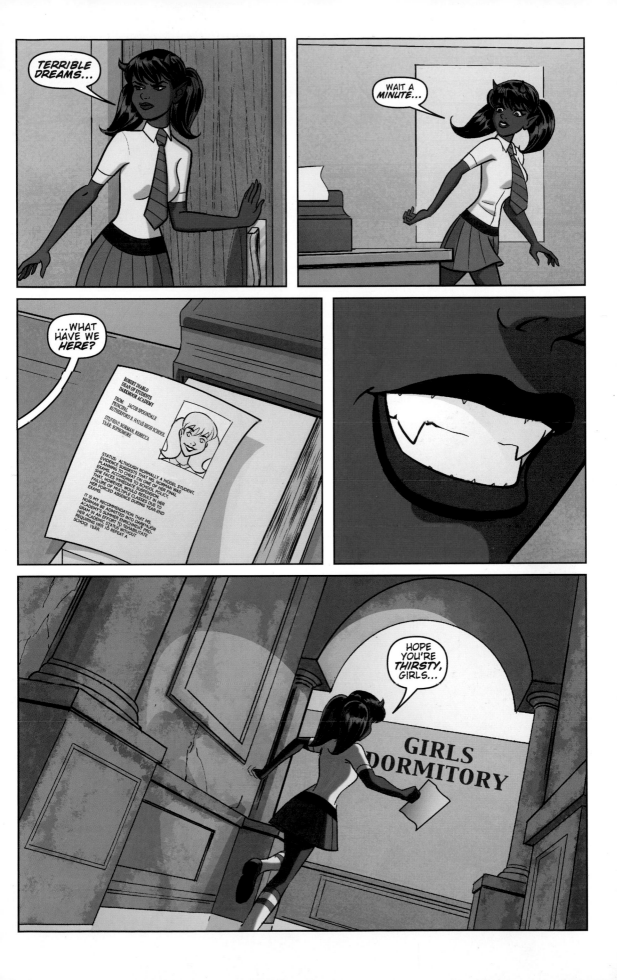

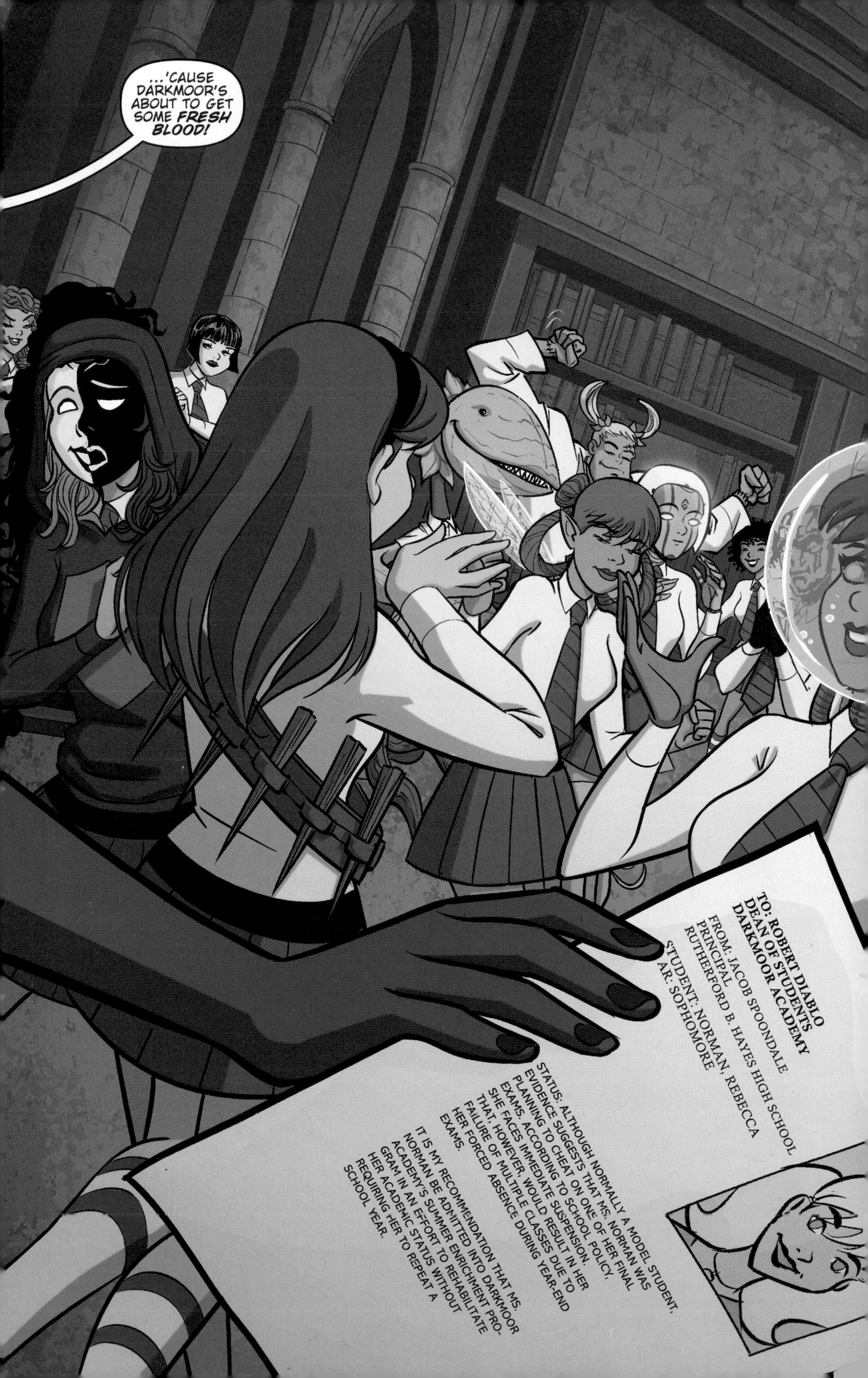
...'CAUSE DARKMOOR'S ABOUT TO GET SOME *FRESH BLOOD!*
TO: ROBERT DIABLO
DEAN OF STUDENTS
DARKMOOR ACADEMY
FROM: JACOB SPOONDALE
PRINCIPAL
RUTHERFORD B. HAYES HIGH SCHOOL
STUDENT: NORMAN, REBECCA
AR: SOPHOMORE
STATUS: ALTHOUGH NORMALLY A MODEL STUDENT, EVIDENCE SUGGESTS THAT MS. NORMAN WAS PLANNING TO CHEAT ON ONE OF HER FINAL EXAMS. ACCORDING TO SCHOOL POLICY, SHE FACES IMMEDIATE SUSPENSION. THAT, HOWEVER, WOULD RESULT IN HER FAILURE OF MULTIPLE CLASSES DUE TO HER FORCED ABSENCE DURING YEAR-END EXAMS.
IT IS MY RECOMMENDATION THAT MS. NORMAN BE ADMITTED INTO DARKMOOR ACADEMY'S SUMMER ENRICHMENT PROGRAM IN AN EFFORT TO REHABILITATE HER ACADEMIC STATUS WITHOUT REQUIRING HER TO REPEAT A SCHOOL YEAR.

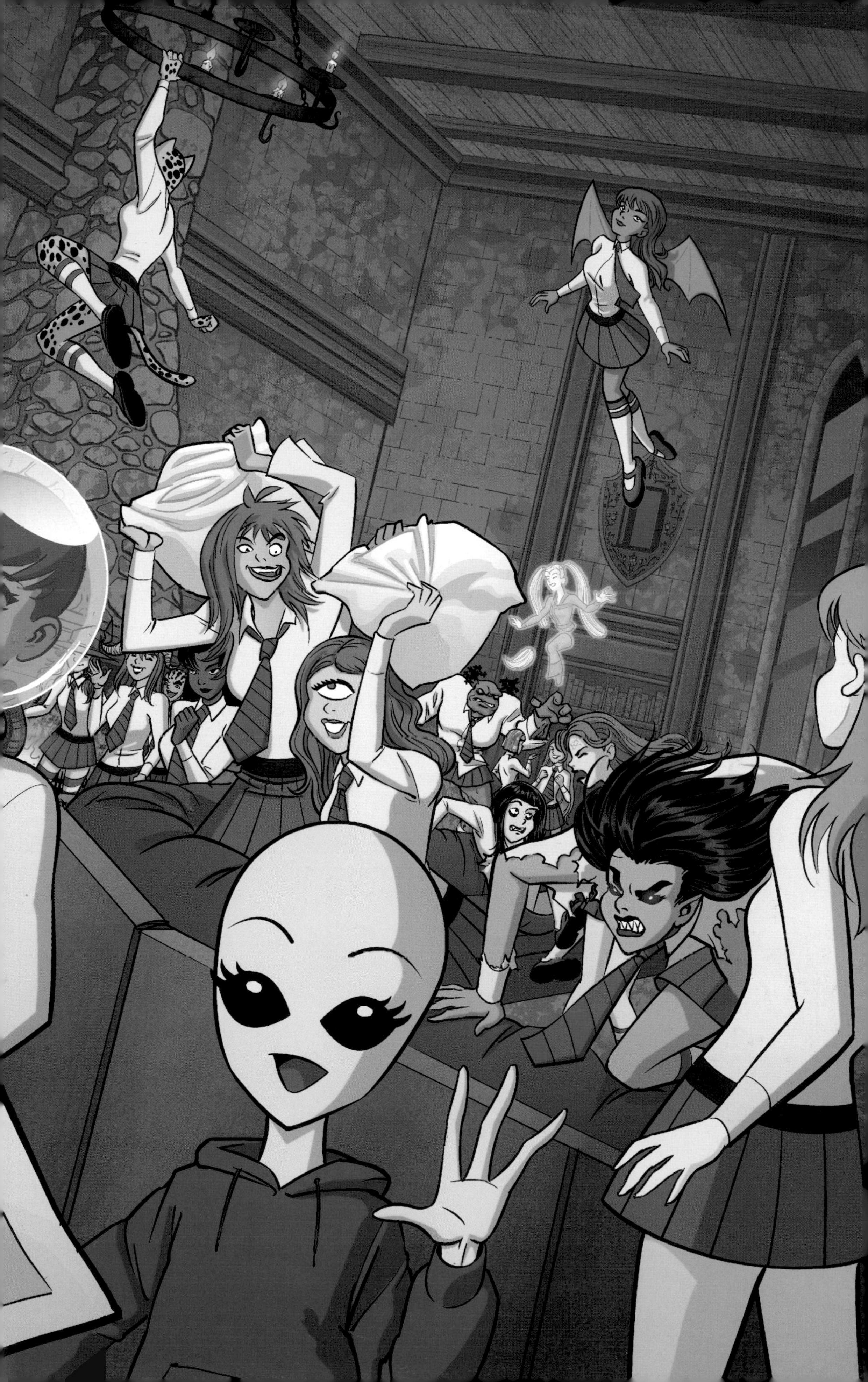

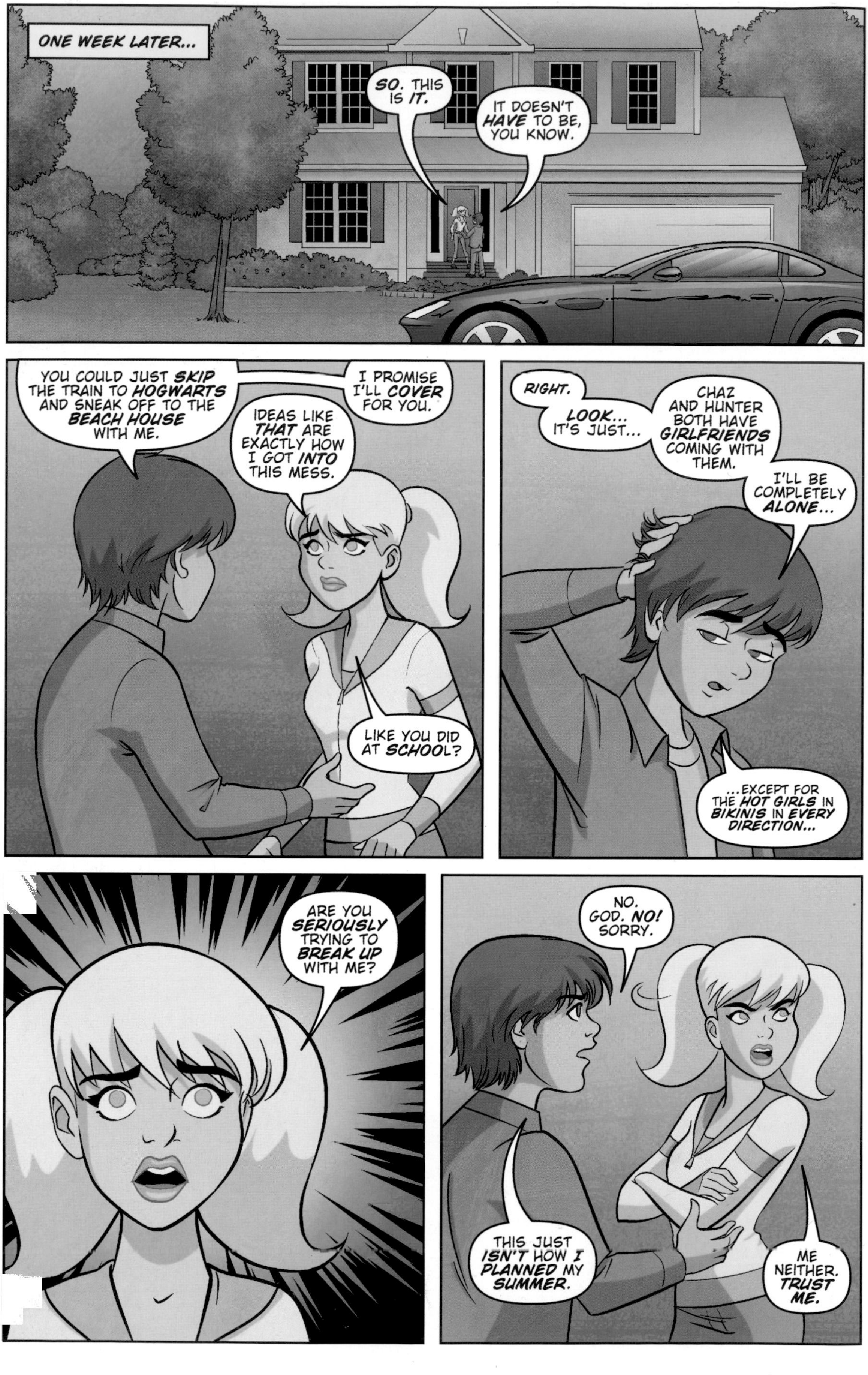
ONE WEEK LATER...
SO. THIS IS IT.
IT DOESN'T HAVE TO BE, YOU KNOW.
YOU COULD JUST SKIP THE TRAIN TO HOGWARTS AND SNEAK OFF TO THE BEACH HOUSE WITH ME.
I PROMISE I'LL COVER FOR YOU.
IDEAS LIKE THAT ARE EXACTLY HOW I GOT INTO THIS MESS.
LIKE YOU DID AT SCHOOL?
RIGHT.
LOOK... IT'S JUST...
CHAZ AND HUNTER BOTH HAVE GIRLFRIENDS COMING WITH THEM.
I'LL BE COMPLETELY ALONE...
...EXCEPT FOR THE HOT GIRLS IN BIKINIS IN EVERY DIRECTION...
ARE YOU SERIOUSLY TRYING TO BREAK UP WITH ME?
NO. GOD. NO! SORRY.
THIS JUST ISN'T HOW I PLANNED MY SUMMER.
ME NEITHER. TRUST ME.

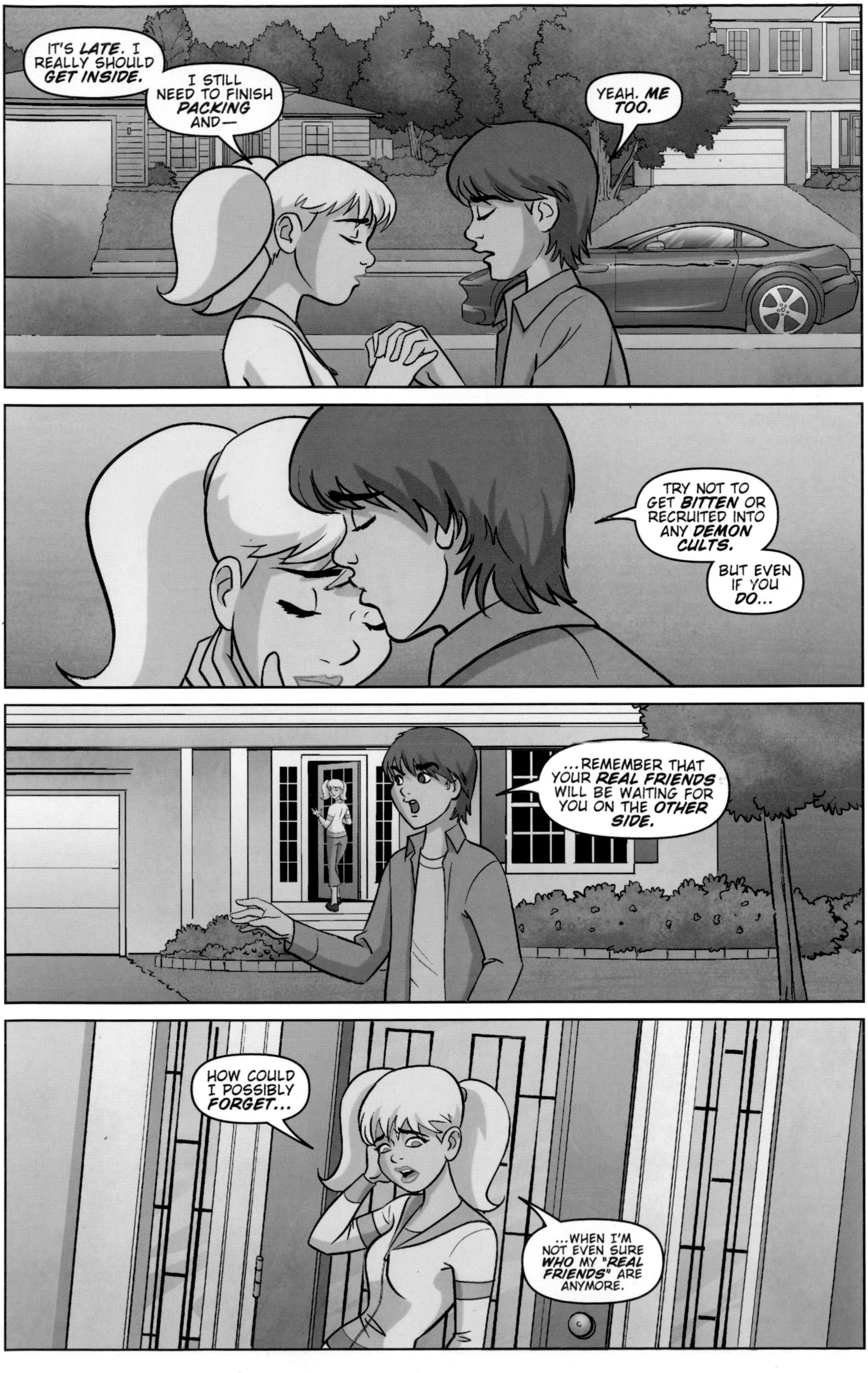
IT'S LATE. I REALLY SHOULD GET INSIDE.
I STILL NEED TO FINISH PACKING AND—
YEAH. ME TOO.
TRY NOT TO GET BITTEN OR RECRUITED INTO ANY DEMON CULTS.
BUT EVEN IF YOU DO...
...REMEMBER THAT YOUR REAL FRIENDS WILL BE WAITING FOR YOU ON THE OTHER SIDE.
HOW COULD I POSSIBLY FORGET...
...WHEN I'M NOT EVEN SURE WHO MY "REAL FRIENDS" ARE ANYMORE.

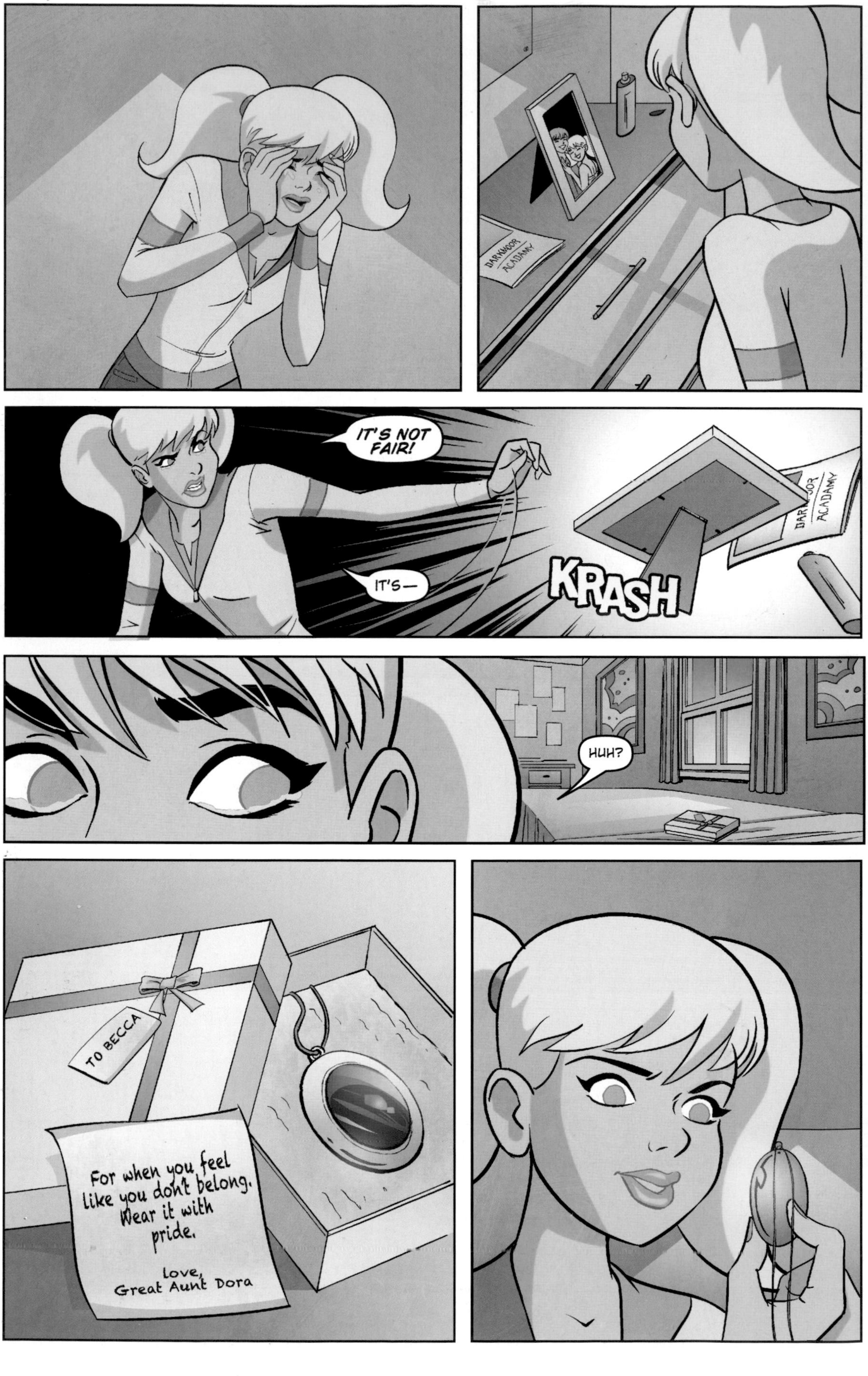
DARKMOOR ACADAMY
IT'S NOT FAIR!
IT'S—
DARKMOOR ACADAMY
KRASH
HUH?
TO BECCA
For when you feel like you don't belong. Wear it with pride.
Love, Great Aunt Dora

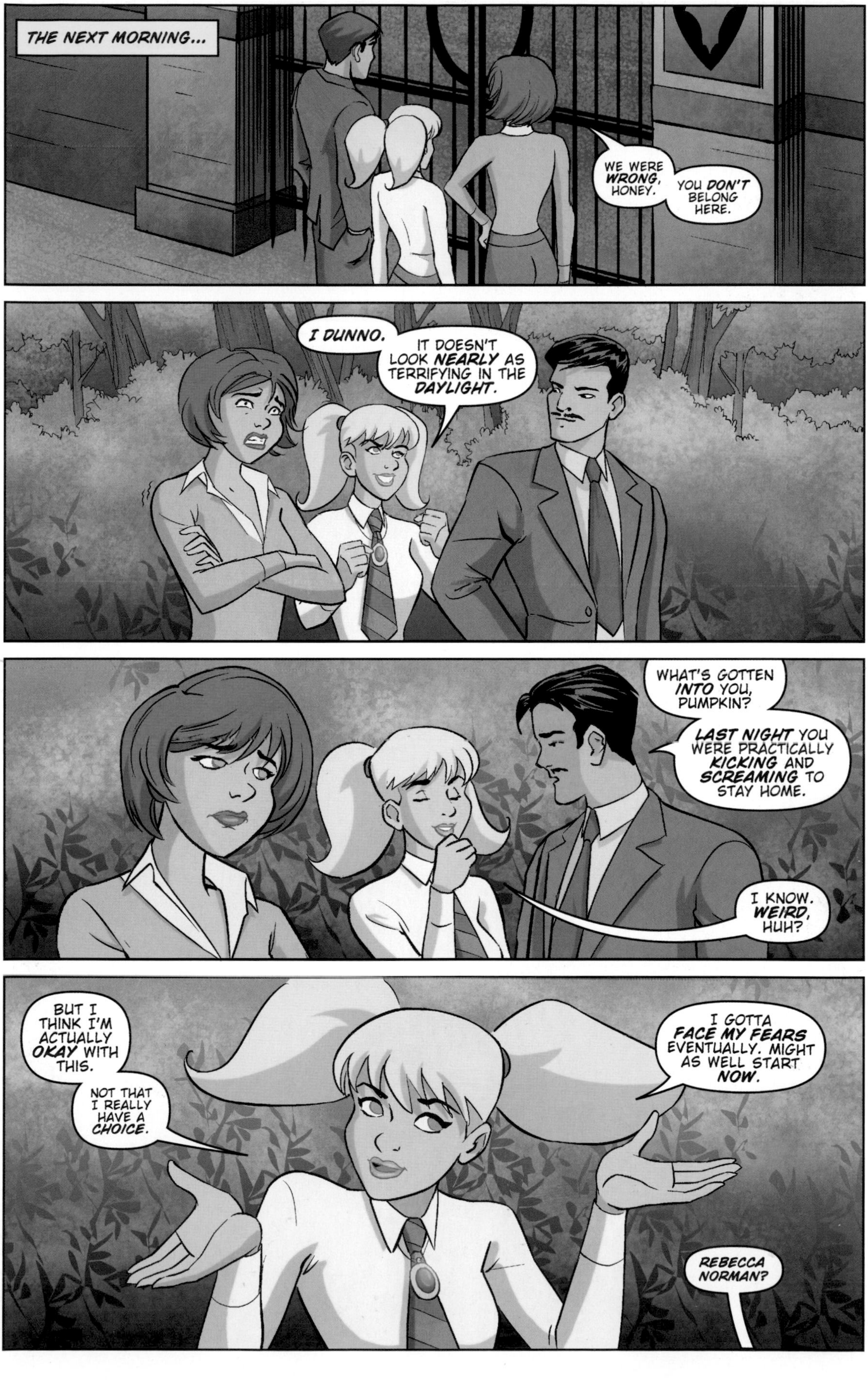
THE NEXT MORNING...
WE WERE WRONG, HONEY.
YOU DON'T BELONG HERE.
I DUNNO.
IT DOESN'T LOOK NEARLY AS TERRIFYING IN THE DAYLIGHT.
WHAT'S GOTTEN INTO YOU, PUMPKIN?
LAST NIGHT YOU WERE PRACTICALLY KICKING AND SCREAMING TO STAY HOME.
I KNOW. WEIRD, HUH?
BUT I THINK I'M ACTUALLY OKAY WITH THIS.
NOT THAT I REALLY HAVE A CHOICE.
I GOTTA FACE MY FEARS EVENTUALLY. MIGHT AS WELL START NOW.
REBECCA NORMAN?

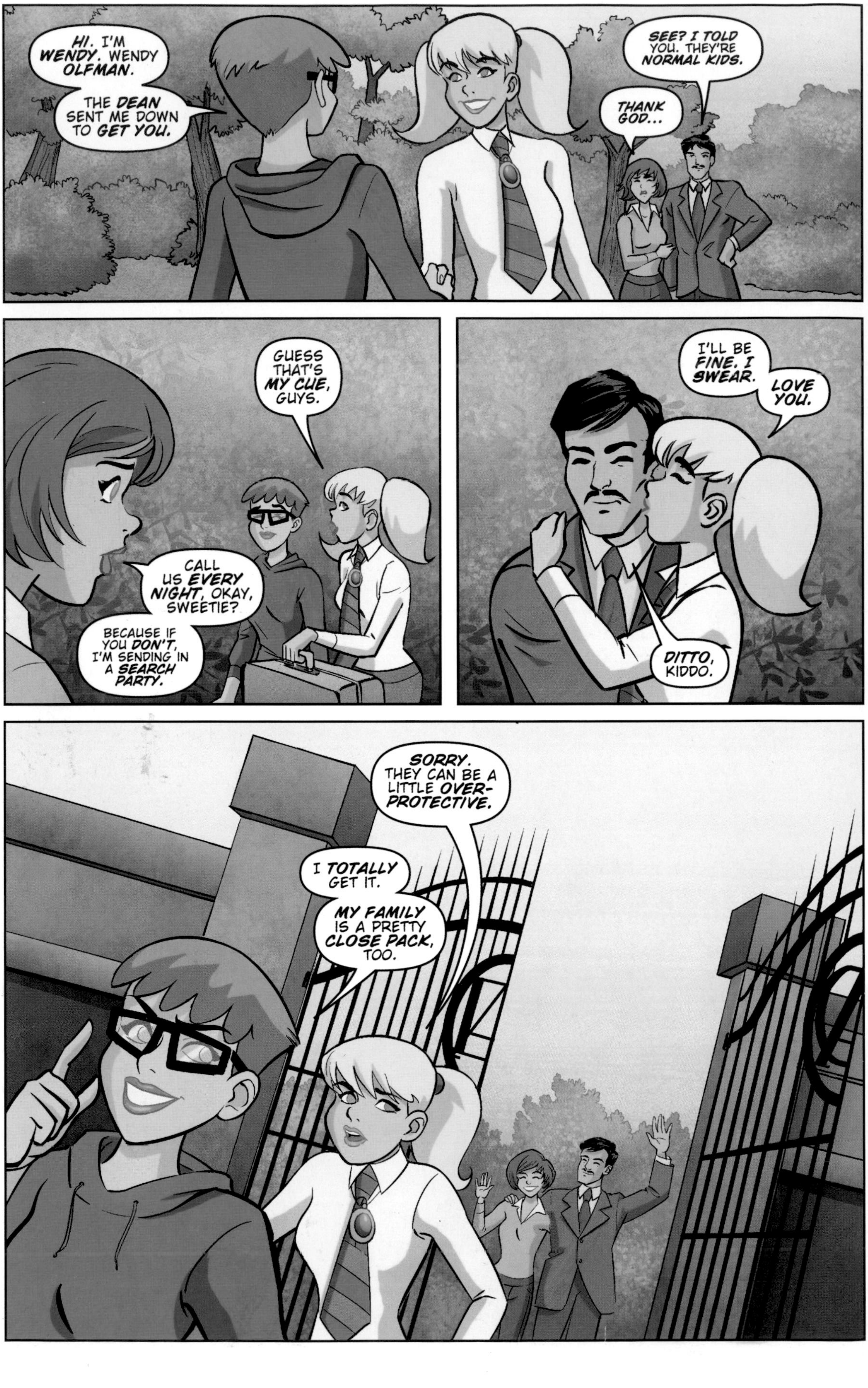
HI. I'M WENDY. WENDY OLFMAN.
THE DEAN SENT ME DOWN TO GET YOU.
SEE? I TOLD YOU. THEY'RE NORMAL KIDS.
THANK GOD...
GUESS THAT'S MY CUE, GUYS.
CALL US EVERY NIGHT, OKAY, SWEETIE?
BECAUSE IF YOU DON'T, I'M SENDING IN A SEARCH PARTY.
I'LL BE FINE. I SWEAR.
LOVE YOU.
DITTO, KIDDO.
SORRY. THEY CAN BE A LITTLE OVER-PROTECTIVE.
I TOTALLY GET IT.
MY FAMILY IS A PRETTY CLOSE PACK, TOO.

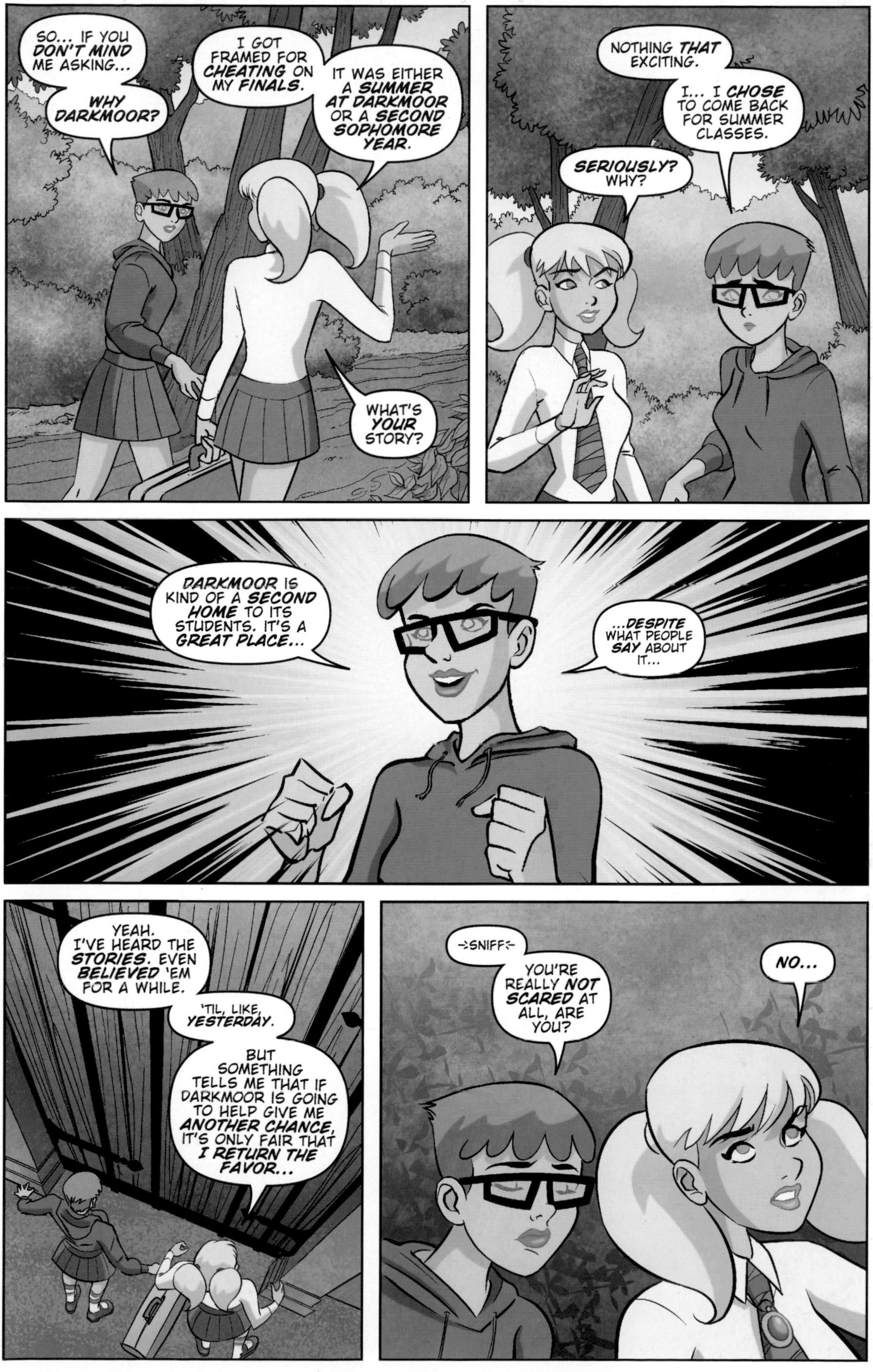
SO... IF YOU DON'T MIND ME ASKING...
WHY DARKMOOR?
I GOT FRAMED FOR CHEATING ON MY FINALS.
IT WAS EITHER A SUMMER AT DARKMOOR OR A SECOND SOPHOMORE YEAR.
WHAT'S YOUR STORY?
NOTHING THAT EXCITING.
I... I CHOSE TO COME BACK FOR SUMMER CLASSES.
SERIOUSLY? WHY?
DARKMOOR IS KIND OF A SECOND HOME TO ITS STUDENTS. IT'S A GREAT PLACE...
...DESPITE WHAT PEOPLE SAY ABOUT IT...
YEAH. I'VE HEARD THE STORIES. EVEN BELIEVED 'EM FOR A WHILE.
'TIL, LIKE, YESTERDAY.
BUT SOMETHING TELLS ME THAT IF DARKMOOR IS GOING TO HELP GIVE ME ANOTHER CHANCE, IT'S ONLY FAIR THAT I RETURN THE FAVOR...
-SNIFF-
YOU'RE REALLY NOT SCARED AT ALL, ARE YOU?
NO...

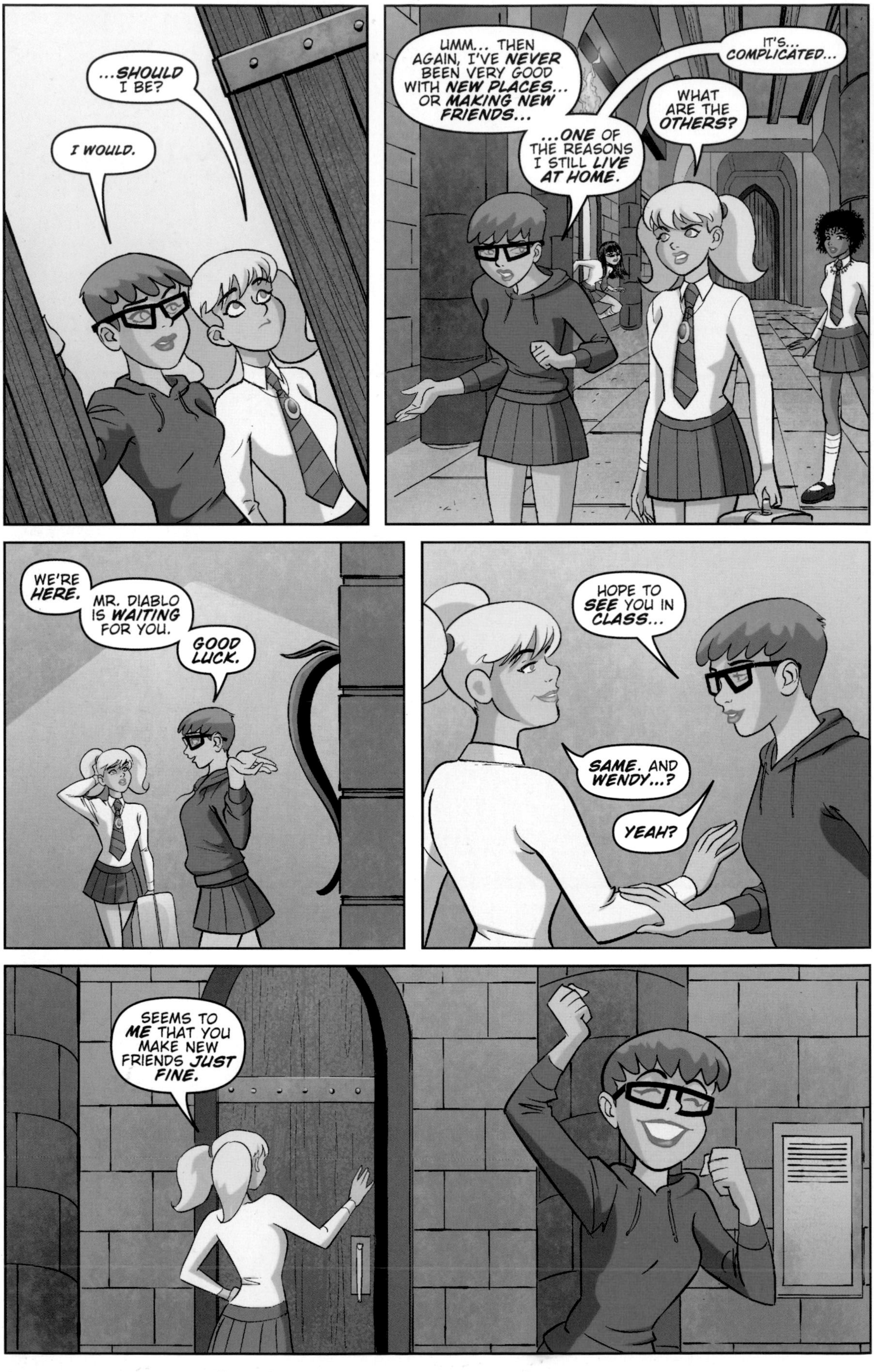
...SHOULD I BE?
I WOULD.
UMM... THEN AGAIN, I'VE NEVER BEEN VERY GOOD WITH NEW PLACES... OR MAKING NEW FRIENDS...
...ONE OF THE REASONS I STILL LIVE AT HOME.
WHAT ARE THE OTHERS?
IT'S... COMPLICATED...
WE'RE HERE.
MR. DIABLO IS WAITING FOR YOU.
GOOD LUCK.
HOPE TO SEE YOU IN CLASS...
SAME. AND WENDY...?
YEAH?
SEEMS TO ME THAT YOU MAKE NEW FRIENDS JUST FINE.

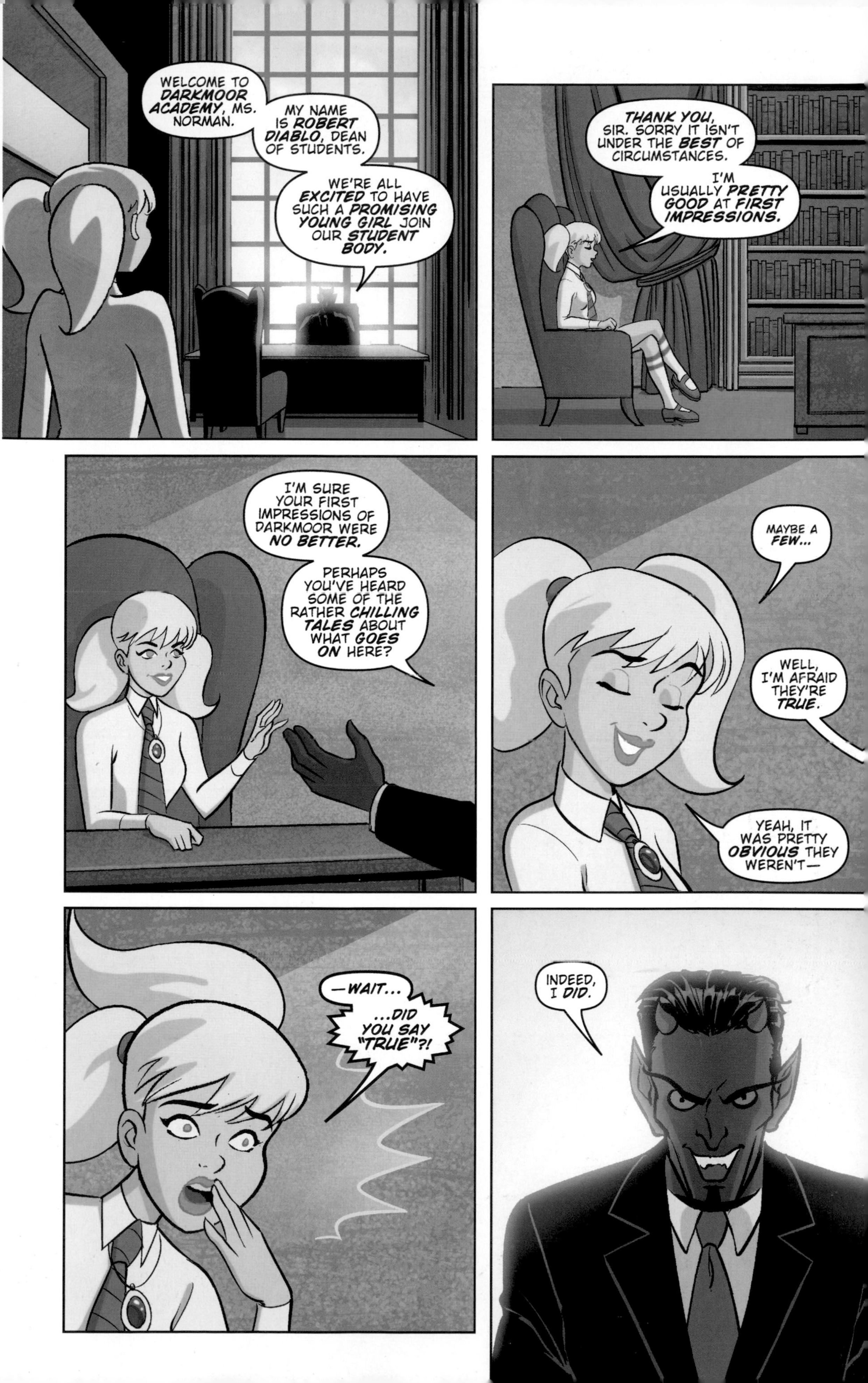

WELCOME TO DARKMOOR ACADEMY, MS. NORMAN.
MY NAME IS ROBERT DIABLO, DEAN OF STUDENTS.
WE'RE ALL EXCITED TO HAVE SUCH A PROMISING YOUNG GIRL JOIN OUR STUDENT BODY.
THANK YOU, SIR. SORRY IT ISN'T UNDER THE BEST OF CIRCUMSTANCES.
I'M USUALLY PRETTY GOOD AT FIRST IMPRESSIONS.
I'M SURE YOUR FIRST IMPRESSIONS OF DARKMOOR WERE NO BETTER.
PERHAPS YOU'VE HEARD SOME OF THE RATHER CHILLING TALES ABOUT WHAT GOES ON HERE?
MAYBE A FEW...
WELL, I'M AFRAID THEY'RE TRUE.
YEAH, IT WAS PRETTY OBVIOUS THEY WEREN'T—
—WAIT...
...DID YOU SAY "TRUE"?!
INDEED, I DID.

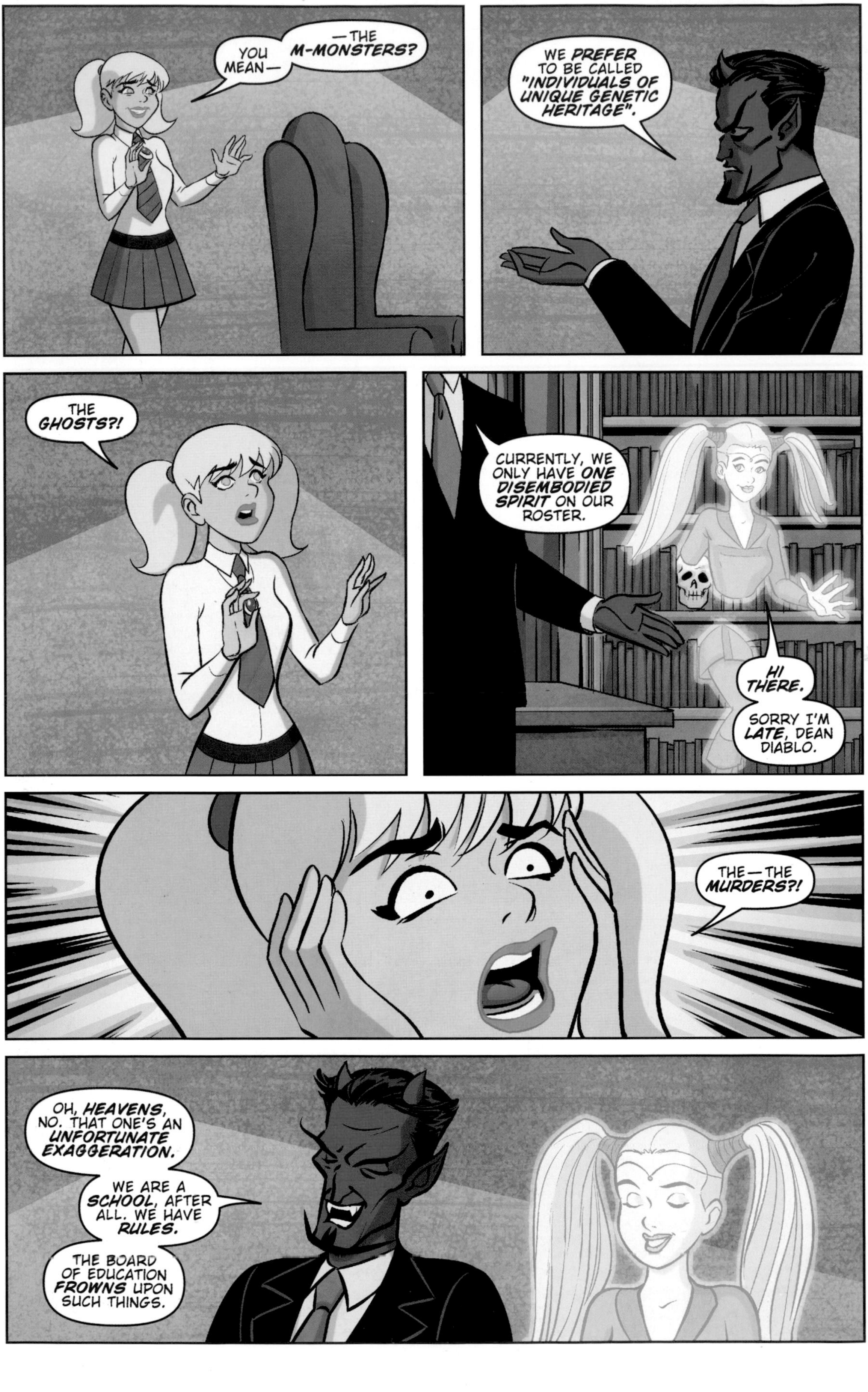
YOU MEAN—
—THE M-MONSTERS?
WE PREFER TO BE CALLED "INDIVIDUALS OF UNIQUE GENETIC HERITAGE".
THE GHOSTS?!
CURRENTLY, WE ONLY HAVE ONE DISEMBODIED SPIRIT ON OUR ROSTER.
HI THERE.
SORRY I'M LATE, DEAN DIABLO.
THE—THE MURDERS?!
OH, HEAVENS, NO. THAT ONE'S AN UNFORTUNATE EXAGGERATION.
WE ARE A SCHOOL, AFTER ALL. WE HAVE RULES.
THE BOARD OF EDUCATION FROWNS UPON SUCH THINGS.

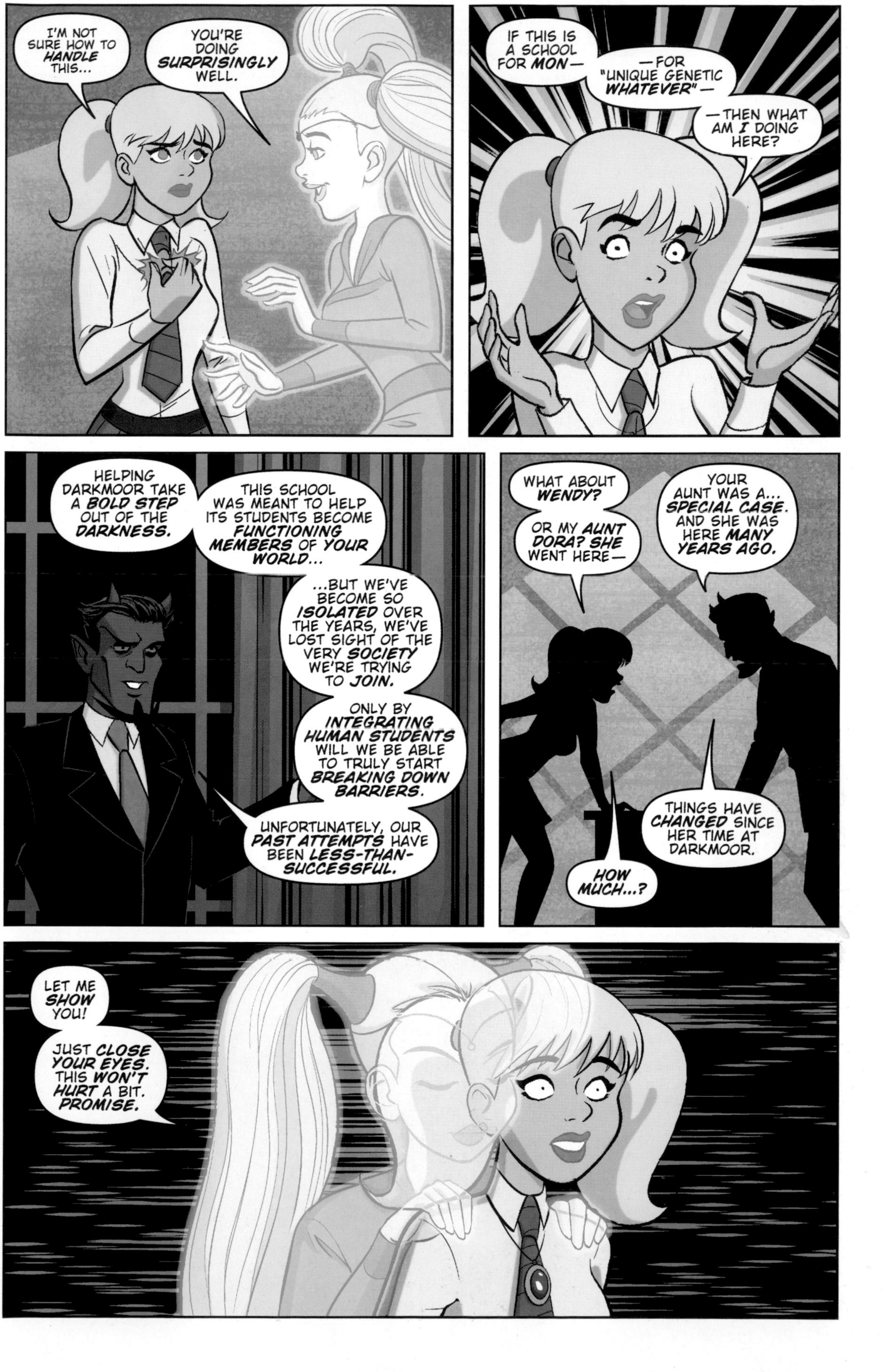

I'M NOT SURE HOW TO HANDLE THIS...
YOU'RE DOING SURPRISINGLY WELL.
IF THIS IS A SCHOOL FOR MON—
—FOR "UNIQUE GENETIC WHATEVER"—
—THEN WHAT AM I DOING HERE?
HELPING DARKMOOR TAKE A BOLD STEP OUT OF THE DARKNESS.
THIS SCHOOL WAS MEANT TO HELP ITS STUDENTS BECOME FUNCTIONING MEMBERS OF YOUR WORLD...
...BUT WE'VE BECOME SO ISOLATED OVER THE YEARS, WE'VE LOST SIGHT OF THE VERY SOCIETY WE'RE TRYING TO JOIN.
ONLY BY INTEGRATING HUMAN STUDENTS WILL WE BE ABLE TO TRULY START BREAKING DOWN BARRIERS.
UNFORTUNATELY, OUR PAST ATTEMPTS HAVE BEEN LESS-THAN-SUCCESSFUL.
WHAT ABOUT WENDY?
OR MY AUNT DORA? SHE WENT HERE—
YOUR AUNT WAS A... SPECIAL CASE. AND SHE WAS HERE MANY YEARS AGO.
THINGS HAVE CHANGED SINCE HER TIME AT DARKMOOR.
HOW MUCH...?
LET ME SHOW YOU!
JUST CLOSE YOUR EYES. THIS WON'T HURT A BIT. PROMISE.

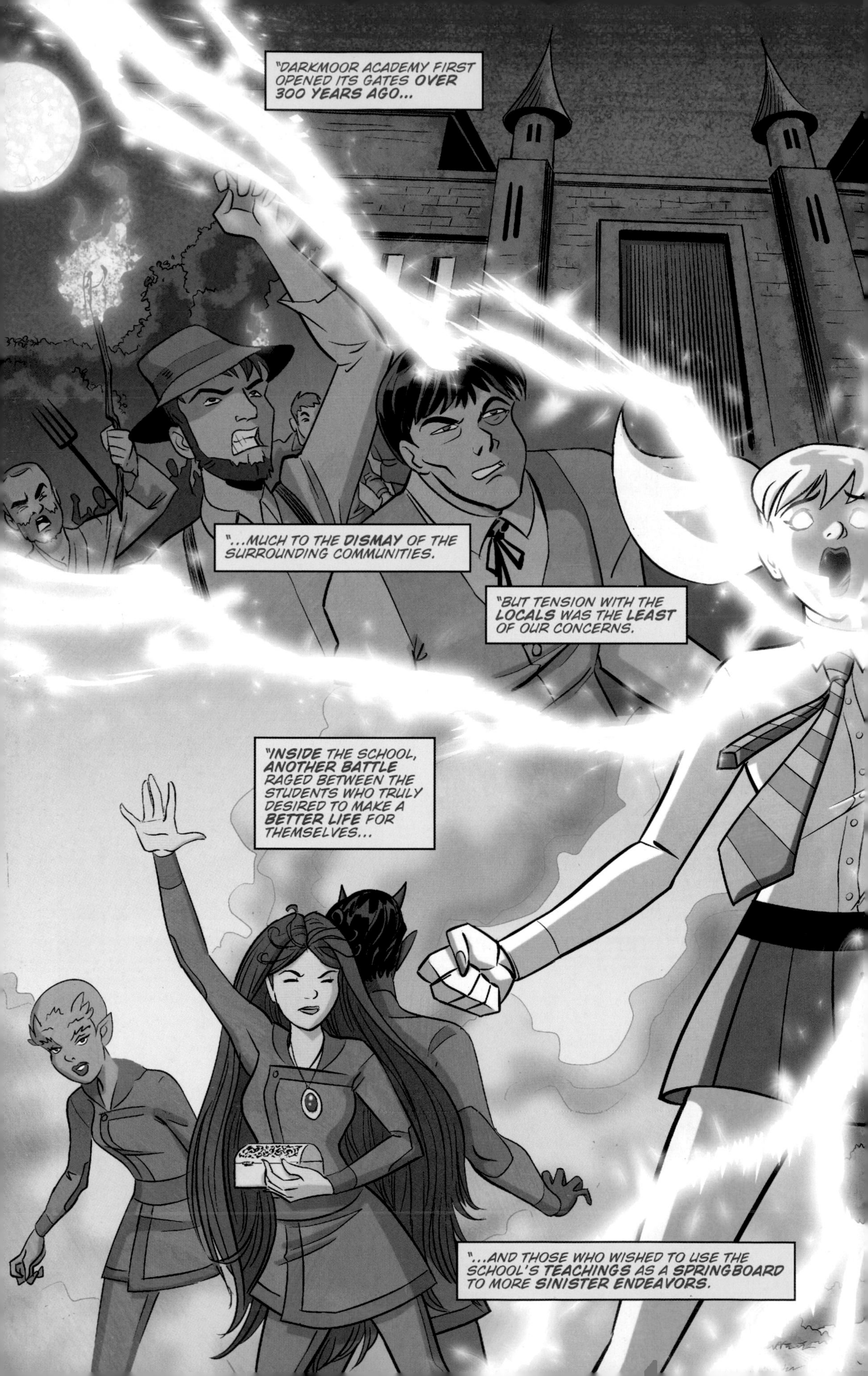
"DARKMOOR ACADEMY FIRST OPENED ITS GATES OVER 300 YEARS AGO...
"...MUCH TO THE DISMAY OF THE SURROUNDING COMMUNITIES.
"BUT TENSION WITH THE LOCALS WAS THE LEAST OF OUR CONCERNS.
"INSIDE THE SCHOOL, ANOTHER BATTLE RAGED BETWEEN THE STUDENTS WHO TRULY DESIRED TO MAKE A BETTER LIFE FOR THEMSELVES...
"...AND THOSE WHO WISHED TO USE THE SCHOOL'S TEACHINGS AS A SPRINGBOARD TO MORE SINISTER ENDEAVORS.

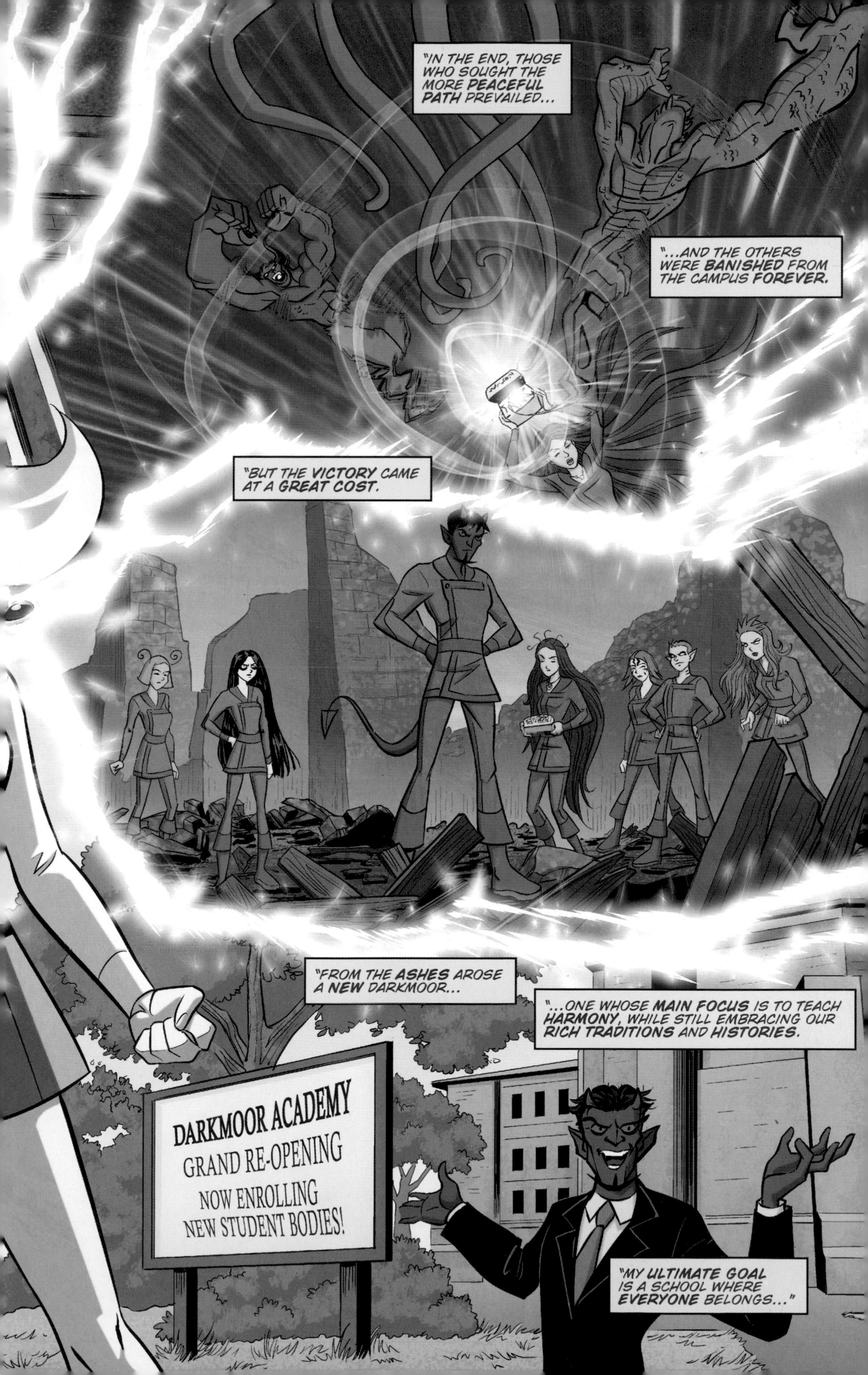
"IN THE END, THOSE WHO SOUGHT THE MORE PEACEFUL PATH PREVAILED...
"...AND THE OTHERS WERE BANISHED FROM THE CAMPUS FOREVER.
"BUT THE VICTORY CAME AT A GREAT COST.
"FROM THE ASHES AROSE A NEW DARKMOOR...
"...ONE WHOSE MAIN FOCUS IS TO TEACH HARMONY, WHILE STILL EMBRACING OUR RICH TRADITIONS AND HISTORIES.
DARKMOOR ACADEMY
GRAND RE-OPENING
NOW ENROLLING
NEW STUDENT BODIES!
"MY ULTIMATE GOAL IS A SCHOOL WHERE EVERYONE BELONGS..."

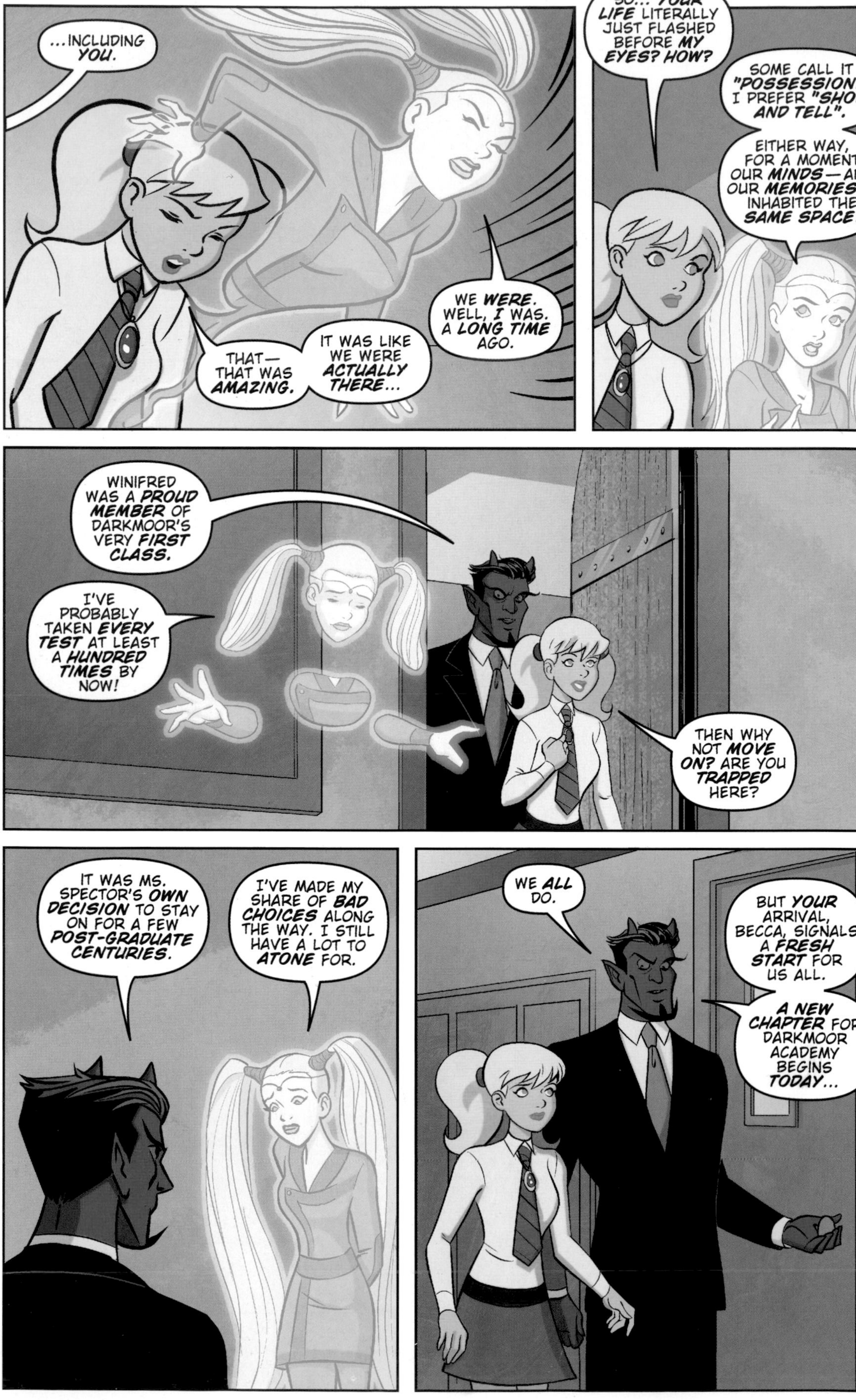
...INCLUDING YOU.
THAT— THAT WAS AMAZING.
IT WAS LIKE WE WERE ACTUALLY THERE...
WE WERE. WELL, I WAS. A LONG TIME AGO.
SO... YOUR LIFE LITERALLY JUST FLASHED BEFORE MY EYES? HOW?
SOME CALL IT "POSSESSION." I PREFER "SHOW AND TELL".
EITHER WAY, FOR A MOMENT OUR MINDS—AND OUR MEMORIES—INHABITED THE SAME SPACE.
WINIFRED WAS A PROUD MEMBER OF DARKMOOR'S VERY FIRST CLASS.
I'VE PROBABLY TAKEN EVERY TEST AT LEAST A HUNDRED TIMES BY NOW!
THEN WHY NOT MOVE ON? ARE YOU TRAPPED HERE?
IT WAS MS. SPECTOR'S OWN DECISION TO STAY ON FOR A FEW POST-GRADUATE CENTURIES.
I'VE MADE MY SHARE OF BAD CHOICES ALONG THE WAY. I STILL HAVE A LOT TO ATONE FOR.
WE ALL DO.
BUT YOUR ARRIVAL, BECCA, SIGNALS A FRESH START FOR US ALL.
A NEW CHAPTER FOR DARKMOOR ACADEMY BEGINS TODAY...

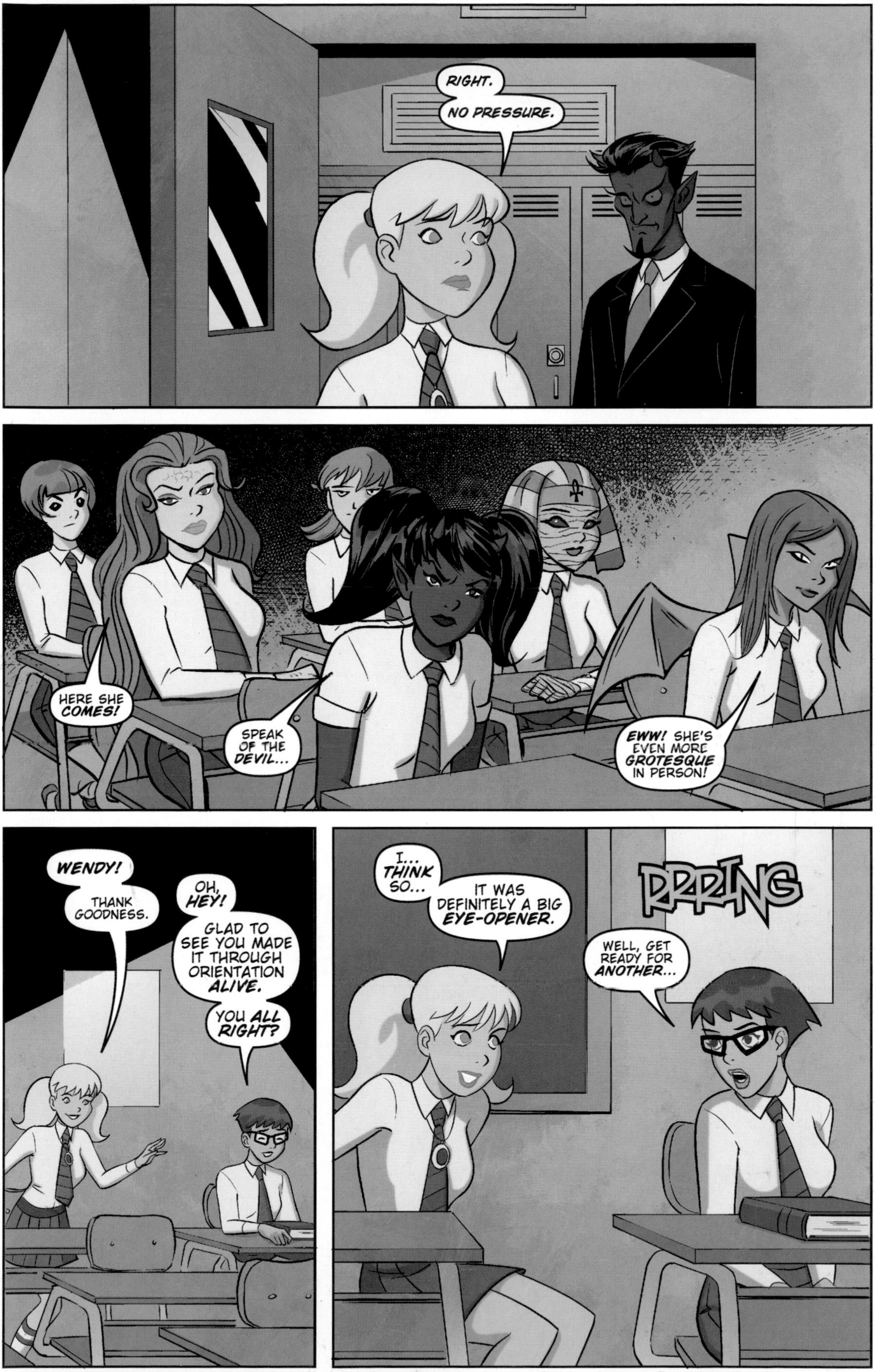
RIGHT.
NO PRESSURE.
HERE SHE COMES!
SPEAK OF THE DEVIL...
EWW! SHE'S EVEN MORE GROTESQUE IN PERSON!
WENDY!
THANK GOODNESS.
OH, HEY!
GLAD TO SEE YOU MADE IT THROUGH ORIENTATION ALIVE.
YOU ALL RIGHT?
I... THINK SO...
IT WAS DEFINITELY A BIG EYE-OPENER.
RRRING
WELL, GET READY FOR ANOTHER...

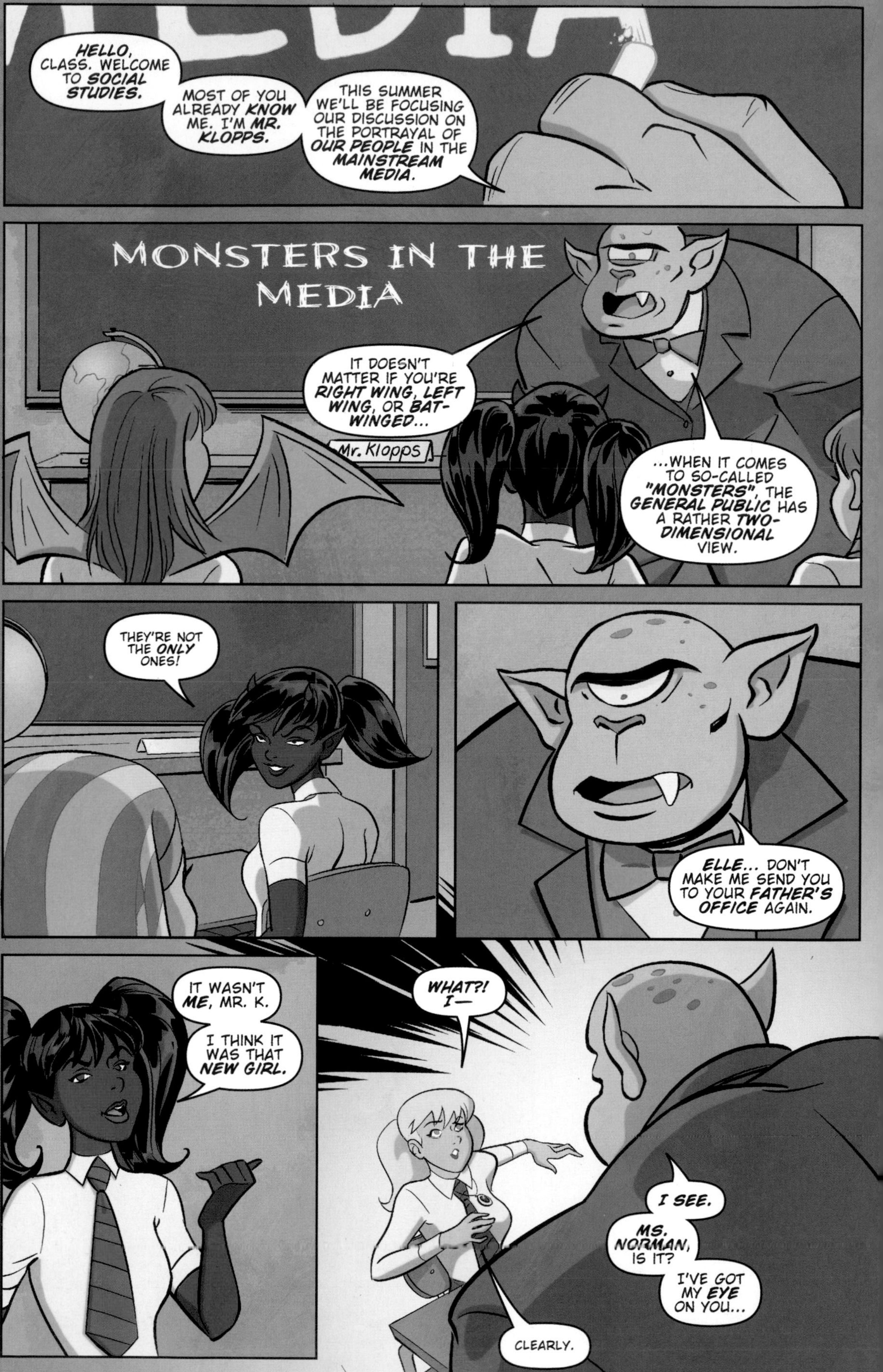
HELLO, CLASS. WELCOME TO SOCIAL STUDIES.
MOST OF YOU ALREADY KNOW ME. I'M MR. KLOPPS.
THIS SUMMER WE'LL BE FOCUSING OUR DISCUSSION ON THE PORTRAYAL OF OUR PEOPLE IN THE MAINSTREAM MEDIA.
MONSTERS IN THE MEDIA
IT DOESN'T MATTER IF YOU'RE RIGHT WING, LEFT WING, OR BAT-WINGED...
Mr. Klopps
...WHEN IT COMES TO SO-CALLED "MONSTERS", THE GENERAL PUBLIC HAS A RATHER TWO-DIMENSIONAL VIEW.
THEY'RE NOT THE ONLY ONES!
ELLE... DON'T MAKE ME SEND YOU TO YOUR FATHER'S OFFICE AGAIN.
IT WASN'T ME, MR. K.
I THINK IT WAS THAT NEW GIRL.
WHAT?! I—
I SEE.
MS. NORMAN, IS IT?
I'VE GOT MY EYE ON YOU...
CLEARLY.

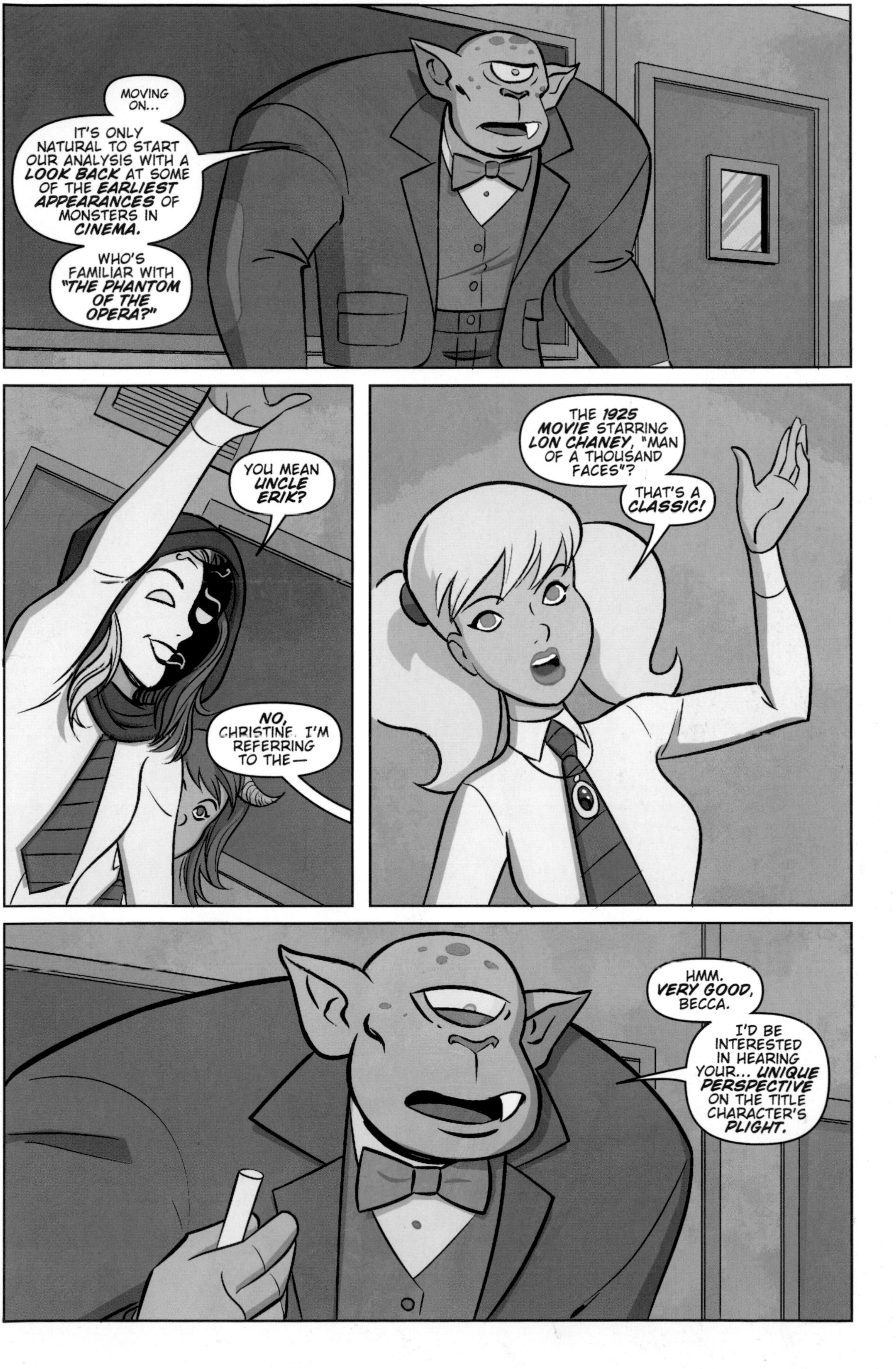
MOVING ON...
IT'S ONLY NATURAL TO START OUR ANALYSIS WITH A LOOK BACK AT SOME OF THE EARLIEST APPEARANCES OF MONSTERS IN CINEMA.
WHO'S FAMILIAR WITH "THE PHANTOM OF THE OPERA?"
YOU MEAN UNCLE ERIK?
NO, CHRISTINE. I'M REFERRING TO THE—
THE 1925 MOVIE STARRING LON CHANEY, "MAN OF A THOUSAND FACES"?
THAT'S A CLASSIC!
HMM. VERY GOOD, BECCA.
I'D BE INTERESTED IN HEARING YOUR... UNIQUE PERSPECTIVE ON THE TITLE CHARACTER'S PLIGHT.

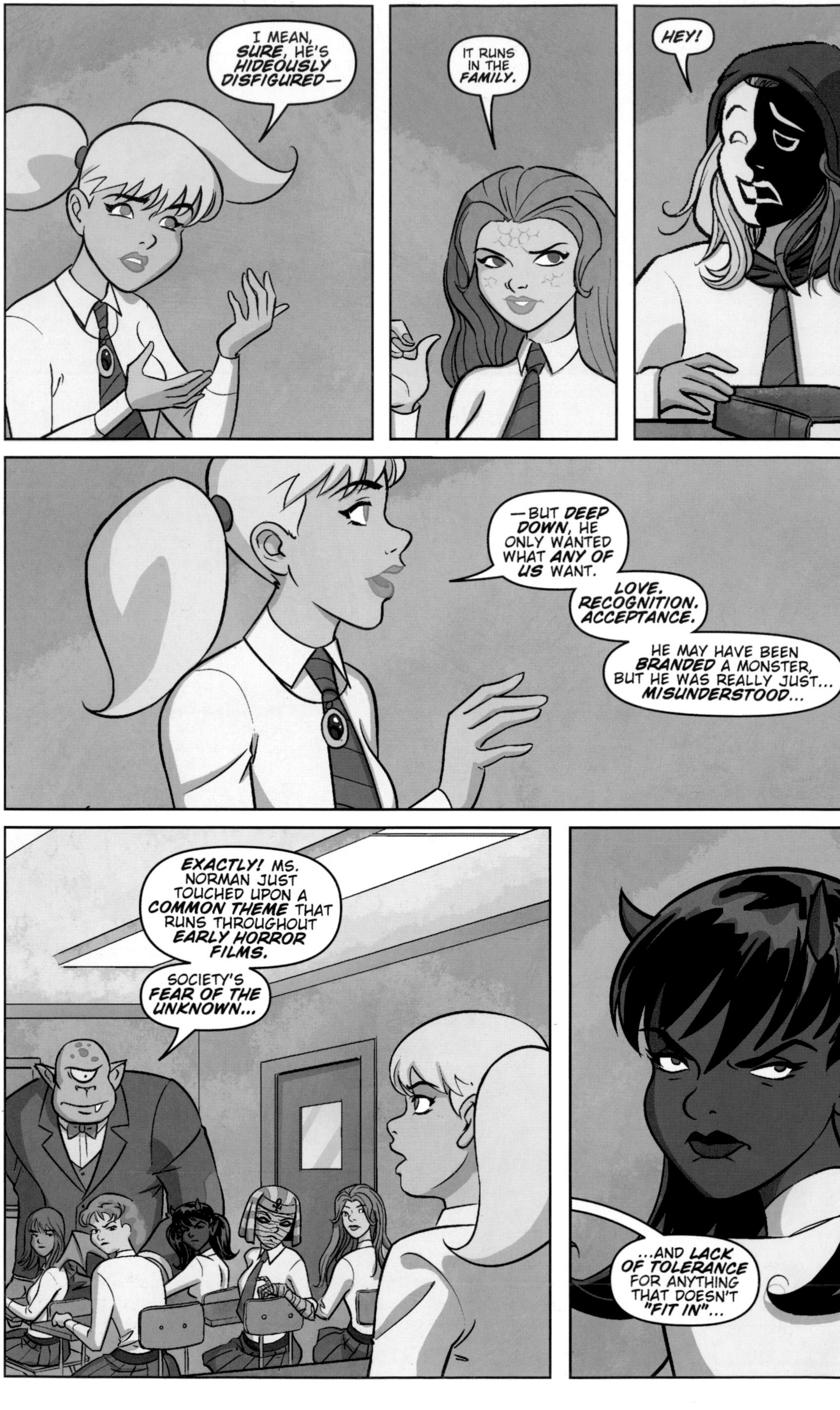
I MEAN, SURE, HE'S HIDEOUSLY DISFIGURED—
IT RUNS IN THE FAMILY.
HEY!
—BUT DEEP DOWN, HE ONLY WANTED WHAT ANY OF US WANT.
LOVE. RECOGNITION. ACCEPTANCE.
HE MAY HAVE BEEN BRANDED A MONSTER, BUT HE WAS REALLY JUST... MISUNDERSTOOD...
EXACTLY! MS. NORMAN JUST TOUCHED UPON A COMMON THEME THAT RUNS THROUGHOUT EARLY HORROR FILMS.
SOCIETY'S FEAR OF THE UNKNOWN...
...AND LACK OF TOLERANCE FOR ANYTHING THAT DOESN'T "FIT IN"...

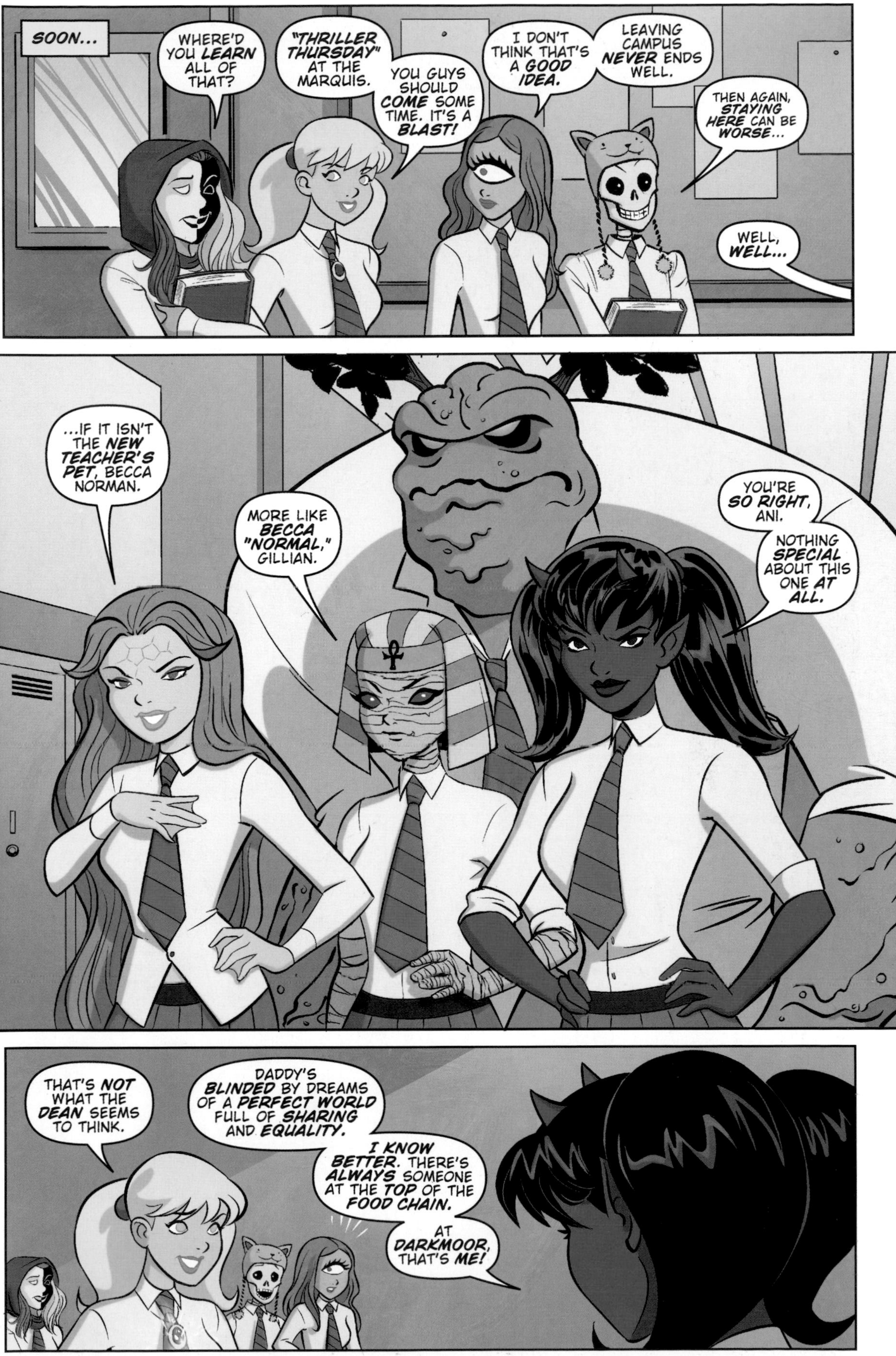
SOON...
WHERE'D YOU LEARN ALL OF THAT?
"THRILLER THURSDAY" AT THE MARQUIS.
YOU GUYS SHOULD COME SOME TIME. IT'S A BLAST!
I DON'T THINK THAT'S A GOOD IDEA.
LEAVING CAMPUS NEVER ENDS WELL.
THEN AGAIN, STAYING HERE CAN BE WORSE...
WELL, WELL...
...IF IT ISN'T THE NEW TEACHER'S PET, BECCA NORMAN.
MORE LIKE BECCA "NORMAL," GILLIAN.
YOU'RE SO RIGHT, ANI.
NOTHING SPECIAL ABOUT THIS ONE AT ALL.
THAT'S NOT WHAT THE DEAN SEEMS TO THINK.
DADDY'S BLINDED BY DREAMS OF A PERFECT WORLD FULL OF SHARING AND EQUALITY.
I KNOW BETTER. THERE'S ALWAYS SOMEONE AT THE TOP OF THE FOOD CHAIN.
AT DARKMOOR, THAT'S ME!

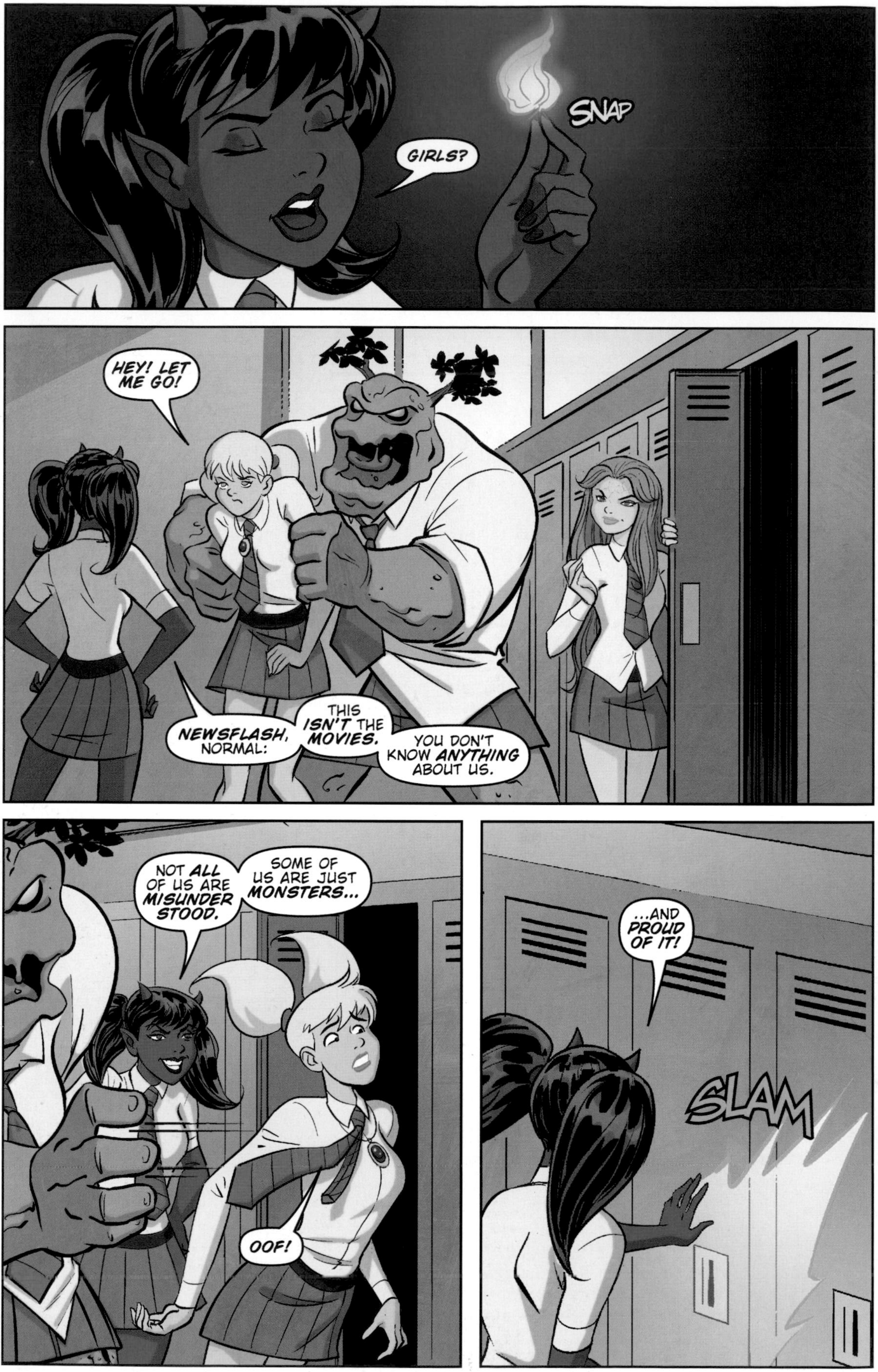
SNAP
GIRLS?
HEY! LET ME GO!
NEWSFLASH, NORMAL:
THIS ISN'T THE MOVIES.
YOU DON'T KNOW ANYTHING ABOUT US.
NOT ALL OF US ARE MISUNDER STOOD.
SOME OF US ARE JUST MONSTERS...
OOF!
...AND PROUD OF IT!
SLAM

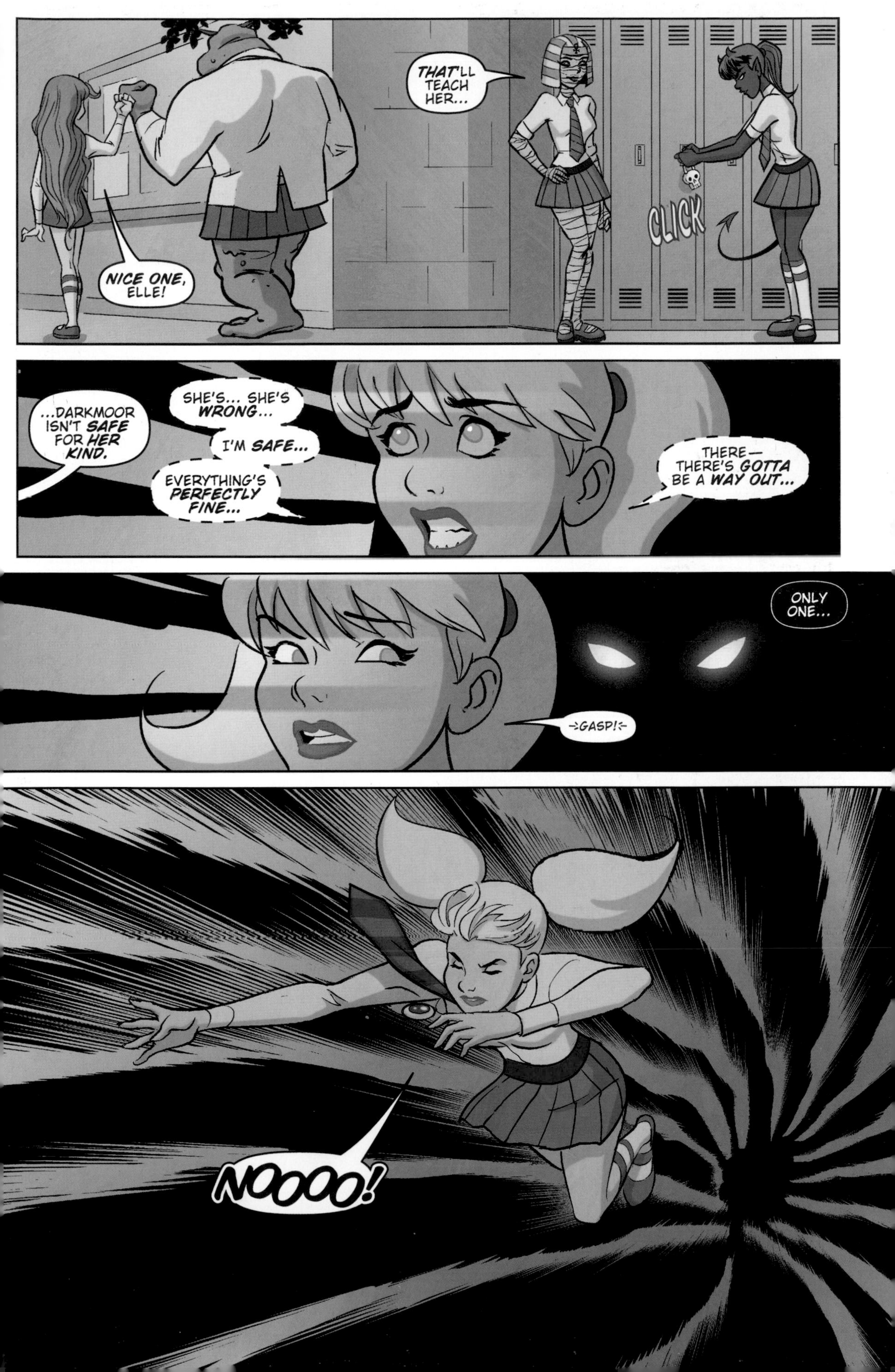
THAT'LL TEACH HER...
NICE ONE, ELLE!
CLICK
...DARKMOOR ISN'T SAFE FOR HER KIND.
SHE'S... SHE'S WRONG...
I'M SAFE...
EVERYTHING'S PERFECTLY FINE...
THERE— THERE'S GOTTA BE A WAY OUT...
ONLY ONE...
GASP!
NOOOO!

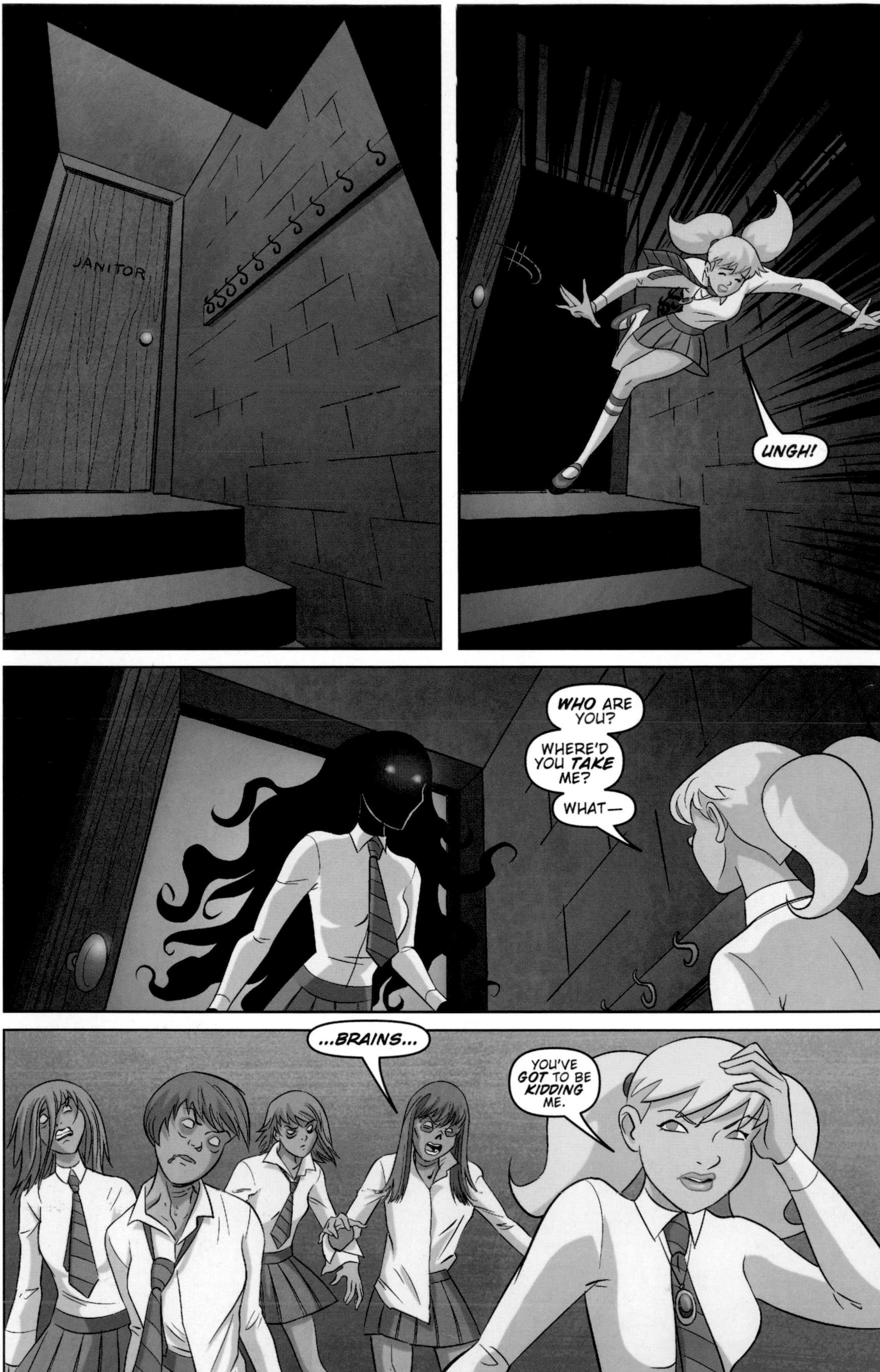
JANITOR
UNGH!
WHO ARE YOU?
WHERE'D YOU TAKE ME?
WHAT—
...BRAINS...
YOU'VE GOT TO BE KIDDING ME.

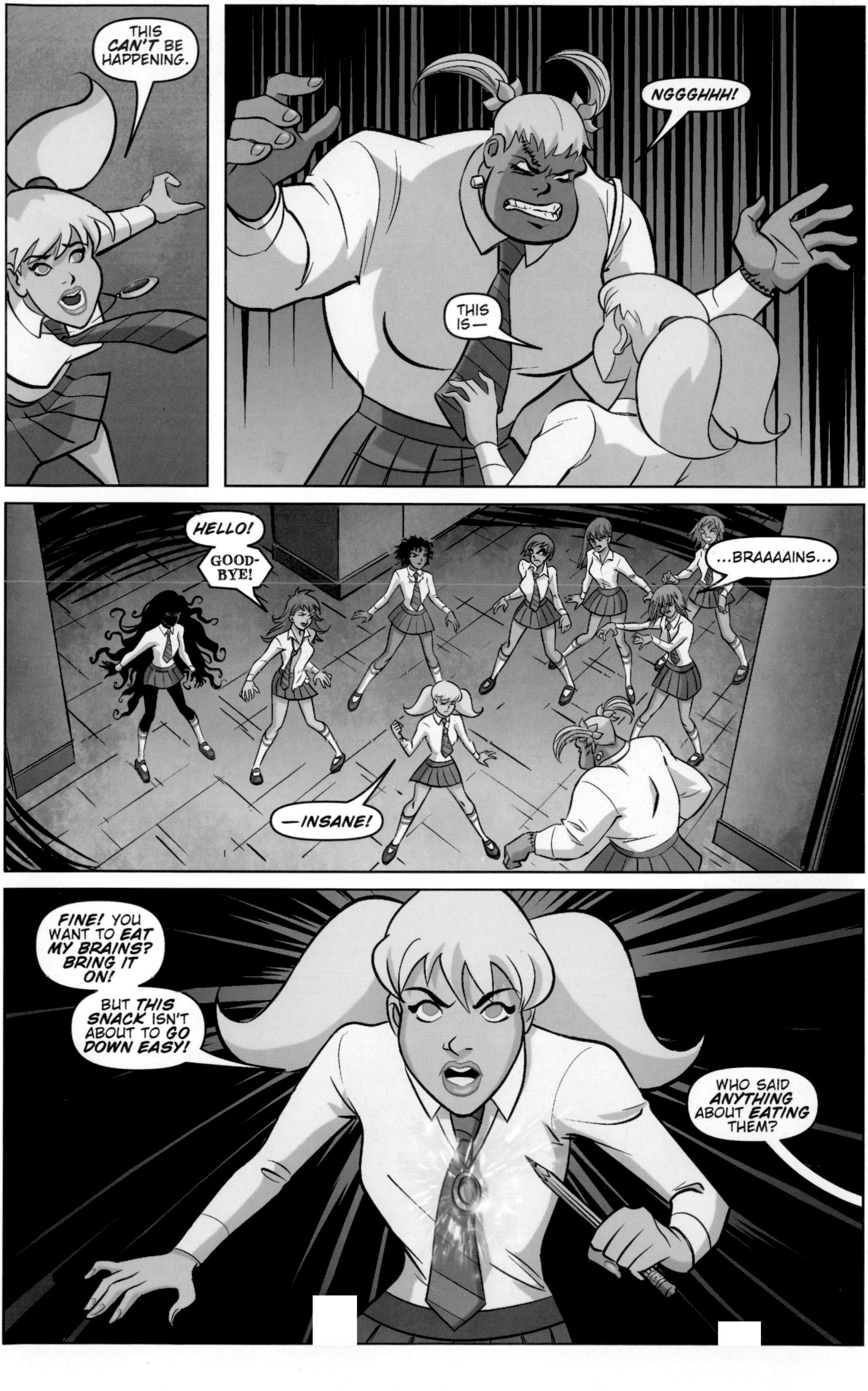
THIS CAN'T BE HAPPENING.
NGGGHHH!
THIS IS—
HELLO!
GOOD-BYE!
...BRAAAAINS...
—INSANE!
FINE! YOU WANT TO EAT MY BRAINS? BRING IT ON!
BUT THIS SNACK ISN'T ABOUT TO GO DOWN EASY!
WHO SAID ANYTHING ABOUT EATING THEM?

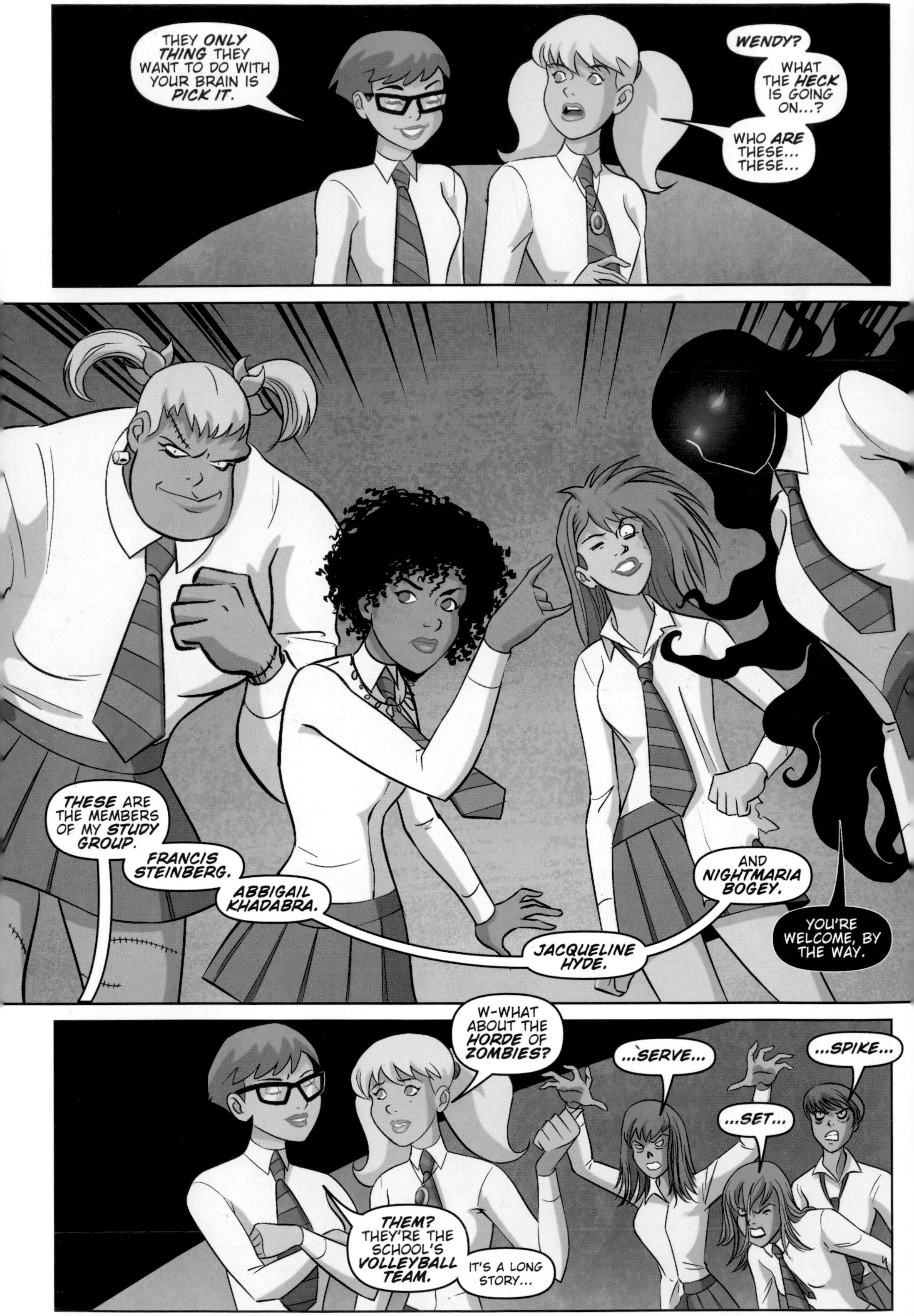
THEY ONLY THING THEY WANT TO DO WITH YOUR BRAIN IS PICK IT.
WENDY?
WHAT THE HECK IS GOING ON...?
WHO ARE THESE... THESE...
THESE ARE THE MEMBERS OF MY STUDY GROUP.
FRANCIS STEINBERG.
ABBIGAIL KHADABRA.
JACQUELINE HYDE.
AND NIGHTMARIA BOGEY.
YOU'RE WELCOME, BY THE WAY.
W-WHAT ABOUT THE HORDE OF ZOMBIES?
...SERVE...
...SPIKE...
...SET...
THEM? THEY'RE THE SCHOOL'S VOLLEYBALL TEAM.
IT'S A LONG STORY...

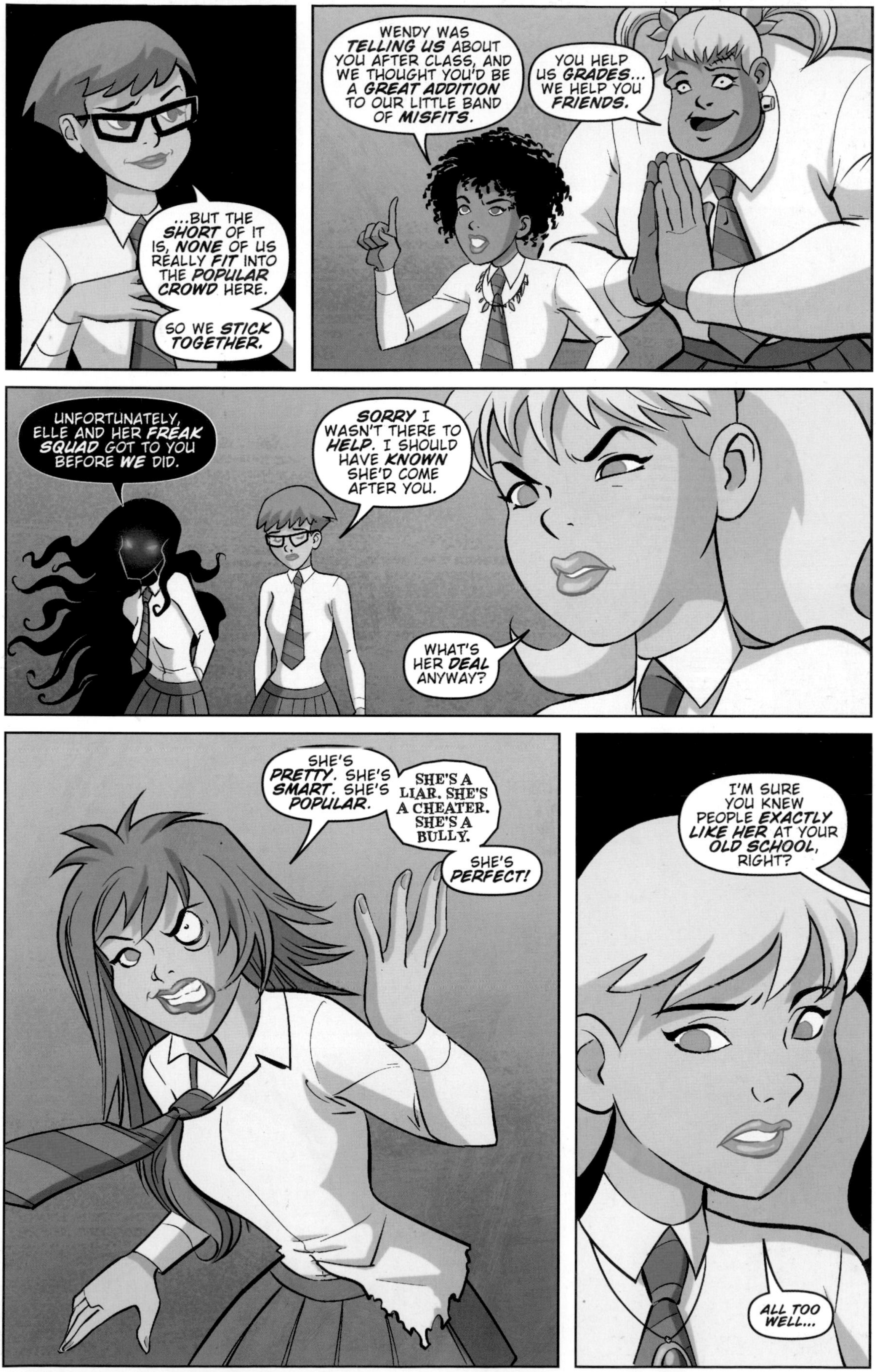
...BUT THE SHORT OF IT IS, NONE OF US REALLY FIT INTO THE POPULAR CROWD HERE.
SO WE STICK TOGETHER.
WENDY WAS TELLING US ABOUT YOU AFTER CLASS, AND WE THOUGHT YOU'D BE A GREAT ADDITION TO OUR LITTLE BAND OF MISFITS.
YOU HELP US GRADES... WE HELP YOU FRIENDS.
UNFORTUNATELY, ELLE AND HER FREAK SQUAD GOT TO YOU BEFORE WE DID.
SORRY I WASN'T THERE TO HELP. I SHOULD HAVE KNOWN SHE'D COME AFTER YOU.
WHAT'S HER DEAL ANYWAY?
SHE'S PRETTY. SHE'S SMART. SHE'S POPULAR.
SHE'S A LIAR. SHE'S A CHEATER. SHE'S A BULLY.
SHE'S PERFECT!
I'M SURE YOU KNEW PEOPLE EXACTLY LIKE HER AT YOUR OLD SCHOOL, RIGHT?
ALL TOO WELL...

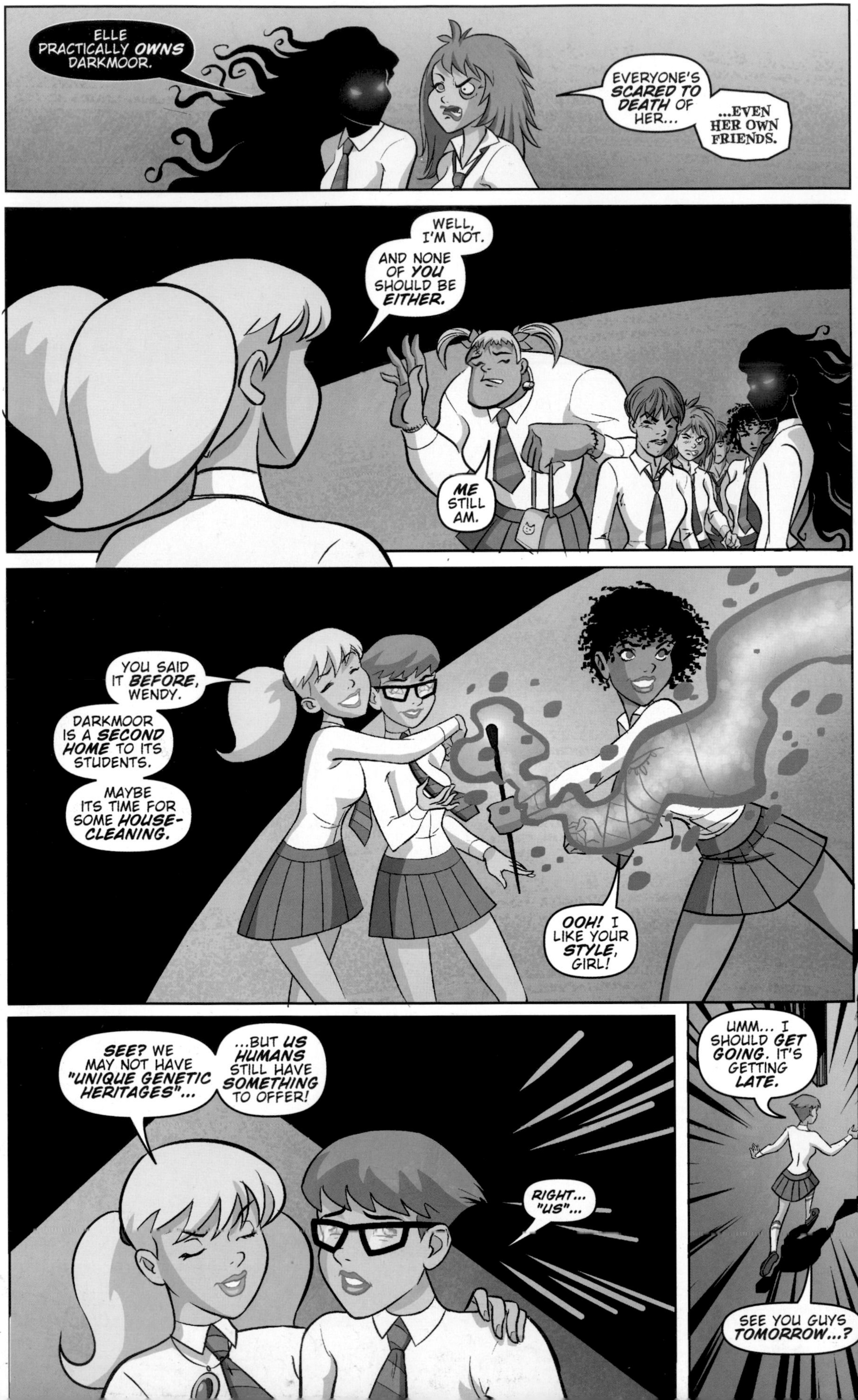
ELLE PRACTICALLY OWNS DARKMOOR.
EVERYONE'S SCARED TO DEATH OF HER...
...EVEN HER OWN FRIENDS.
WELL, I'M NOT.
AND NONE OF YOU SHOULD BE EITHER.
ME STILL AM.
YOU SAID IT BEFORE, WENDY.
DARKMOOR IS A SECOND HOME TO ITS STUDENTS.
MAYBE ITS TIME FOR SOME HOUSE-CLEANING.
OOH! I LIKE YOUR STYLE, GIRL!
SEE? WE MAY NOT HAVE "UNIQUE GENETIC HERITAGES"...
...BUT US HUMANS STILL HAVE SOMETHING TO OFFER!
RIGHT... "US"...
UMM... I SHOULD GET GOING. IT'S GETTING LATE.
SEE YOU GUYS TOMORROW...?

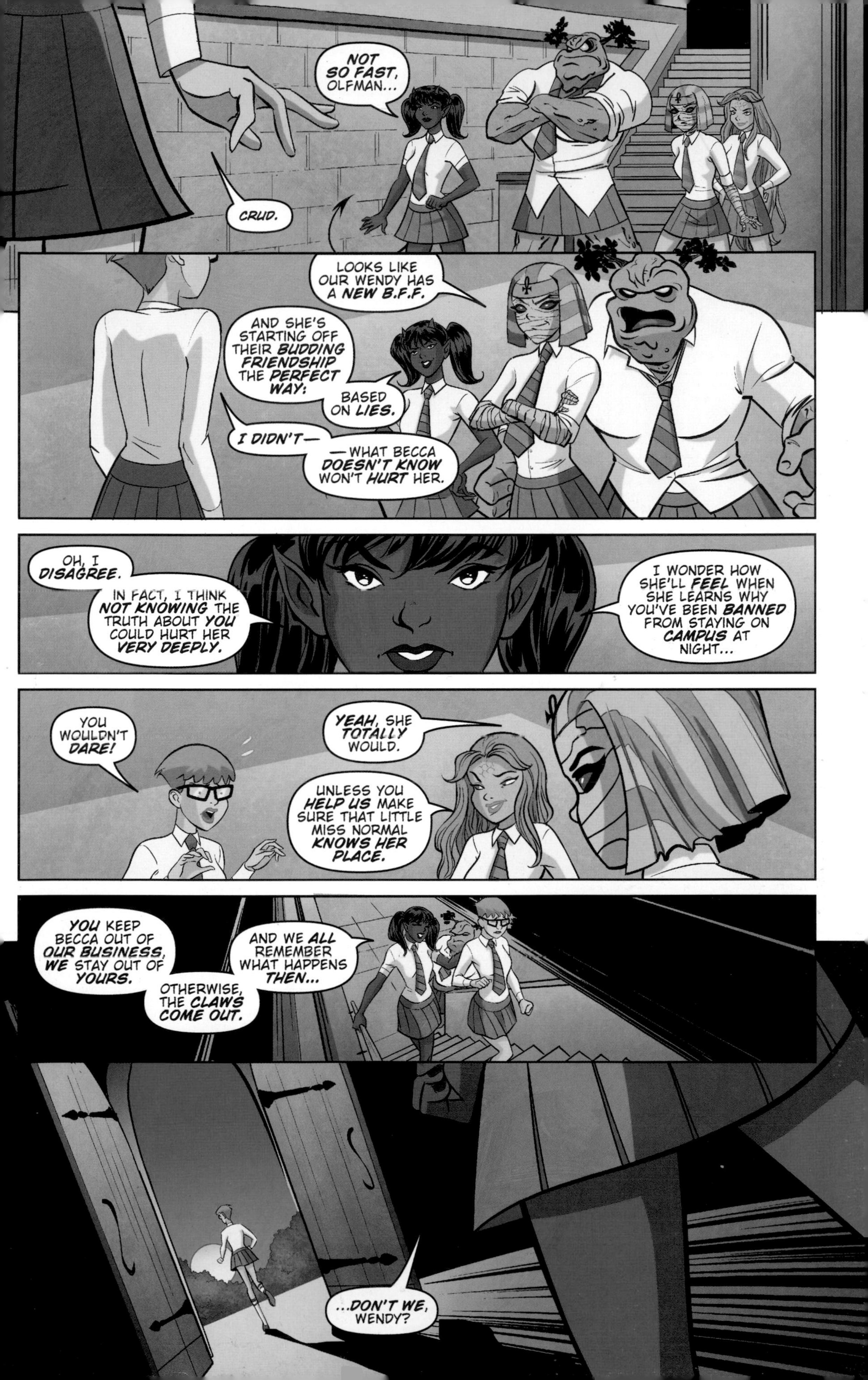
NOT SO FAST, OLFMAN...
CRUD.
LOOKS LIKE OUR WENDY HAS A NEW B.F.F.
AND SHE'S STARTING OFF THEIR BUDDING FRIENDSHIP THE PERFECT WAY:
BASED ON LIES.
I DIDN'T—
—WHAT BECCA DOESN'T KNOW WON'T HURT HER.
OH, I DISAGREE.
IN FACT, I THINK NOT KNOWING THE TRUTH ABOUT YOU COULD HURT HER VERY DEEPLY.
I WONDER HOW SHE'LL FEEL WHEN SHE LEARNS WHY YOU'VE BEEN BANNED FROM STAYING ON CAMPUS AT NIGHT...
YOU WOULDN'T DARE!
YEAH, SHE TOTALLY WOULD.
UNLESS YOU HELP US MAKE SURE THAT LITTLE MISS NORMAL KNOWS HER PLACE.
YOU KEEP BECCA OUT OF OUR BUSINESS, WE STAY OUT OF YOURS.
OTHERWISE, THE CLAWS COME OUT.
AND WE ALL REMEMBER WHAT HAPPENS THEN...
...DON'T WE, WENDY?

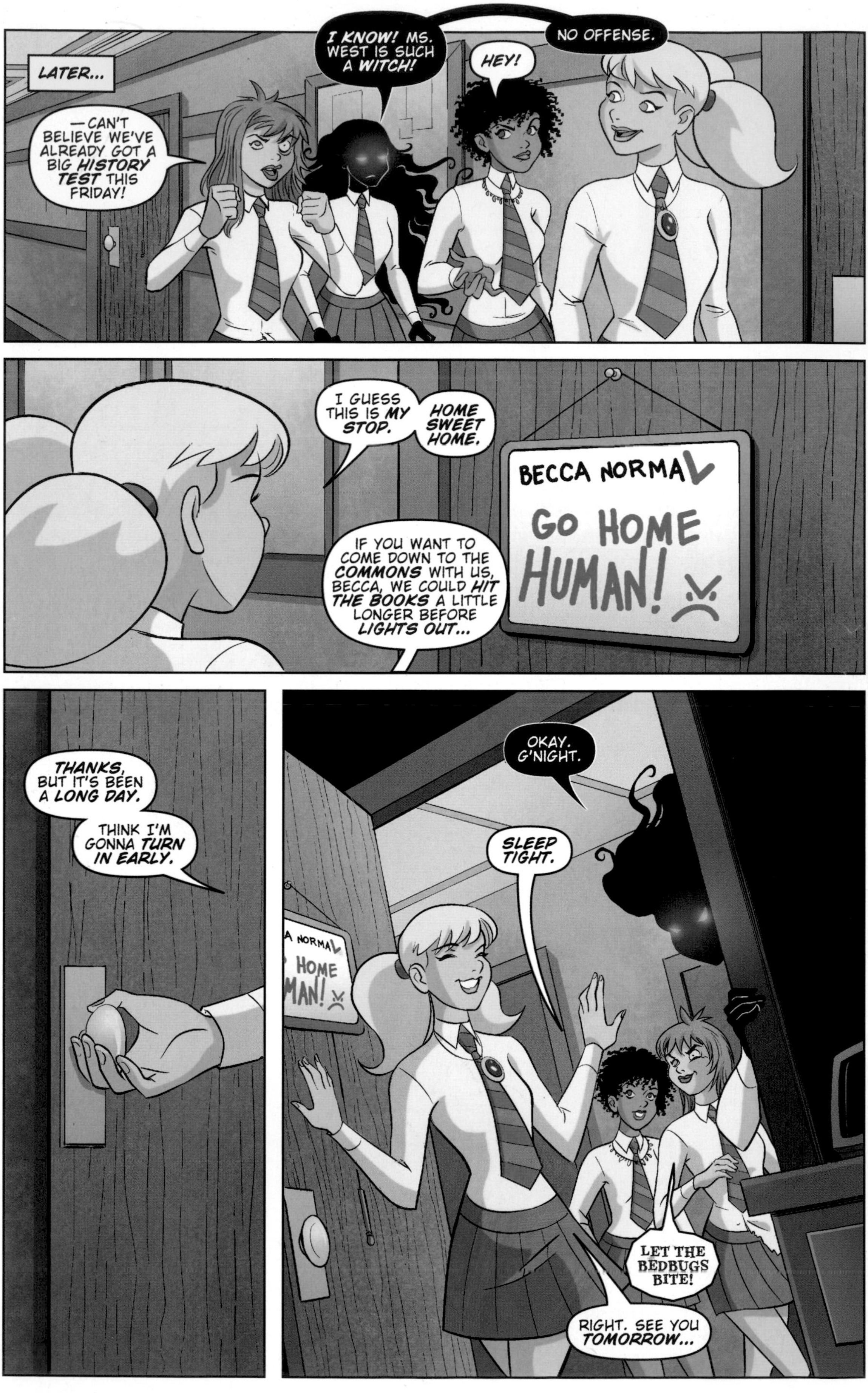

LATER...
—CAN'T BELIEVE WE'VE ALREADY GOT A BIG HISTORY TEST THIS FRIDAY!
I KNOW! MS. WEST IS SUCH A WITCH!
NO OFFENSE.
HEY!
I GUESS THIS IS MY STOP.
HOME SWEET HOME.
BECCA NORMAL
GO HOME HUMAN!
IF YOU WANT TO COME DOWN TO THE COMMONS WITH US, BECCA, WE COULD HIT THE BOOKS A LITTLE LONGER BEFORE LIGHTS OUT...
THANKS, BUT IT'S BEEN A LONG DAY.
THINK I'M GONNA TURN IN EARLY.
OKAY. G'NIGHT.
SLEEP TIGHT.
LET THE BEDBUGS BITE!
RIGHT. SEE YOU TOMORROW...

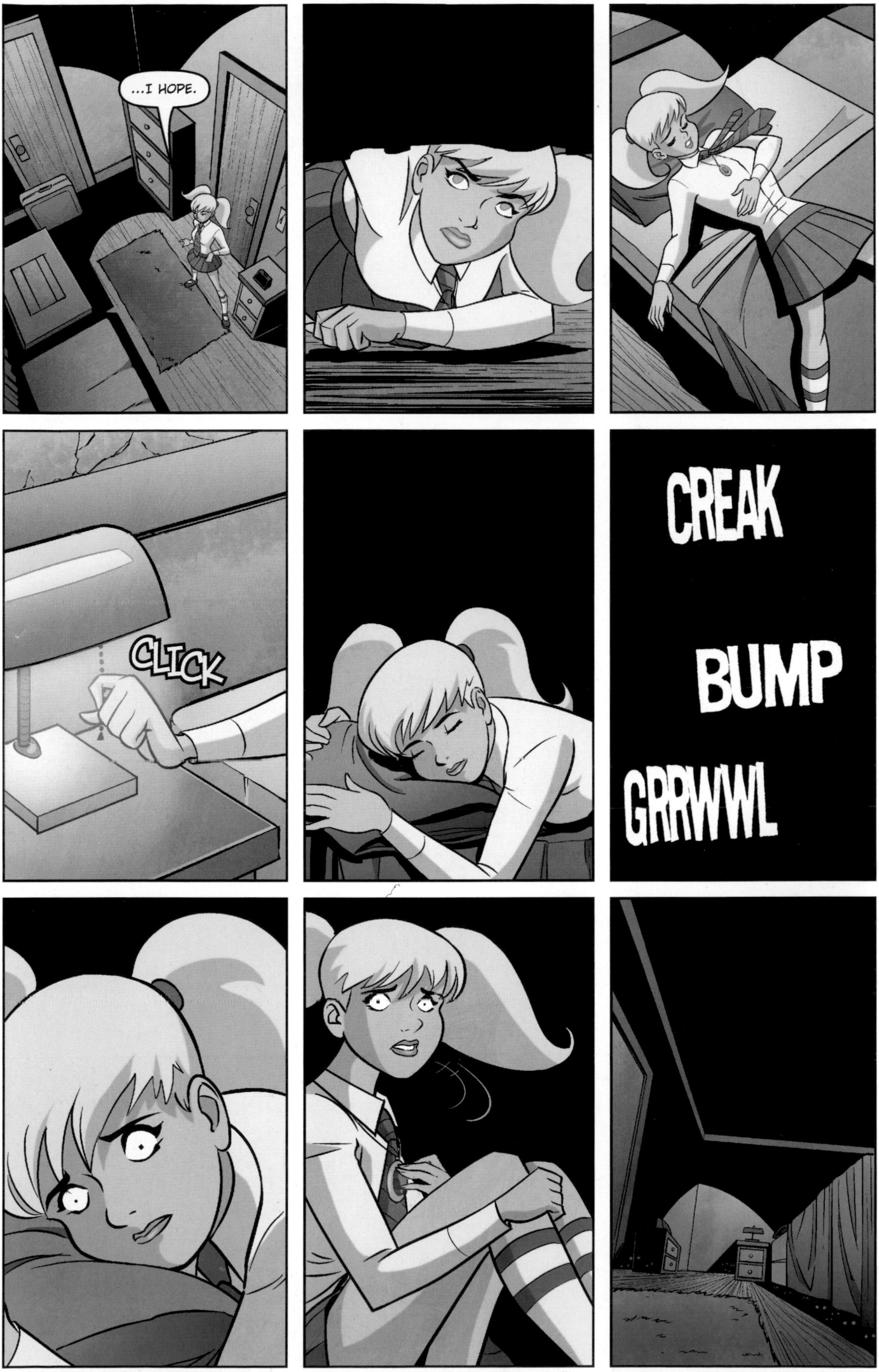
...I HOPE.
CLICK
CREAK
BUMP
GRRWWL

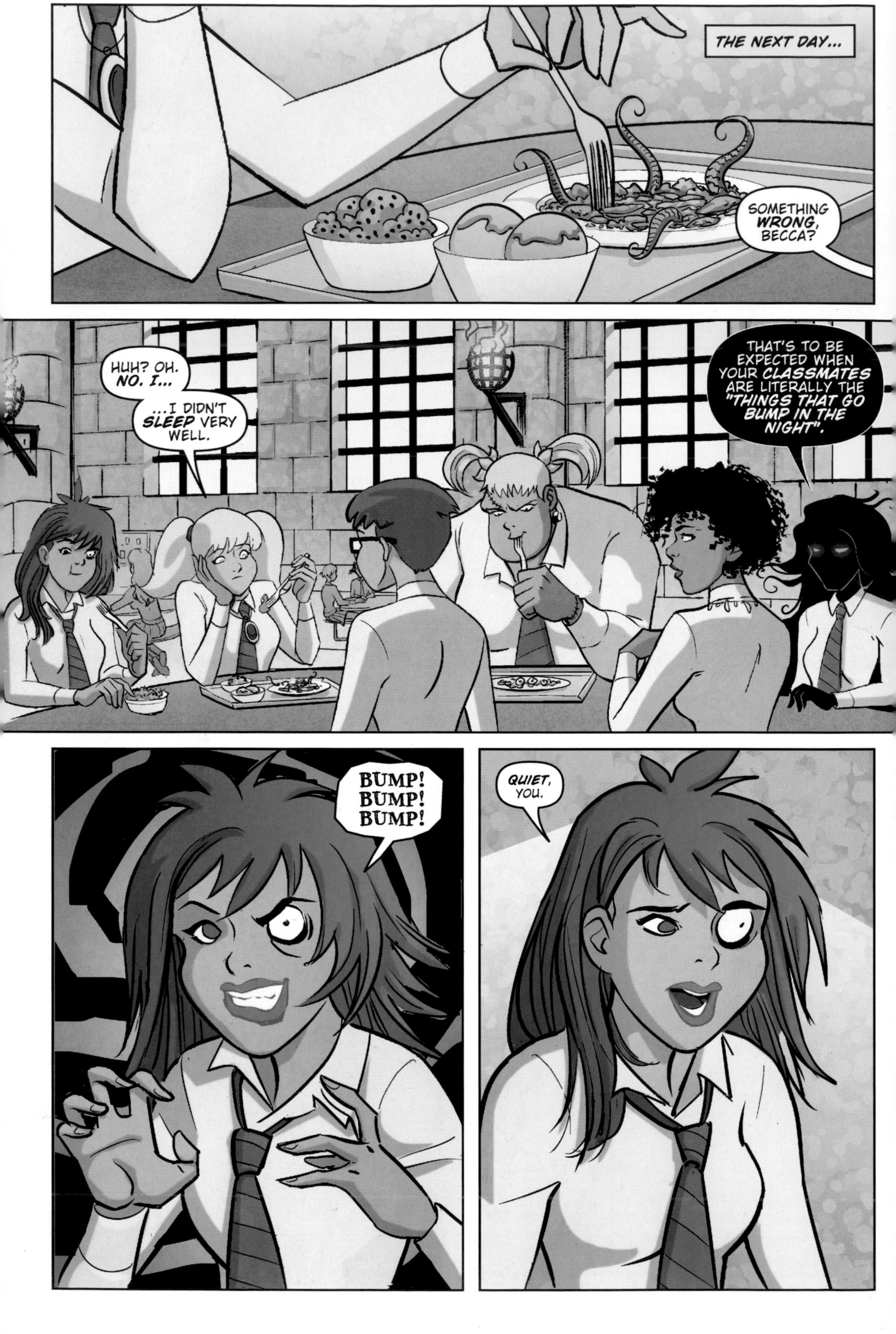
THE NEXT DAY...
SOMETHING WRONG, BECCA?
HUH? OH. NO. I...
...I DIDN'T SLEEP VERY WELL.
THAT'S TO BE EXPECTED WHEN YOUR CLASSMATES ARE LITERALLY THE "THINGS THAT GO BUMP IN THE NIGHT".
BUMP! BUMP! BUMP!
QUIET, YOU.

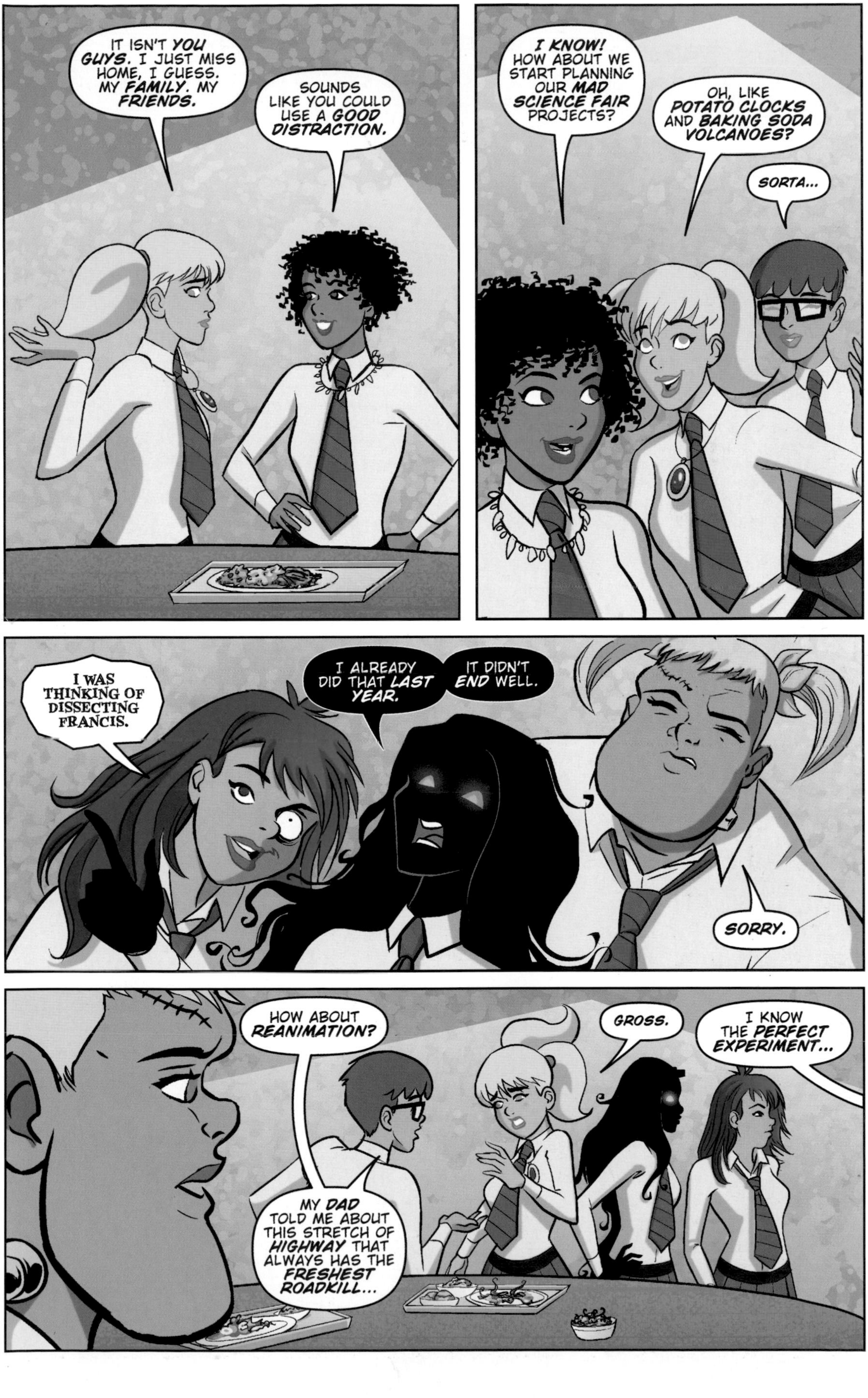
IT ISN'T YOU GUYS. I JUST MISS HOME, I GUESS. MY FAMILY. MY FRIENDS.
SOUNDS LIKE YOU COULD USE A GOOD DISTRACTION.
I KNOW! HOW ABOUT WE START PLANNING OUR MAD SCIENCE FAIR PROJECTS?
OH, LIKE POTATO CLOCKS AND BAKING SODA VOLCANOES?
SORTA...
I WAS THINKING OF DISSECTING FRANCIS.
I ALREADY DID THAT LAST YEAR.
IT DIDN'T END WELL.
SORRY.
HOW ABOUT REANIMATION?
MY DAD TOLD ME ABOUT THIS STRETCH OF HIGHWAY THAT ALWAYS HAS THE FRESHEST ROADKILL...
GROSS.
I KNOW THE PERFECT EXPERIMENT...

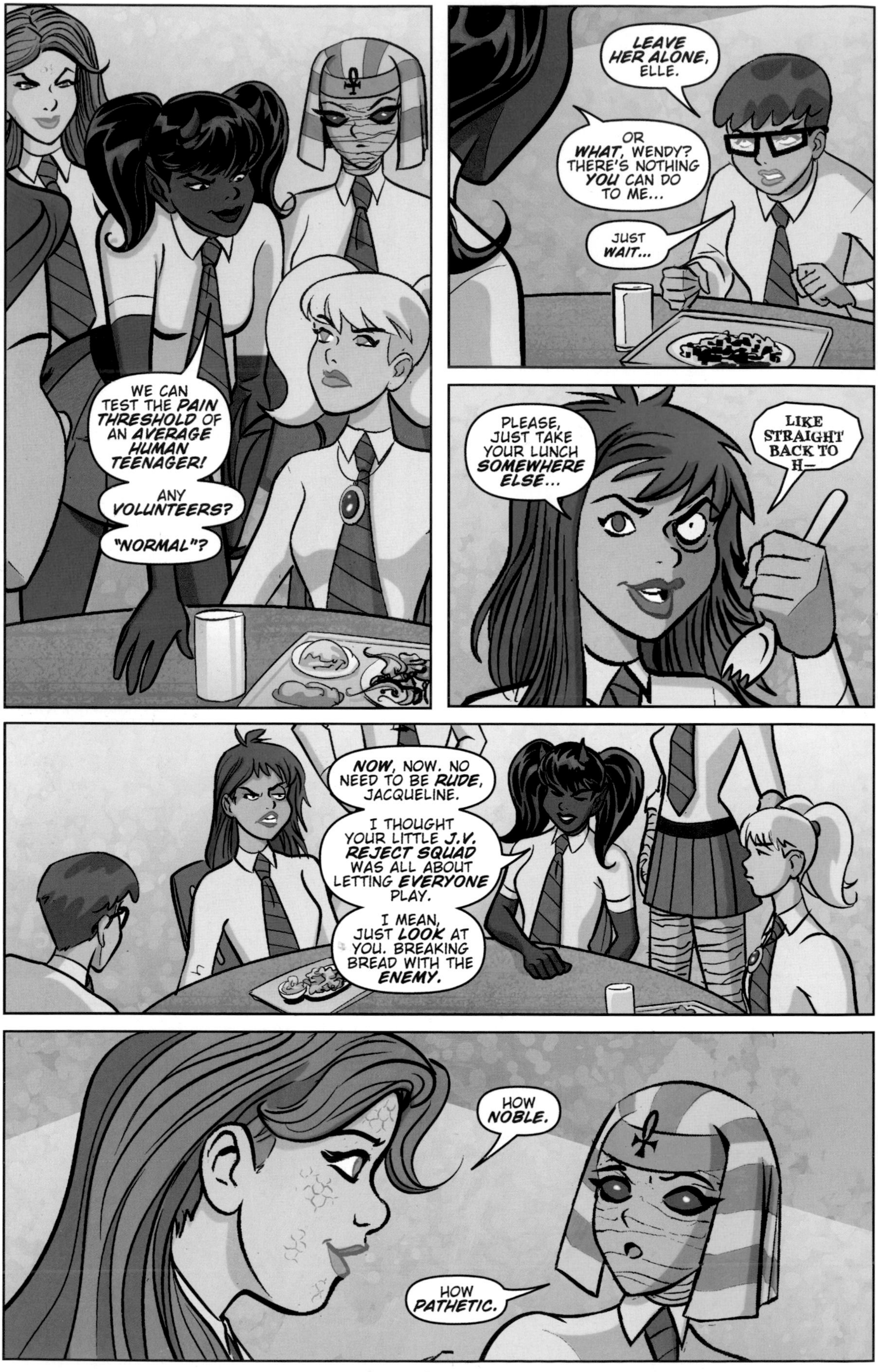
WE CAN TEST THE PAIN THRESHOLD OF AN AVERAGE HUMAN TEENAGER!
ANY VOLUNTEERS?
"NORMAL"?
LEAVE HER ALONE, ELLE.
OR WHAT, WENDY? THERE'S NOTHING YOU CAN DO TO ME...
JUST WAIT...
PLEASE, JUST TAKE YOUR LUNCH SOMEWHERE ELSE...
LIKE STRAIGHT BACK TO H—
NOW, NOW. NO NEED TO BE RUDE, JACQUELINE.
I THOUGHT YOUR LITTLE J.V. REJECT SQUAD WAS ALL ABOUT LETTING EVERYONE PLAY.
I MEAN, JUST LOOK AT YOU. BREAKING BREAD WITH THE ENEMY.
HOW NOBLE.
HOW PATHETIC.

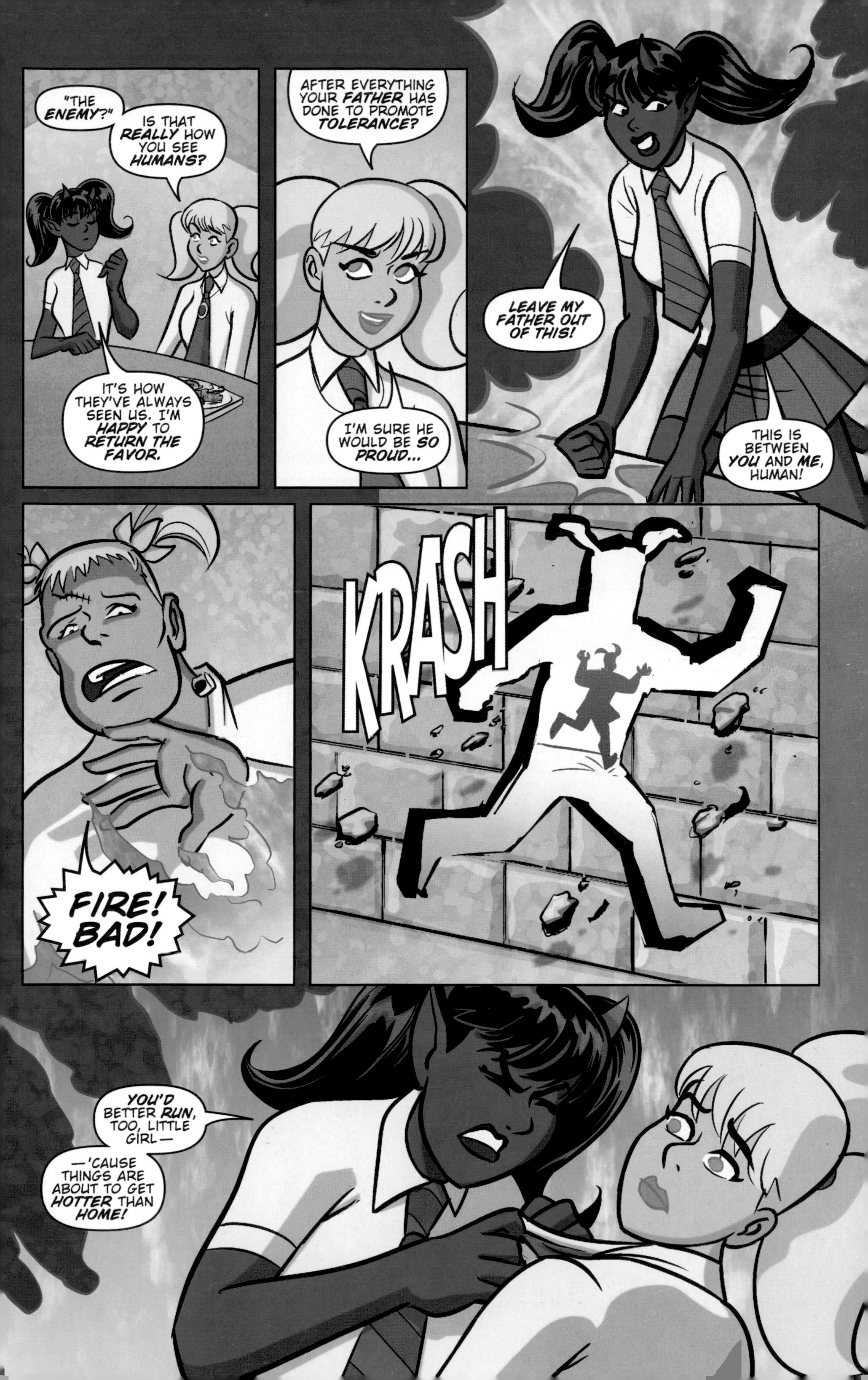
"THE ENEMY?"
IS THAT REALLY HOW YOU SEE HUMANS?
IT'S HOW THEY'VE ALWAYS SEEN US. I'M HAPPY TO RETURN THE FAVOR.
AFTER EVERYTHING YOUR FATHER HAS DONE TO PROMOTE TOLERANCE?
I'M SURE HE WOULD BE SO PROUD...
LEAVE MY FATHER OUT OF THIS!
THIS IS BETWEEN YOU AND ME, HUMAN!
FIRE! BAD!
KRASH
YOU'D BETTER RUN, TOO, LITTLE GIRL—
—'CAUSE THINGS ARE ABOUT TO GET HOTTER THAN HOME!

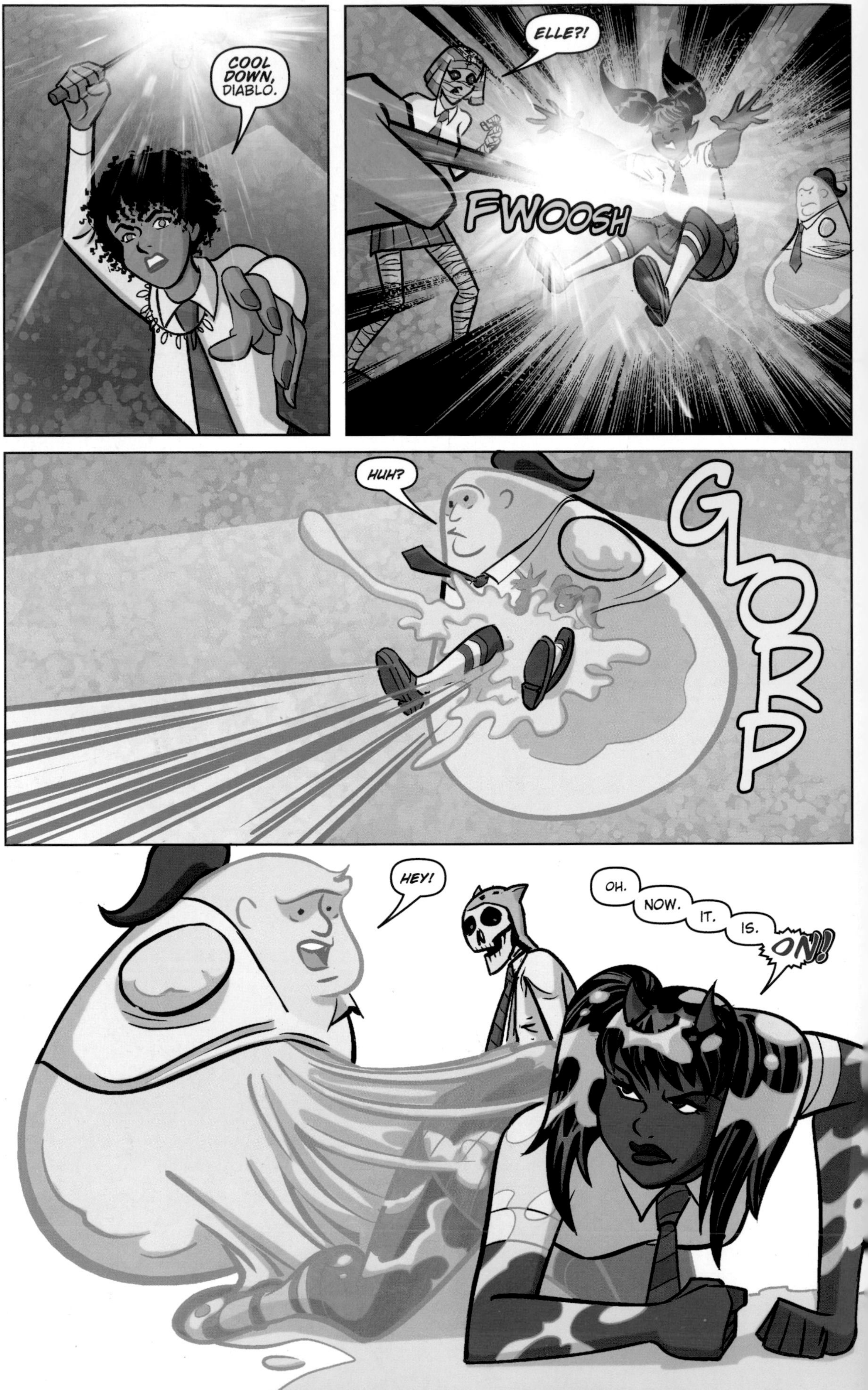
COOL DOWN, DIABLO.
ELLE?!
FWOOSH
HUH?
GLORP
HEY!
OH.
NOW.
IT.
IS.
ON!!

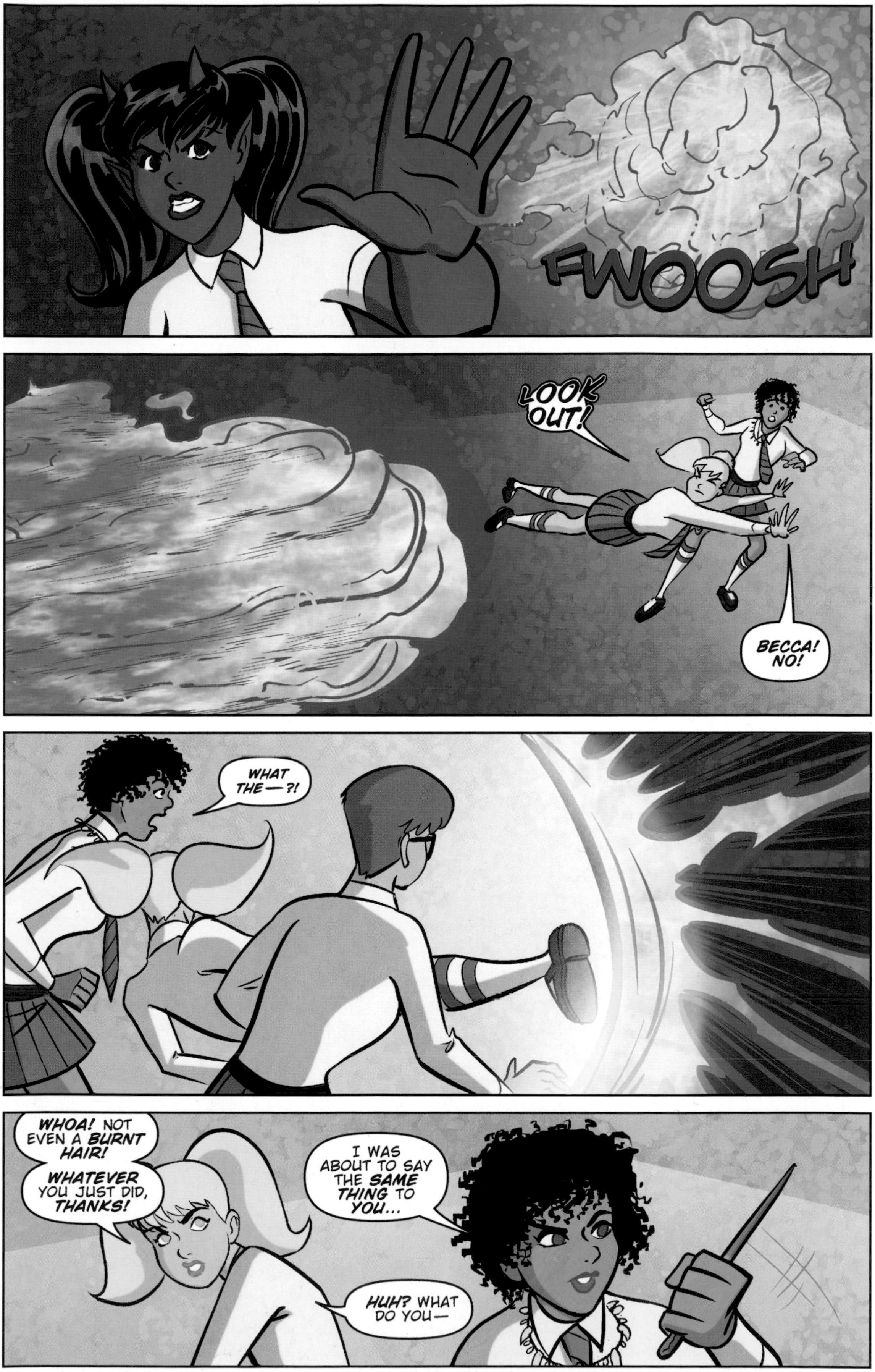
FWOOSH
LOOK OUT!
BECCA! NO!
WHAT THE—?!
WHOA! NOT EVEN A BURNT HAIR!
WHATEVER YOU JUST DID, THANKS!
I WAS ABOUT TO SAY THE SAME THING TO YOU...
HUH? WHAT DO YOU—

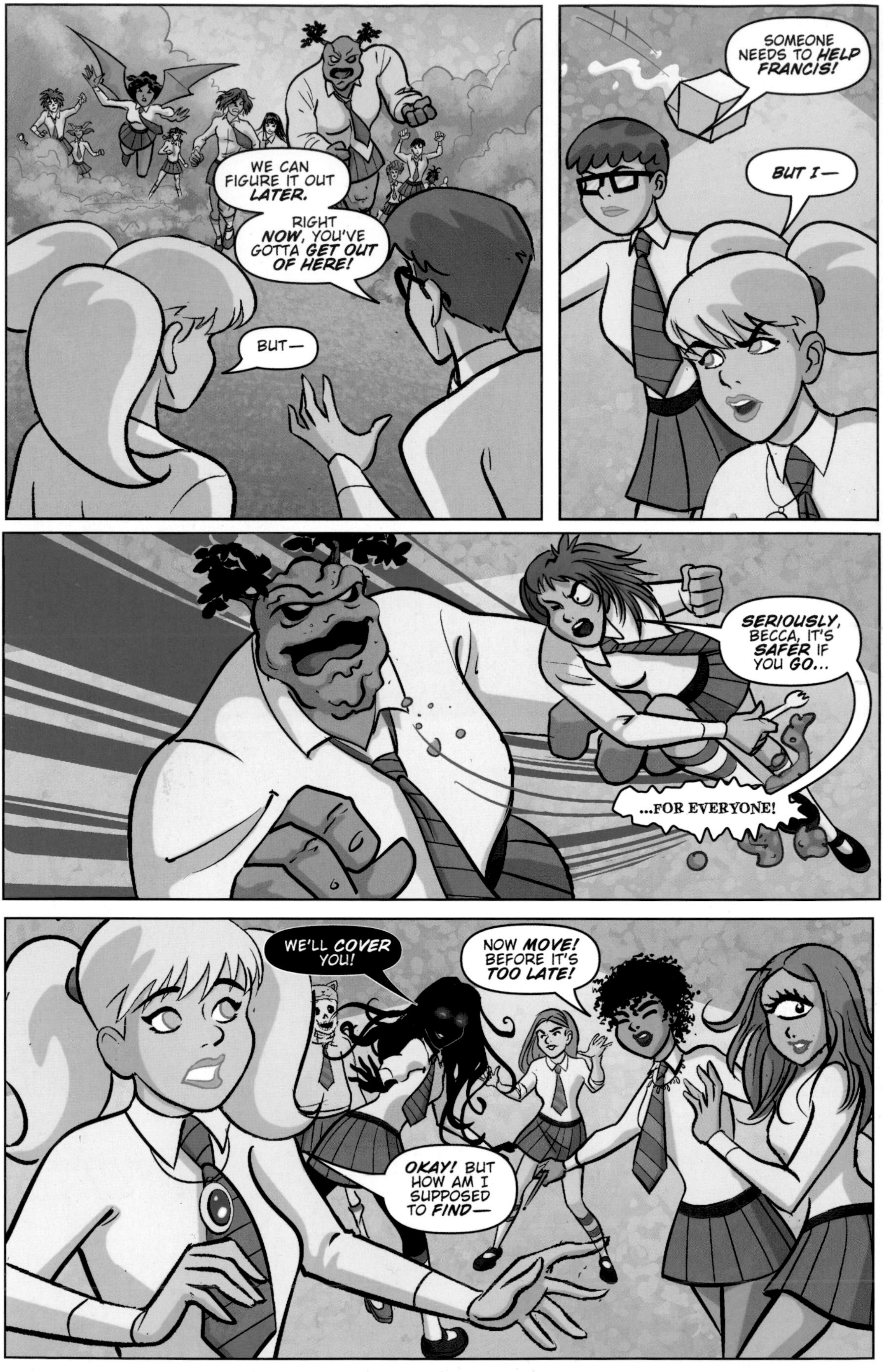
WE CAN FIGURE IT OUT LATER.
RIGHT NOW, YOU'VE GOTTA GET OUT OF HERE!
BUT—
SOMEONE NEEDS TO HELP FRANCIS!
BUT I—
SERIOUSLY, BECCA, IT'S SAFER IF YOU GO...
...FOR EVERYONE!
WE'LL COVER YOU!
NOW MOVE! BEFORE IT'S TOO LATE!
OKAY! BUT HOW AM I SUPPOSED TO FIND—

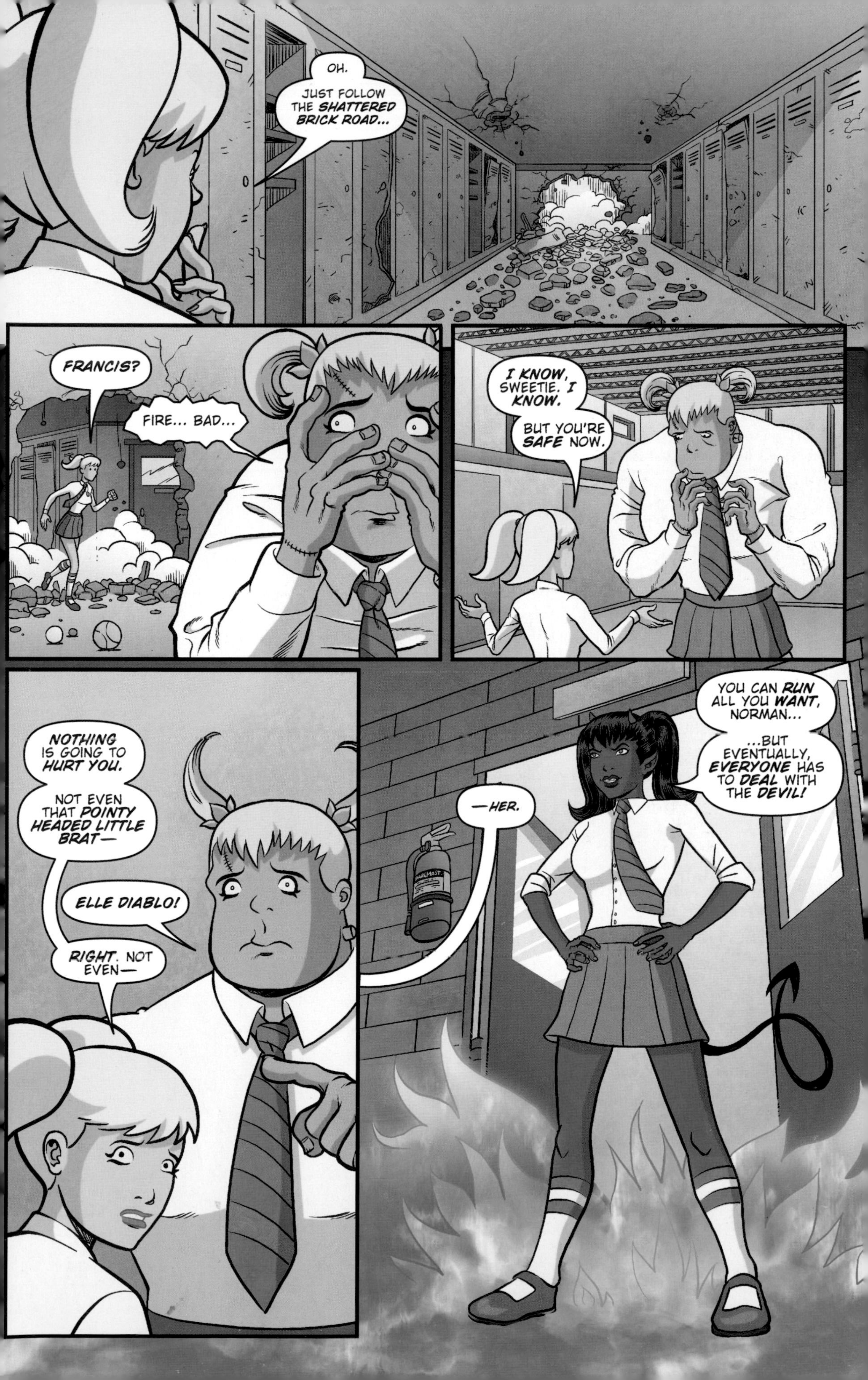
OH.
JUST FOLLOW THE SHATTERED BRICK ROAD...
FRANCIS?
FIRE... BAD...
I KNOW, SWEETIE. I KNOW.
BUT YOU'RE SAFE NOW.
NOTHING IS GOING TO HURT YOU.
NOT EVEN THAT POINTY HEADED LITTLE BRAT—
ELLE DIABLO!
RIGHT. NOT EVEN—
—HER.
YOU CAN RUN ALL YOU WANT, NORMAN...
...BUT EVENTUALLY, EVERYONE HAS TO DEAL WITH THE DEVIL!

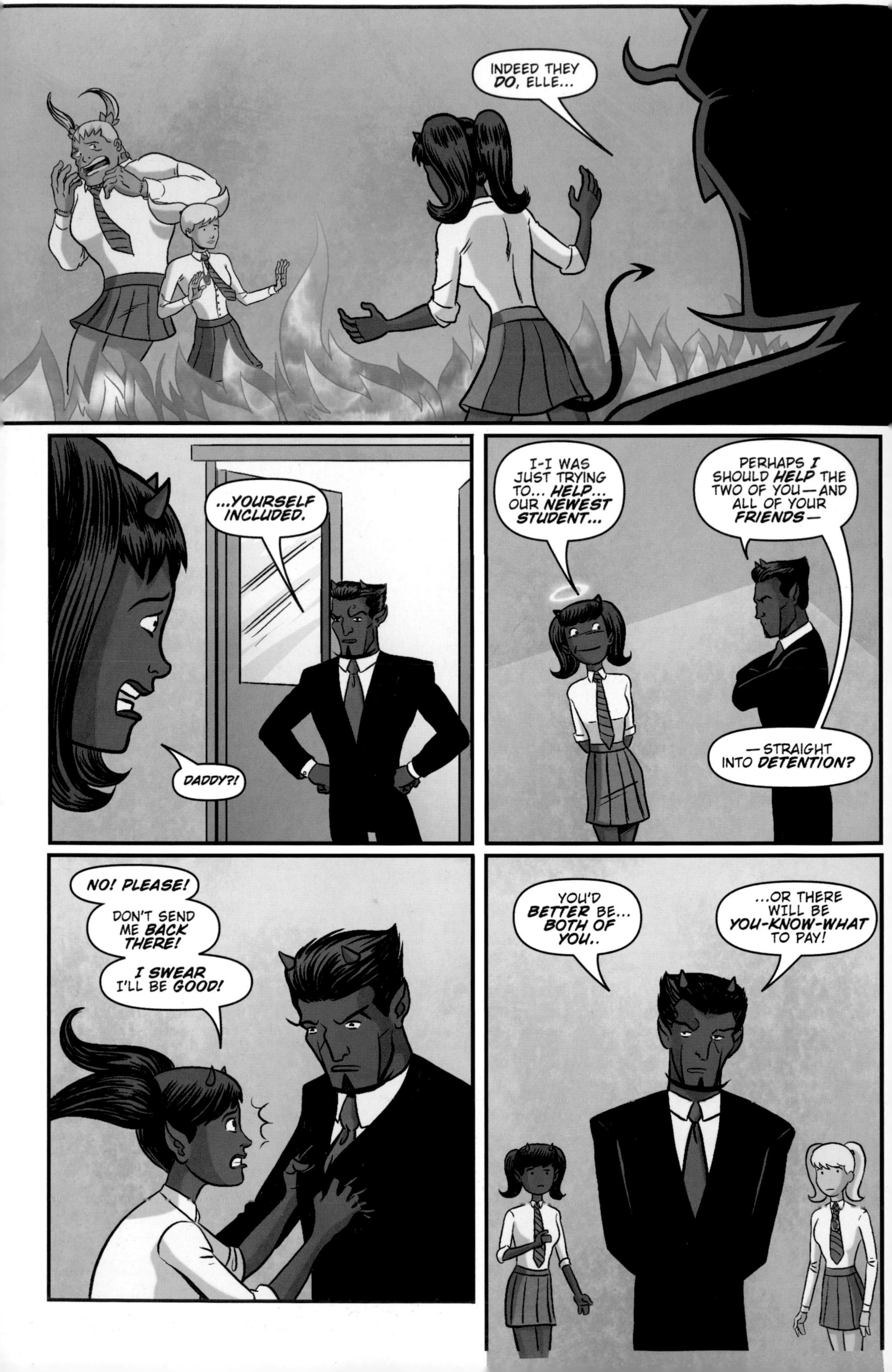
INDEED THEY DO, ELLE...
...YOURSELF INCLUDED.
DADDY?!
I-I WAS JUST TRYING TO... HELP... OUR NEWEST STUDENT...
PERHAPS I SHOULD HELP THE TWO OF YOU—AND ALL OF YOUR FRIENDS—
—STRAIGHT INTO DETENTION?
NO! PLEASE!
DON'T SEND ME BACK THERE!
I SWEAR I'LL BE GOOD!
YOU'D BETTER BE... BOTH OF YOU..
...OR THERE WILL BE YOU-KNOW-WHAT TO PAY!

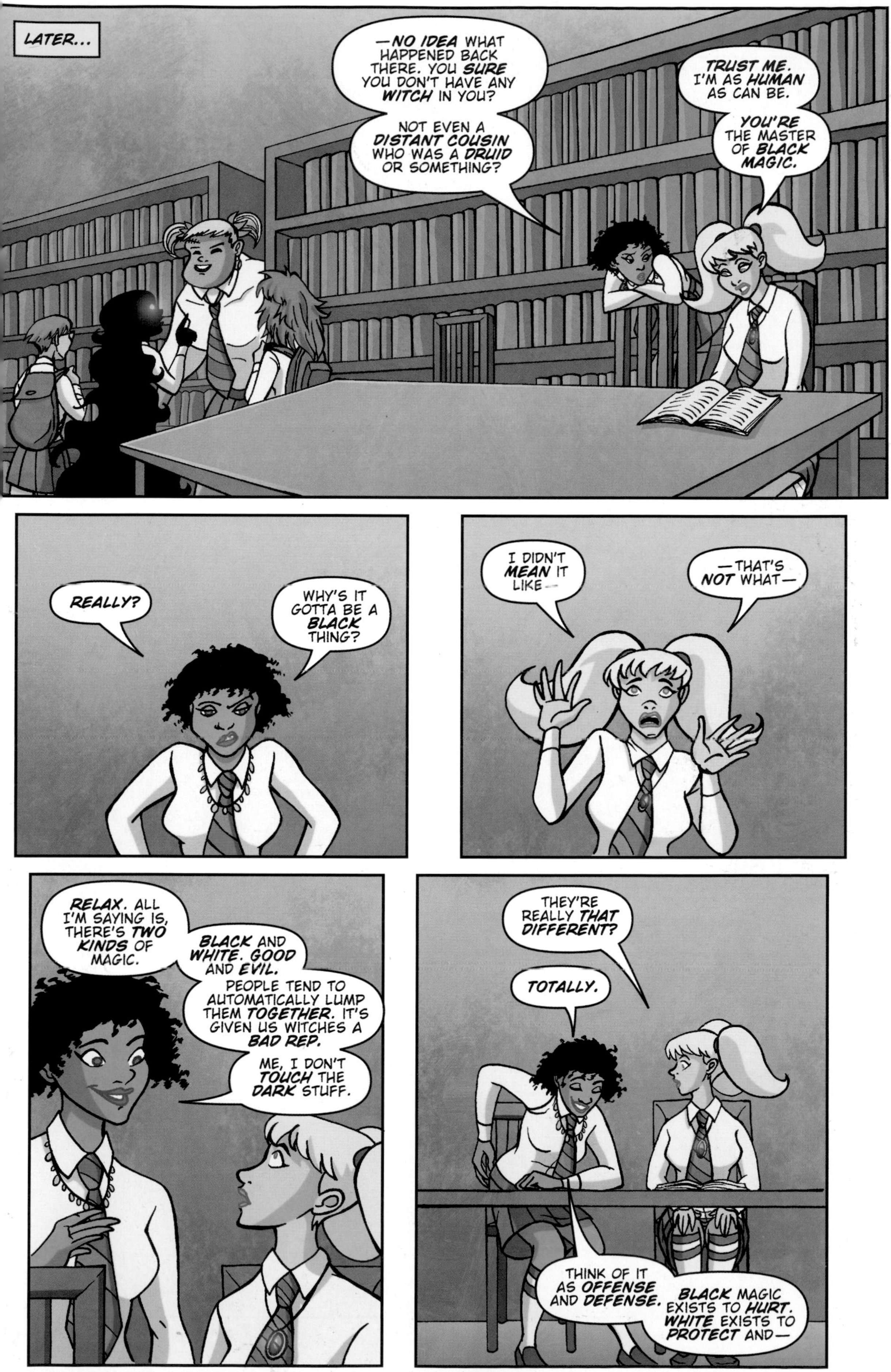
LATER...
—NO IDEA WHAT HAPPENED BACK THERE. YOU SURE YOU DON'T HAVE ANY WITCH IN YOU?
NOT EVEN A DISTANT COUSIN WHO WAS A DRUID OR SOMETHING?
TRUST ME. I'M AS HUMAN AS CAN BE.
YOU'RE THE MASTER OF BLACK MAGIC.
REALLY?
WHY'S IT GOTTA BE A BLACK THING?
I DIDN'T MEAN IT LIKE—
—THAT'S NOT WHAT—
RELAX. ALL I'M SAYING IS, THERE'S TWO KINDS OF MAGIC.
BLACK AND WHITE. GOOD AND EVIL.
PEOPLE TEND TO AUTOMATICALLY LUMP THEM TOGETHER. IT'S GIVEN US WITCHES A BAD REP.
ME, I DON'T TOUCH THE DARK STUFF.
THEY'RE REALLY THAT DIFFERENT?
TOTALLY.
THINK OF IT AS OFFENSE AND DEFENSE.
BLACK MAGIC EXISTS TO HURT. WHITE EXISTS TO PROTECT AND—

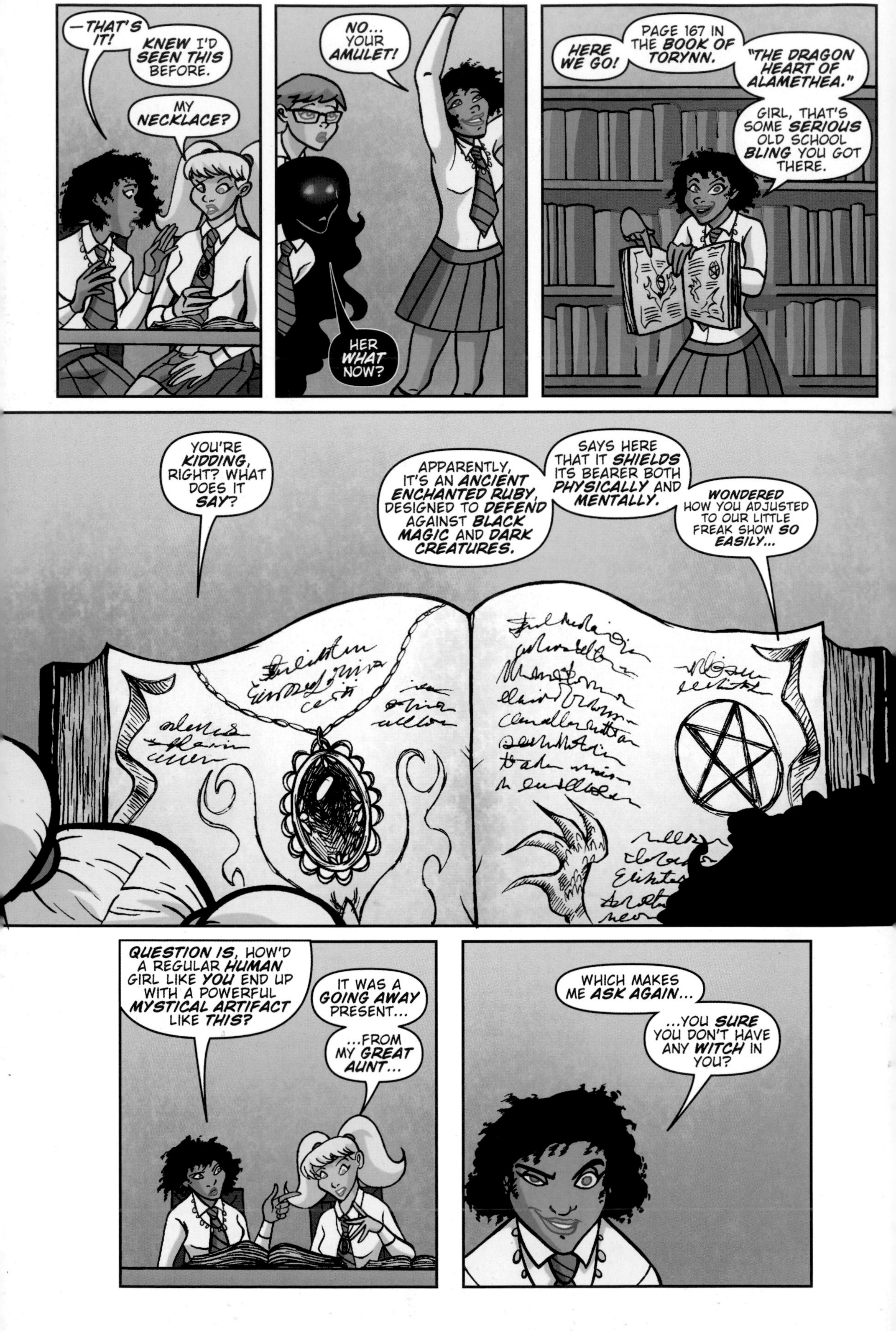
—THAT'S IT!
KNEW I'D SEEN THIS BEFORE.
MY NECKLACE?
NO... YOUR AMULET!
HER WHAT NOW?
HERE WE GO!
PAGE 167 IN THE BOOK OF TORYNN.
"THE DRAGON HEART OF ALAMETHEA."
GIRL, THAT'S SOME SERIOUS OLD SCHOOL BLING YOU GOT THERE.
YOU'RE KIDDING, RIGHT? WHAT DOES IT SAY?
APPARENTLY, IT'S AN ANCIENT ENCHANTED RUBY, DESIGNED TO DEFEND AGAINST BLACK MAGIC AND DARK CREATURES.
SAYS HERE THAT IT SHIELDS ITS BEARER BOTH PHYSICALLY AND MENTALLY.
WONDERED HOW YOU ADJUSTED TO OUR LITTLE FREAK SHOW SO EASILY...
QUESTION IS, HOW'D A REGULAR HUMAN GIRL LIKE YOU END UP WITH A POWERFUL MYSTICAL ARTIFACT LIKE THIS?
IT WAS A GOING AWAY PRESENT...
...FROM MY GREAT AUNT...
WHICH MAKES ME ASK AGAIN...
...YOU SURE YOU DON'T HAVE ANY WITCH IN YOU?

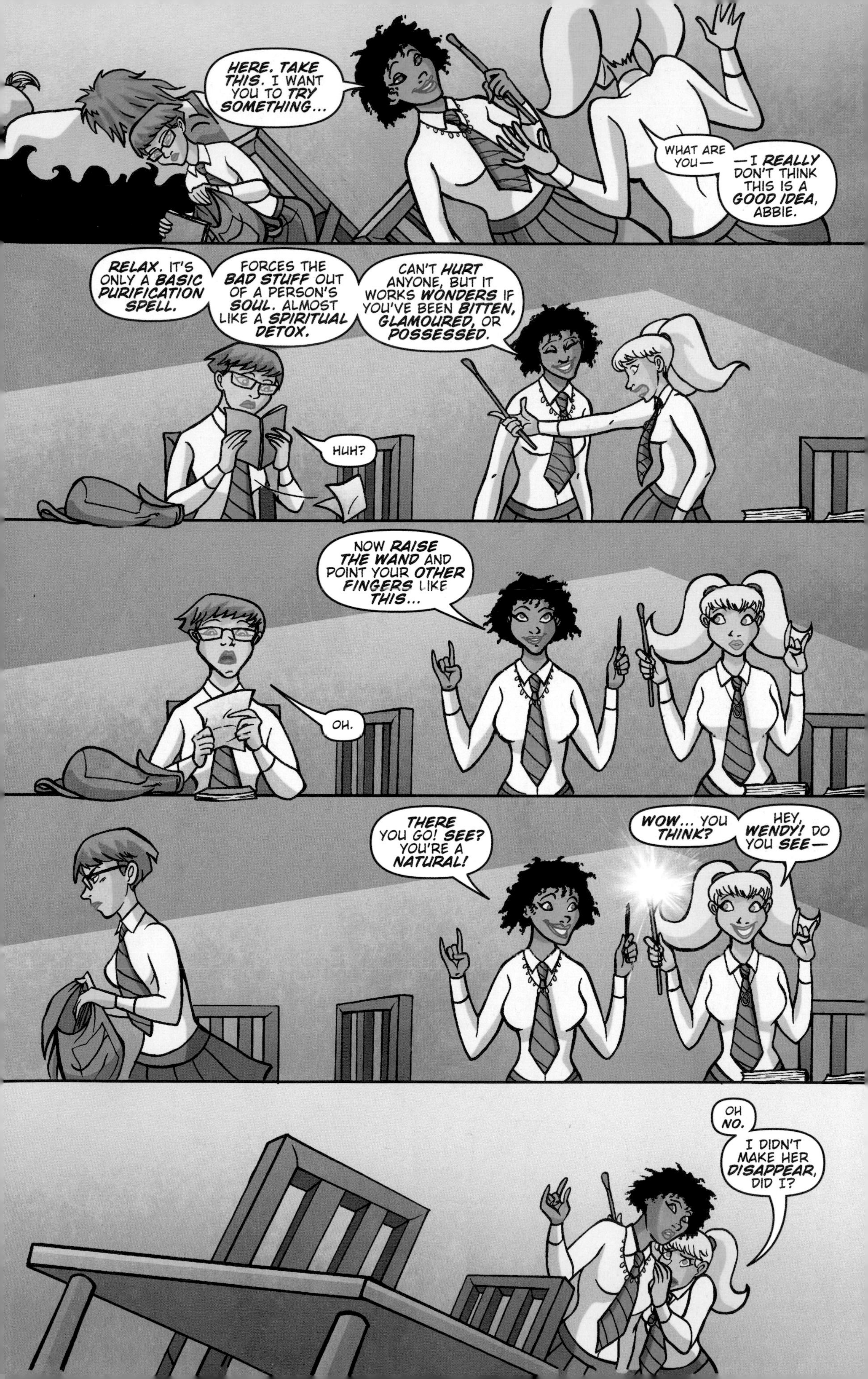
HERE. TAKE THIS. I WANT YOU TO TRY SOMETHING...
WHAT ARE YOU—
—I REALLY DON'T THINK THIS IS A GOOD IDEA, ABBIE.
RELAX. IT'S ONLY A BASIC PURIFICATION SPELL.
FORCES THE BAD STUFF OUT OF A PERSON'S SOUL. ALMOST LIKE A SPIRITUAL DETOX.
CAN'T HURT ANYONE, BUT IT WORKS WONDERS IF YOU'VE BEEN BITTEN, GLAMOURED, OR POSSESSED.
HUH?
NOW RAISE THE WAND AND POINT YOUR OTHER FINGERS LIKE THIS...
OH.
THERE YOU GO! SEE? YOU'RE A NATURAL!
WOW... YOU THINK?
HEY, WENDY! DO YOU SEE—
OH NO.
I DIDN'T MAKE HER DISAPPEAR, DID I?

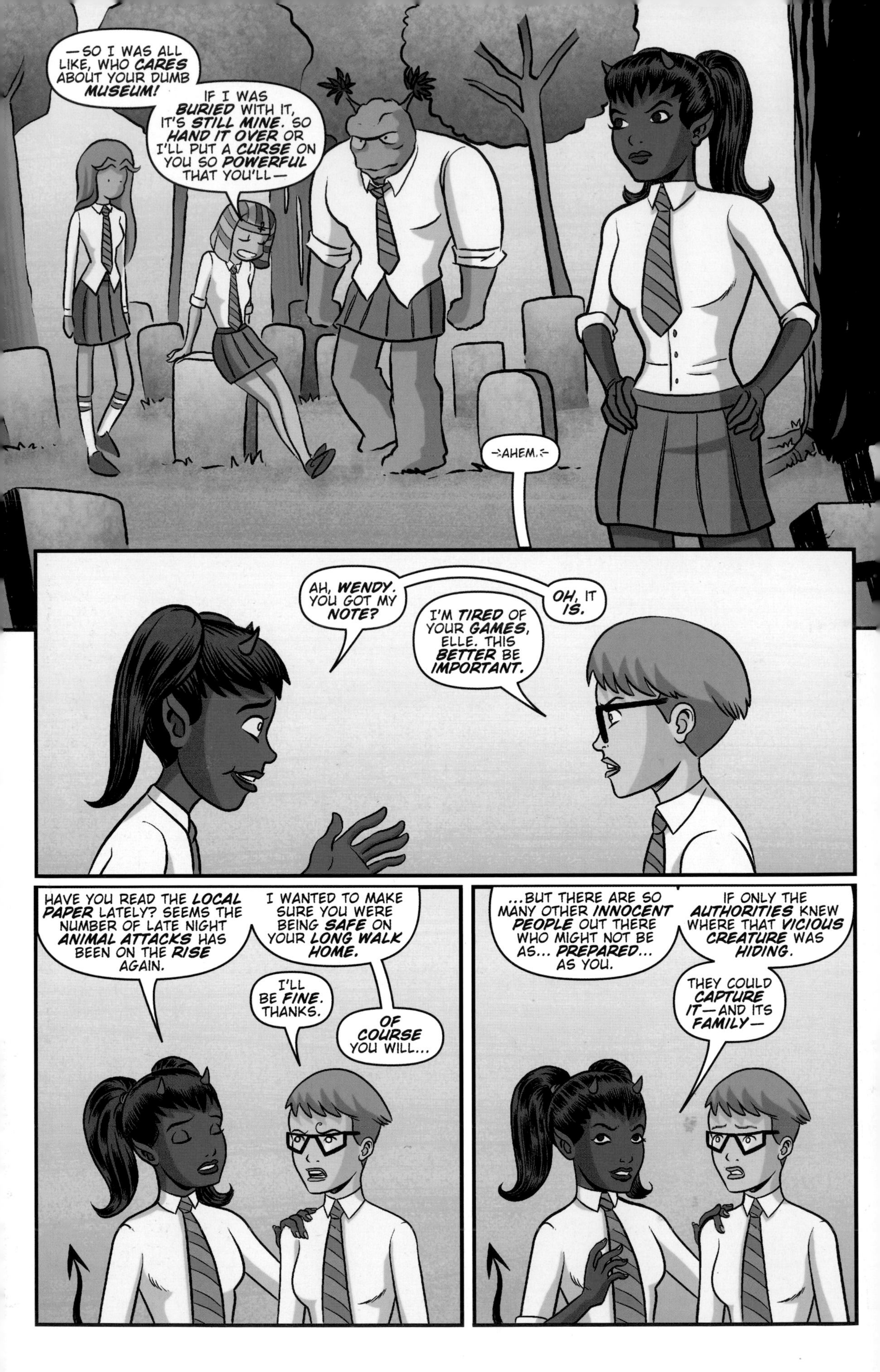

—SO I WAS ALL LIKE, WHO CARES ABOUT YOUR DUMB MUSEUM!
IF I WAS BURIED WITH IT, IT'S STILL MINE. SO HAND IT OVER OR I'LL PUT A CURSE ON YOU SO POWERFUL THAT YOU'LL—
AHEM.
AH, WENDY. YOU GOT MY NOTE?
OH, IT IS.
I'M TIRED OF YOUR GAMES, ELLE. THIS BETTER BE IMPORTANT.
HAVE YOU READ THE LOCAL PAPER LATELY? SEEMS THE NUMBER OF LATE NIGHT ANIMAL ATTACKS HAS BEEN ON THE RISE AGAIN.
I WANTED TO MAKE SURE YOU WERE BEING SAFE ON YOUR LONG WALK HOME.
I'LL BE FINE. THANKS.
OF COURSE YOU WILL...
...BUT THERE ARE SO MANY OTHER INNOCENT PEOPLE OUT THERE WHO MIGHT NOT BE AS... PREPARED... AS YOU.
IF ONLY THE AUTHORITIES KNEW WHERE THAT VICIOUS CREATURE WAS HIDING.
THEY COULD CAPTURE IT—AND ITS FAMILY—

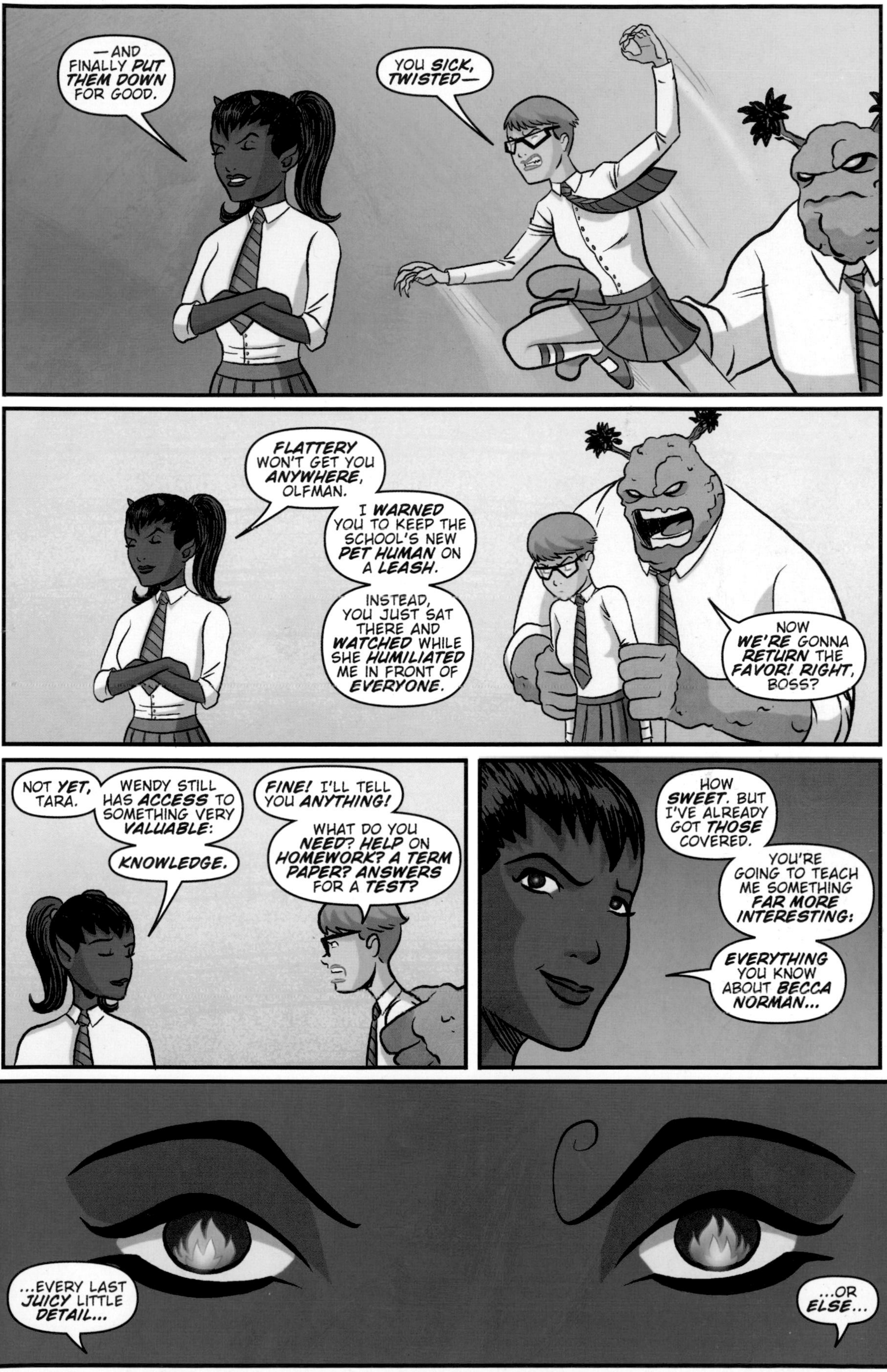
—AND FINALLY PUT THEM DOWN FOR GOOD.
YOU SICK, TWISTED—
FLATTERY WON'T GET YOU ANYWHERE, OLFMAN.
I WARNED YOU TO KEEP THE SCHOOL'S NEW PET HUMAN ON A LEASH.
INSTEAD, YOU JUST SAT THERE AND WATCHED WHILE SHE HUMILIATED ME IN FRONT OF EVERYONE.
NOW WE'RE GONNA RETURN THE FAVOR! RIGHT, BOSS?
NOT YET, TARA.
WENDY STILL HAS ACCESS TO SOMETHING VERY VALUABLE:
KNOWLEDGE.
FINE! I'LL TELL YOU ANYTHING!
WHAT DO YOU NEED? HELP ON HOMEWORK? A TERM PAPER? ANSWERS FOR A TEST?
HOW SWEET. BUT I'VE ALREADY GOT THOSE COVERED.
YOU'RE GOING TO TEACH ME SOMETHING FAR MORE INTERESTING:
EVERYTHING YOU KNOW ABOUT BECCA NORMAN...
...EVERY LAST JUICY LITTLE DETAIL...
...OR ELSE...

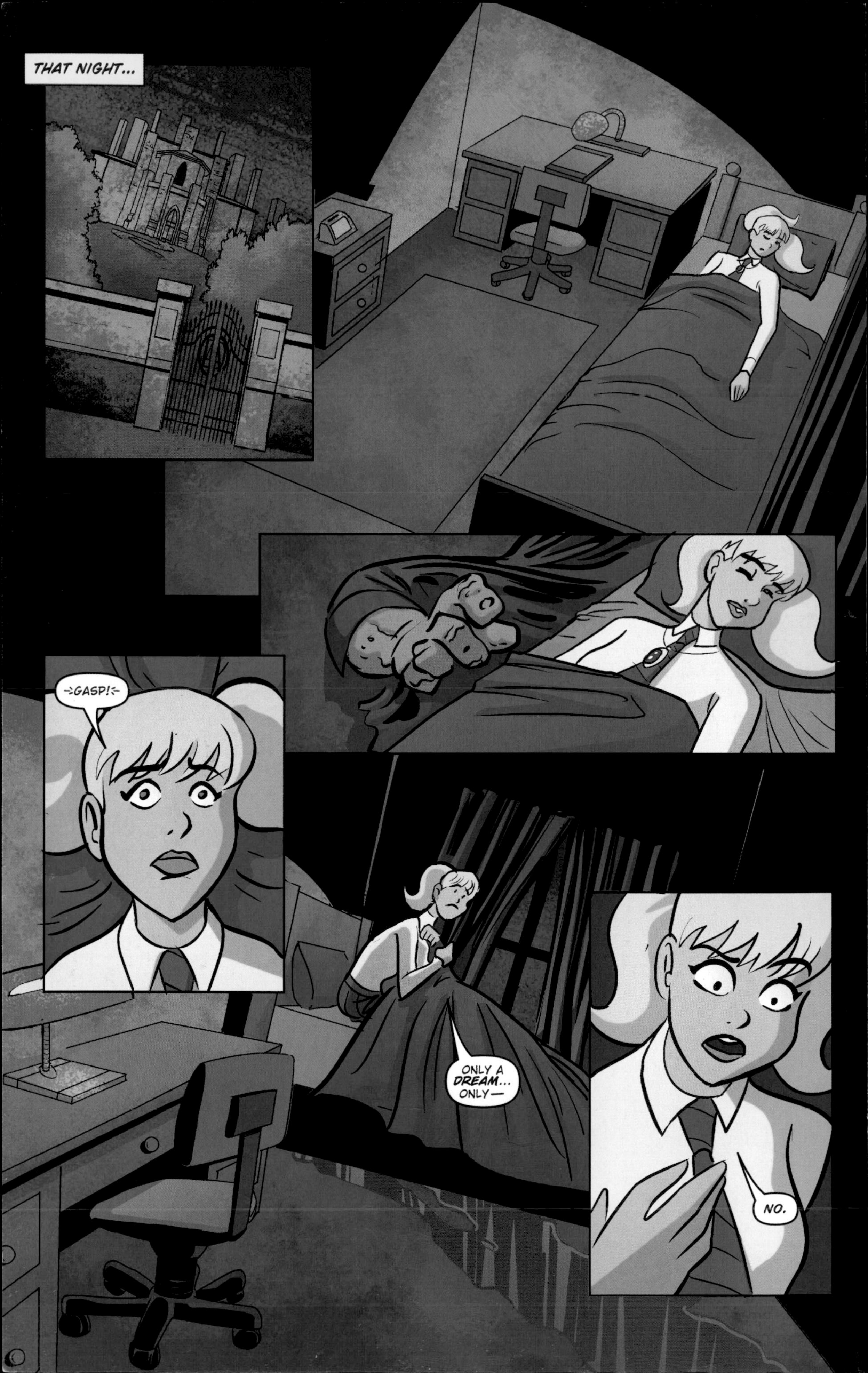
THAT NIGHT...
–GASP!–
ONLY A DREAM... ONLY—
NO.

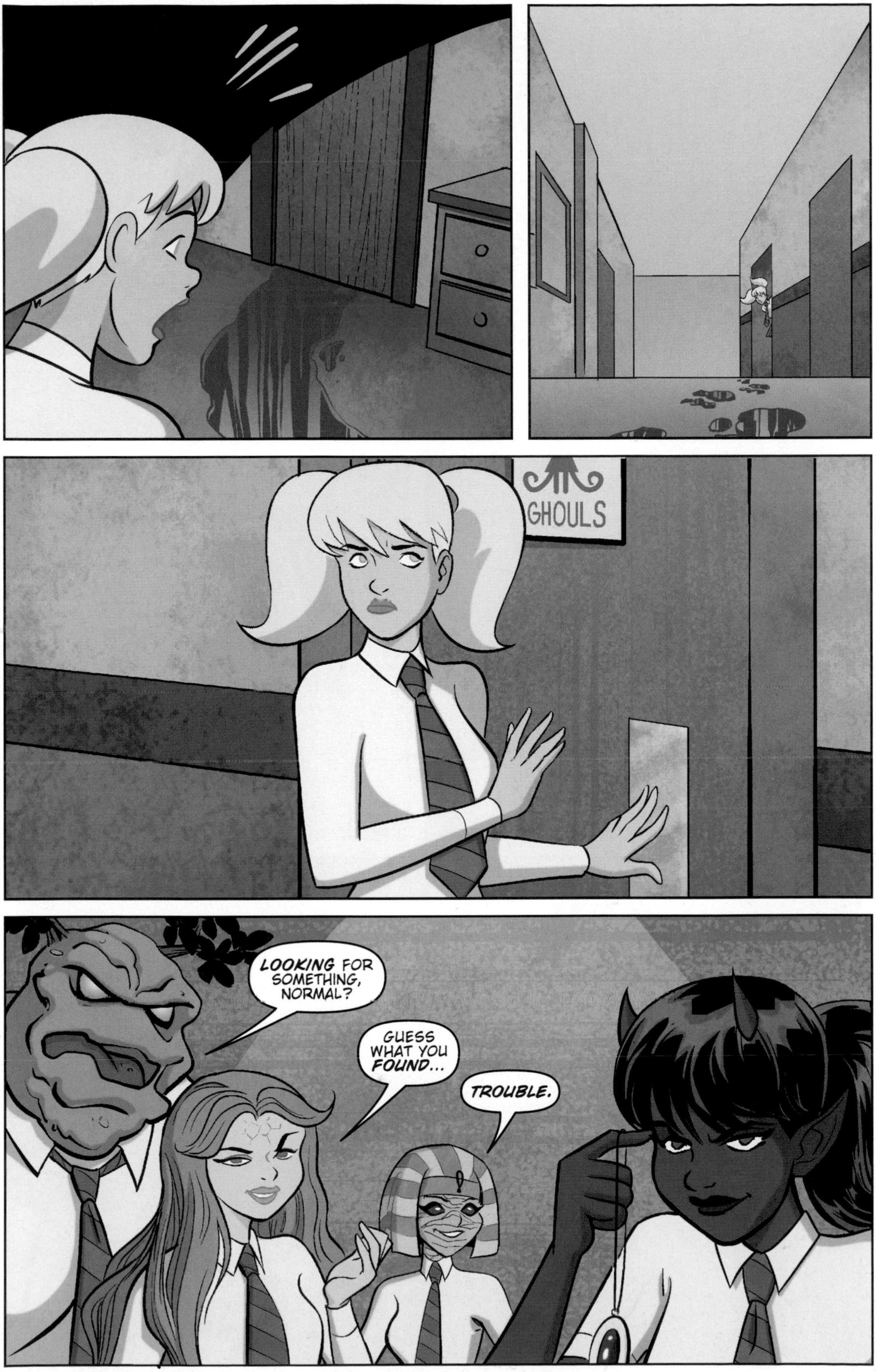
GHOULS
LOOKING FOR SOMETHING, NORMAL?
GUESS WHAT YOU FOUND...
TROUBLE.

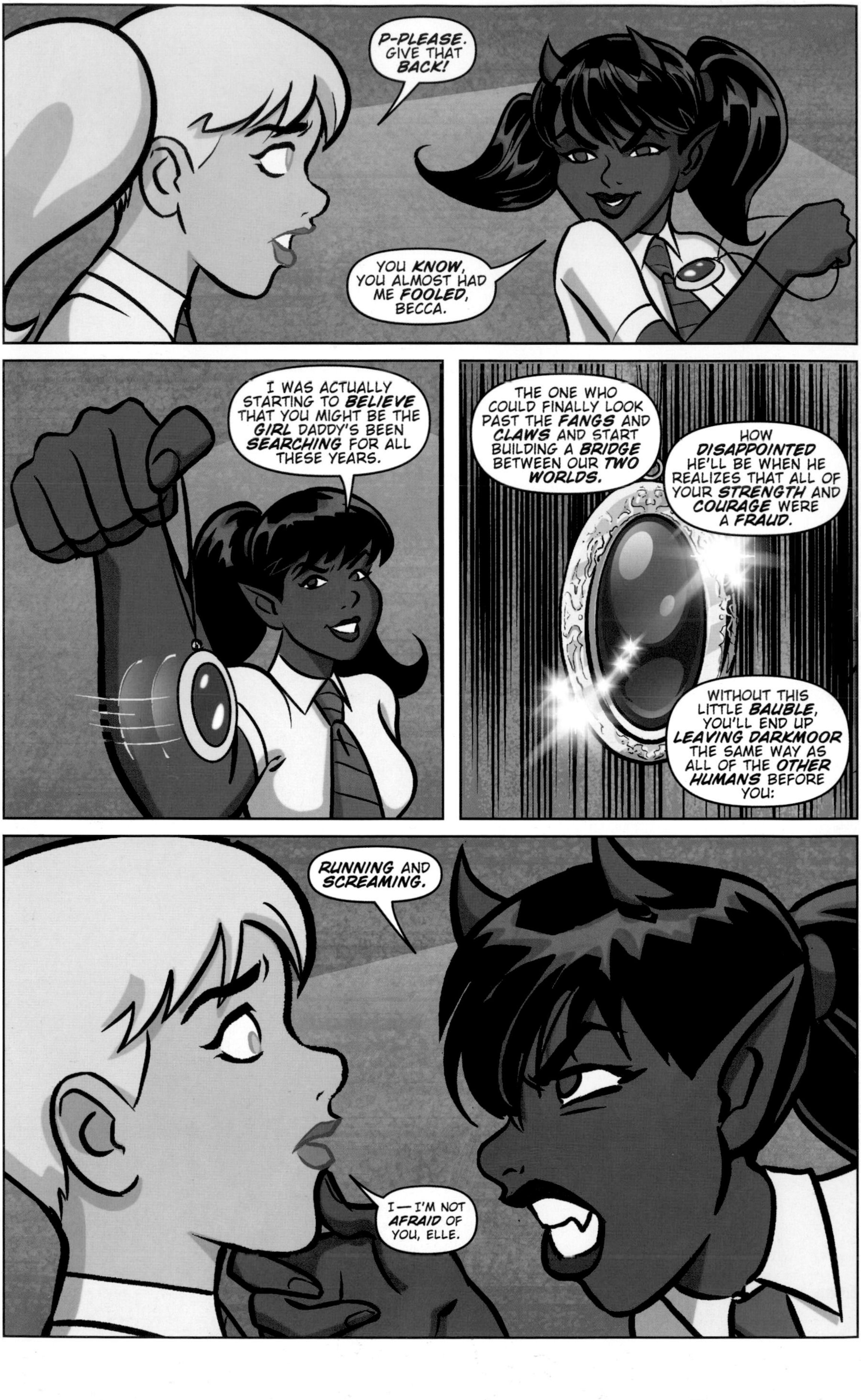
P-PLEASE. GIVE THAT BACK!
YOU KNOW, YOU ALMOST HAD ME FOOLED, BECCA.
I WAS ACTUALLY STARTING TO BELIEVE THAT YOU MIGHT BE THE GIRL DADDY'S BEEN SEARCHING FOR ALL THESE YEARS.
THE ONE WHO COULD FINALLY LOOK PAST THE FANGS AND CLAWS AND START BUILDING A BRIDGE BETWEEN OUR TWO WORLDS.
HOW DISAPPOINTED HE'LL BE WHEN HE REALIZES THAT ALL OF YOUR STRENGTH AND COURAGE WERE A FRAUD.
WITHOUT THIS LITTLE BAUBLE, YOU'LL END UP LEAVING DARKMOOR THE SAME WAY AS ALL OF THE OTHER HUMANS BEFORE YOU:
RUNNING AND SCREAMING.
I— I'M NOT AFRAID OF YOU, ELLE.

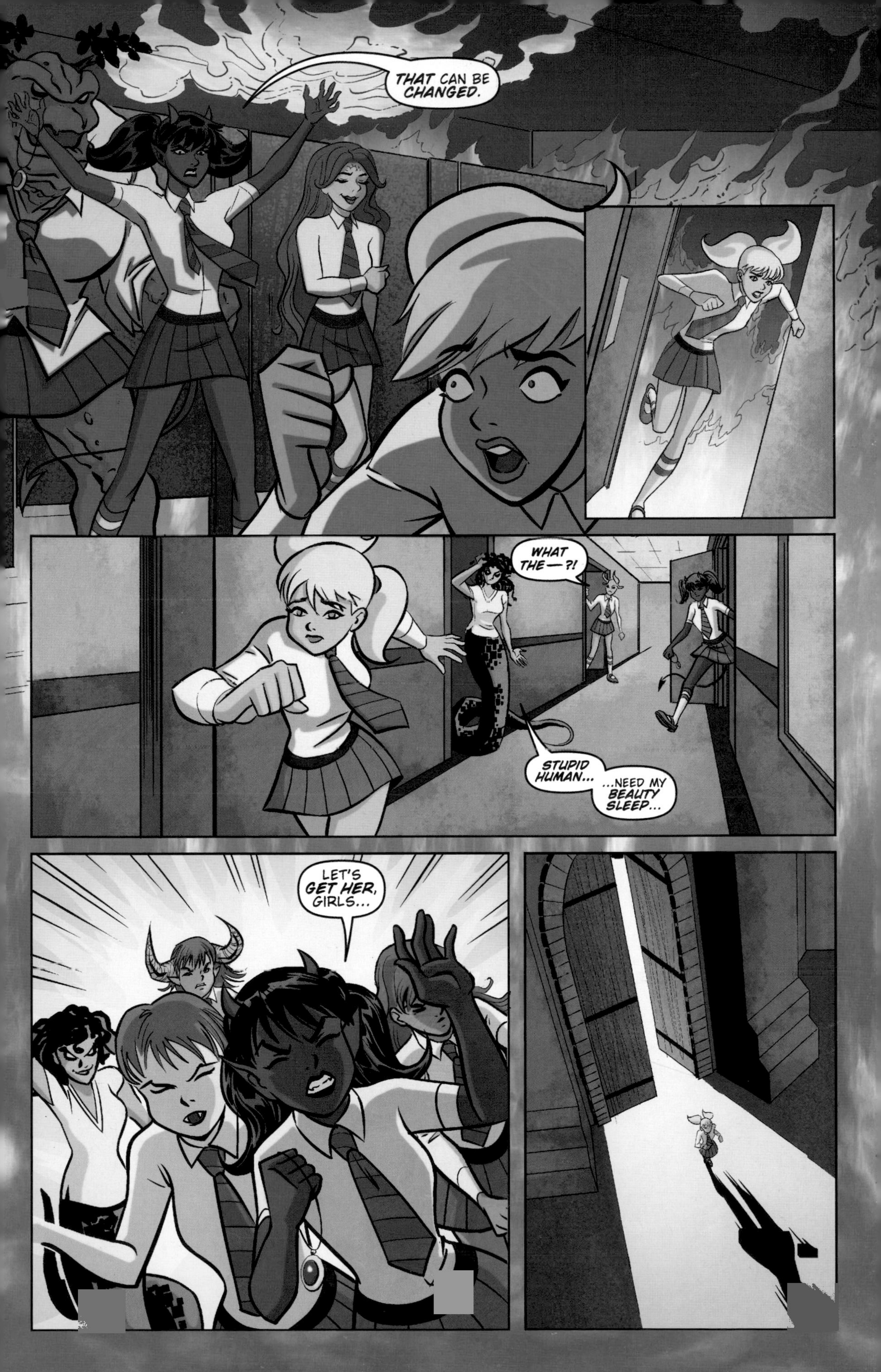
THAT CAN BE CHANGED.
WHAT THE—?!
STUPID HUMAN...
...NEED MY BEAUTY SLEEP...
LET'S GET HER, GIRLS...

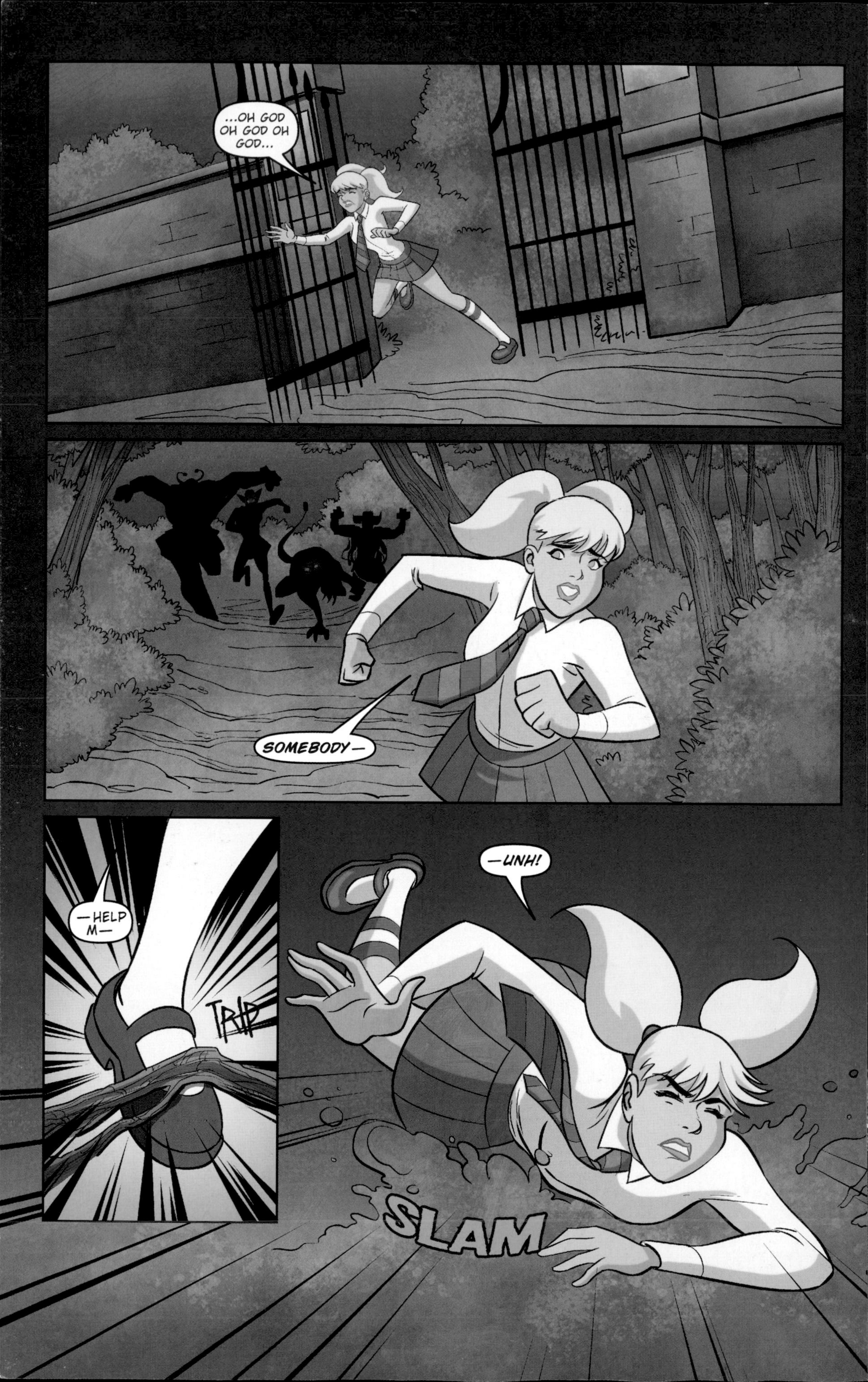
...OH GOD
OH GOD OH
GOD...
SOMEBODY—
—HELP
M—
TRIP
—UNH!
SLAM

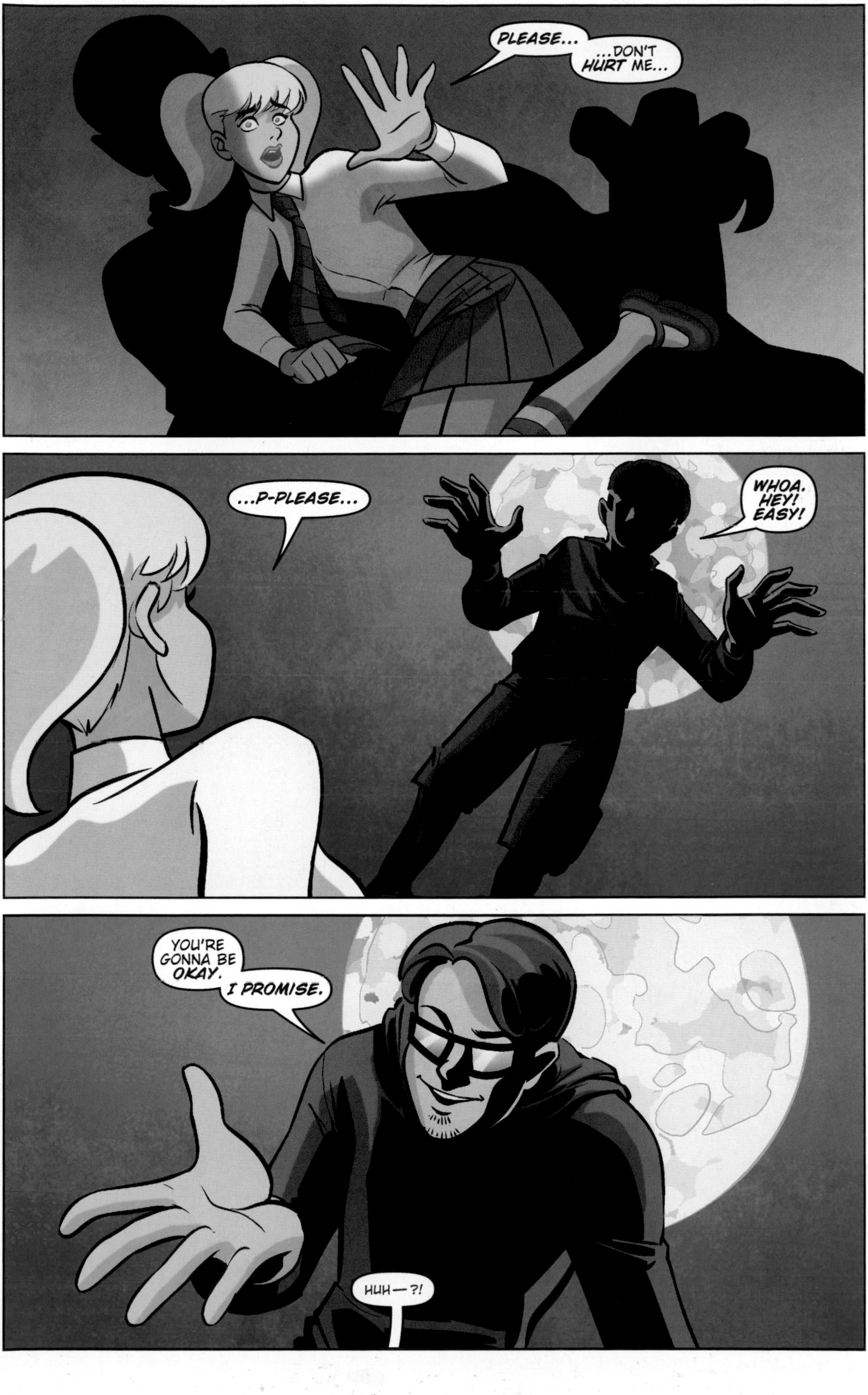
PLEASE...
...DON'T HURT ME...
...P-PLEASE...
WHOA. HEY! EASY!
YOU'RE GONNA BE OKAY.
I PROMISE.
HUH—?!

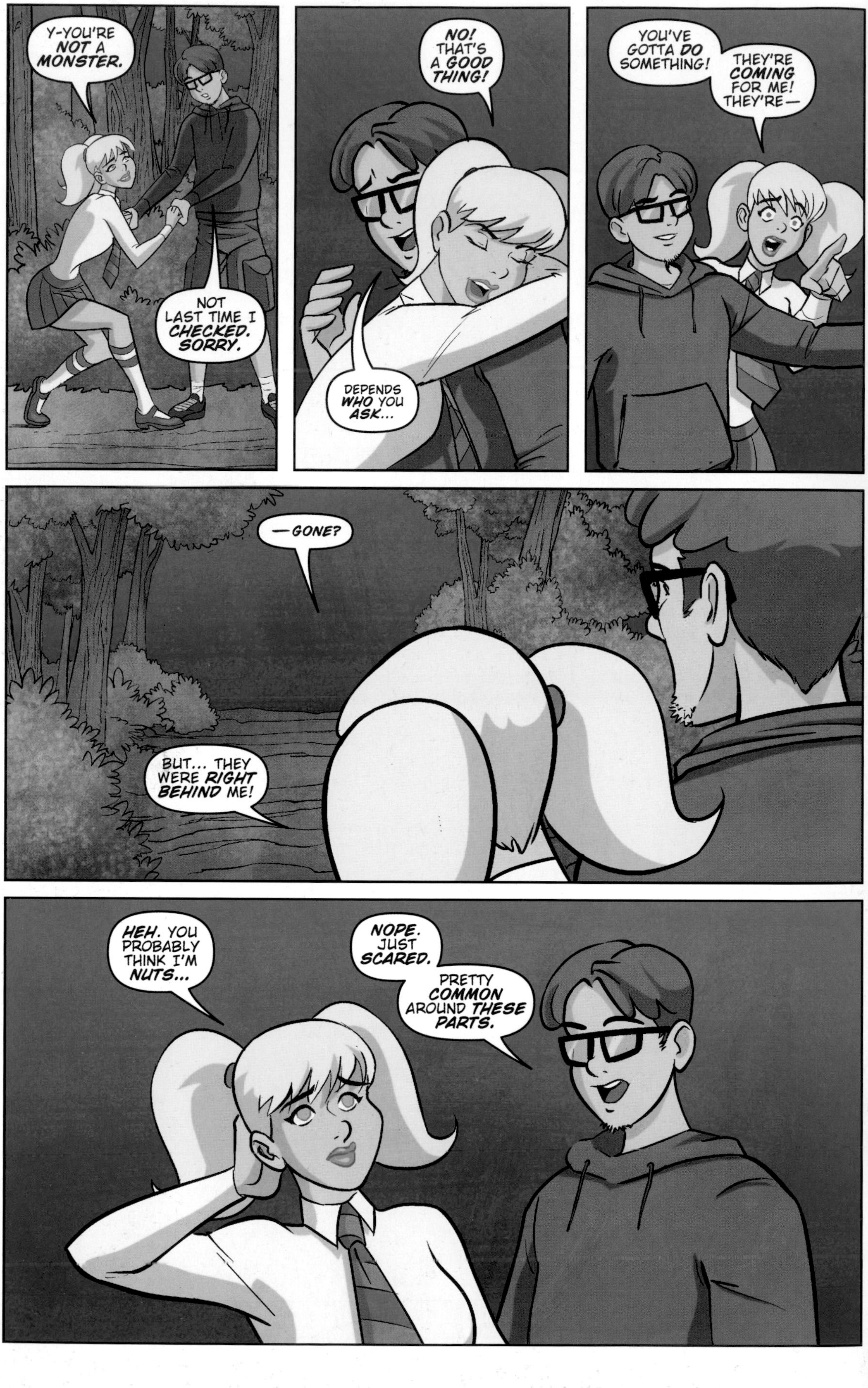
Y-YOU'RE NOT A MONSTER.
NOT LAST TIME I CHECKED. SORRY.
NO! THAT'S A GOOD THING!
DEPENDS WHO YOU ASK...
YOU'VE GOTTA DO SOMETHING!
THEY'RE COMING FOR ME! THEY'RE—
—GONE?
BUT... THEY WERE RIGHT BEHIND ME!
HEH. YOU PROBABLY THINK I'M NUTS...
NOPE. JUST SCARED.
PRETTY COMMON AROUND THESE PARTS.

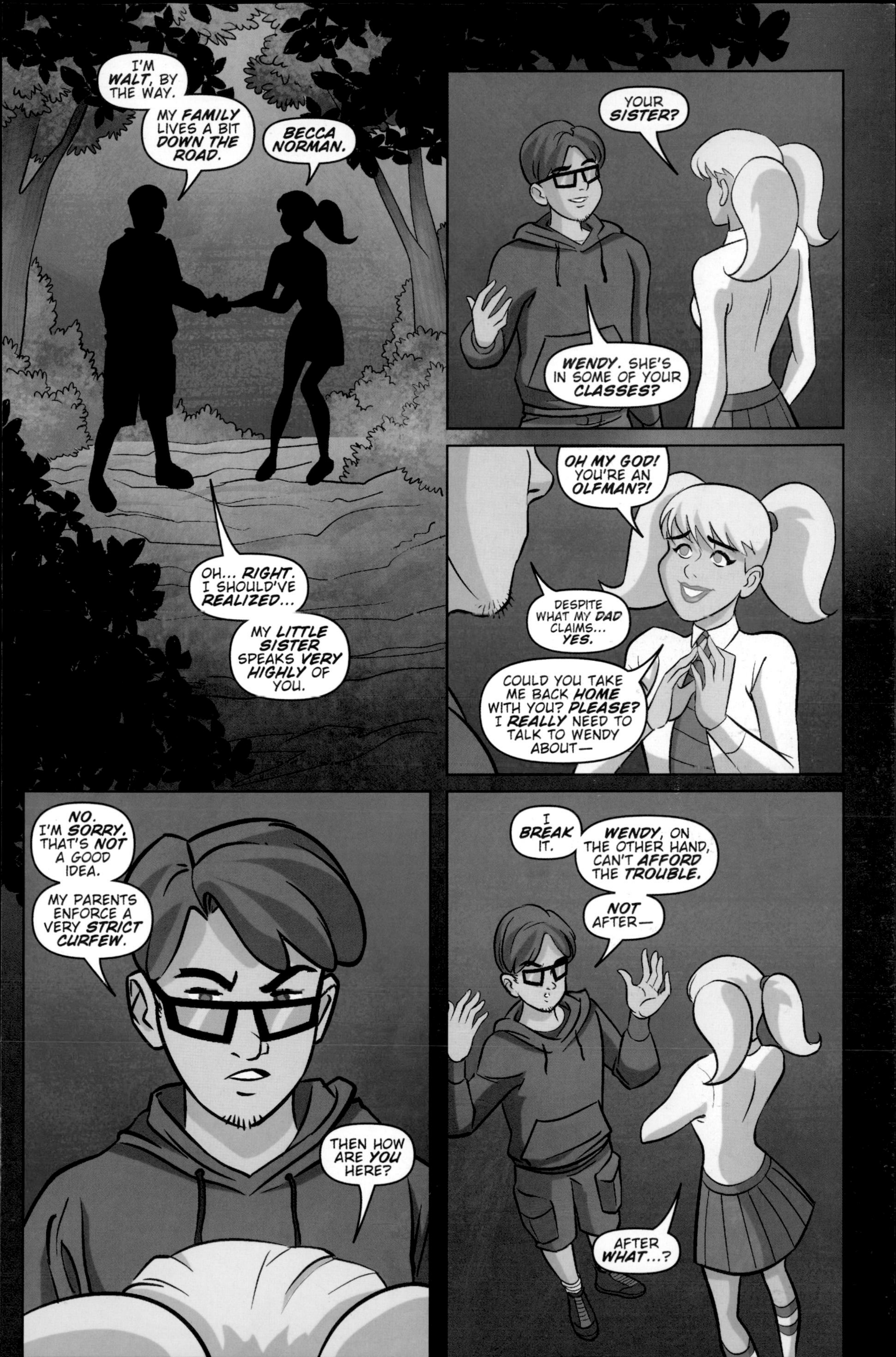
I'M WALT, BY THE WAY.
MY FAMILY LIVES A BIT DOWN THE ROAD.
BECCA NORMAN.
OH... RIGHT. I SHOULD'VE REALIZED...
MY LITTLE SISTER SPEAKS VERY HIGHLY OF YOU.
YOUR SISTER?
WENDY. SHE'S IN SOME OF YOUR CLASSES?
OH MY GOD! YOU'RE AN OLFMAN?!
DESPITE WHAT MY DAD CLAIMS... YES.
COULD YOU TAKE ME BACK HOME WITH YOU? PLEASE? I REALLY NEED TO TALK TO WENDY ABOUT—
NO. I'M SORRY. THAT'S NOT A GOOD IDEA.
MY PARENTS ENFORCE A VERY STRICT CURFEW.
THEN HOW ARE YOU HERE?
I BREAK IT.
WENDY, ON THE OTHER HAND, CAN'T AFFORD THE TROUBLE.
NOT AFTER—
AFTER WHAT...?

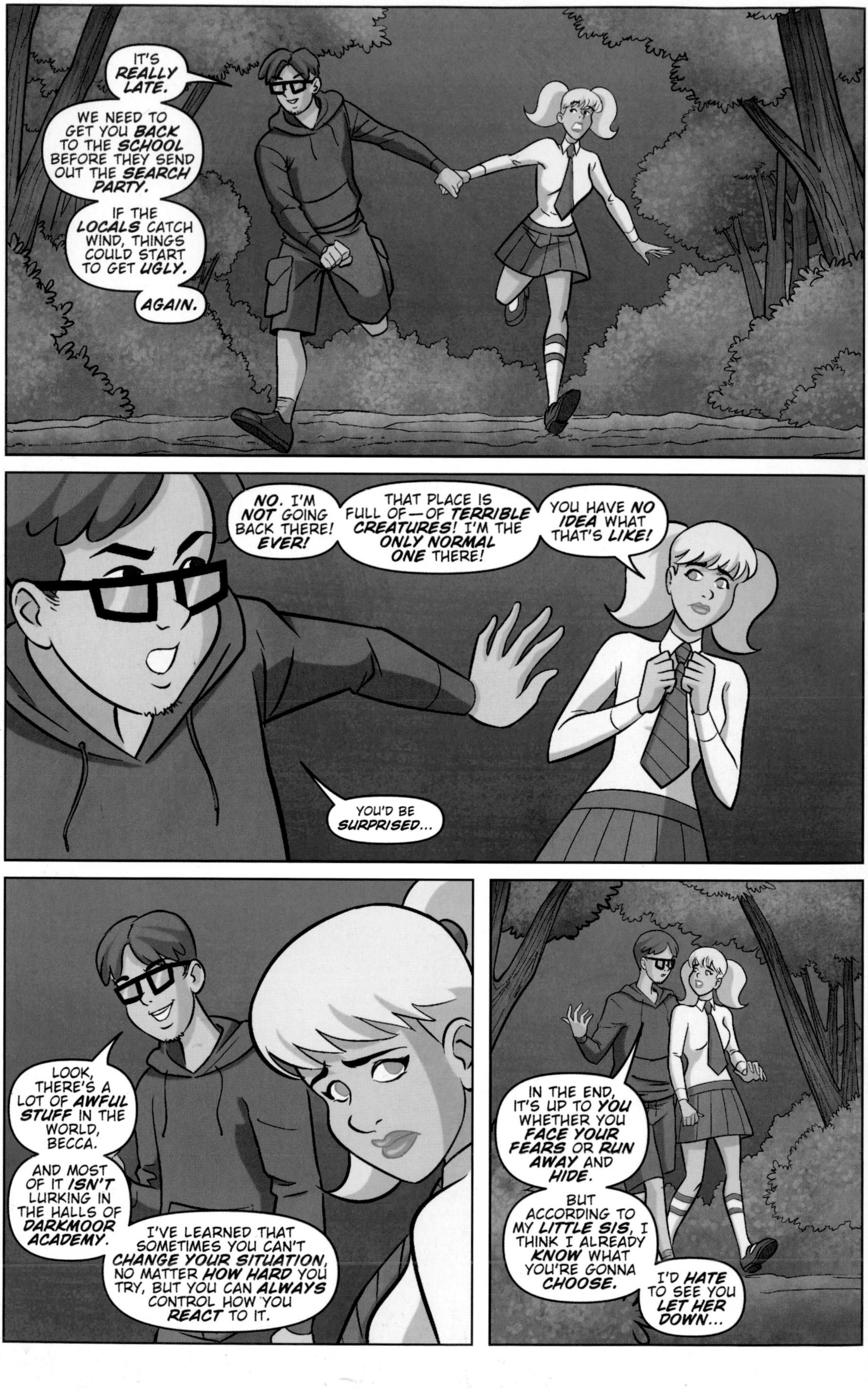
IT'S REALLY LATE.
WE NEED TO GET YOU BACK TO THE SCHOOL BEFORE THEY SEND OUT THE SEARCH PARTY.
IF THE LOCALS CATCH WIND, THINGS COULD START TO GET UGLY.
AGAIN.
NO. I'M NOT GOING BACK THERE! EVER!
THAT PLACE IS FULL OF—OF TERRIBLE CREATURES! I'M THE ONLY NORMAL ONE THERE!
YOU HAVE NO IDEA WHAT THAT'S LIKE!
YOU'D BE SURPRISED...
LOOK, THERE'S A LOT OF AWFUL STUFF IN THE WORLD, BECCA.
AND MOST OF IT ISN'T LURKING IN THE HALLS OF DARKMOOR ACADEMY.
I'VE LEARNED THAT SOMETIMES YOU CAN'T CHANGE YOUR SITUATION, NO MATTER HOW HARD YOU TRY, BUT YOU CAN ALWAYS CONTROL HOW YOU REACT TO IT.
IN THE END, IT'S UP TO YOU WHETHER YOU FACE YOUR FEARS OR RUN AWAY AND HIDE.
BUT ACCORDING TO MY LITTLE SIS, I THINK I ALREADY KNOW WHAT YOU'RE GONNA CHOOSE.
I'D HATE TO SEE YOU LET HER DOWN...

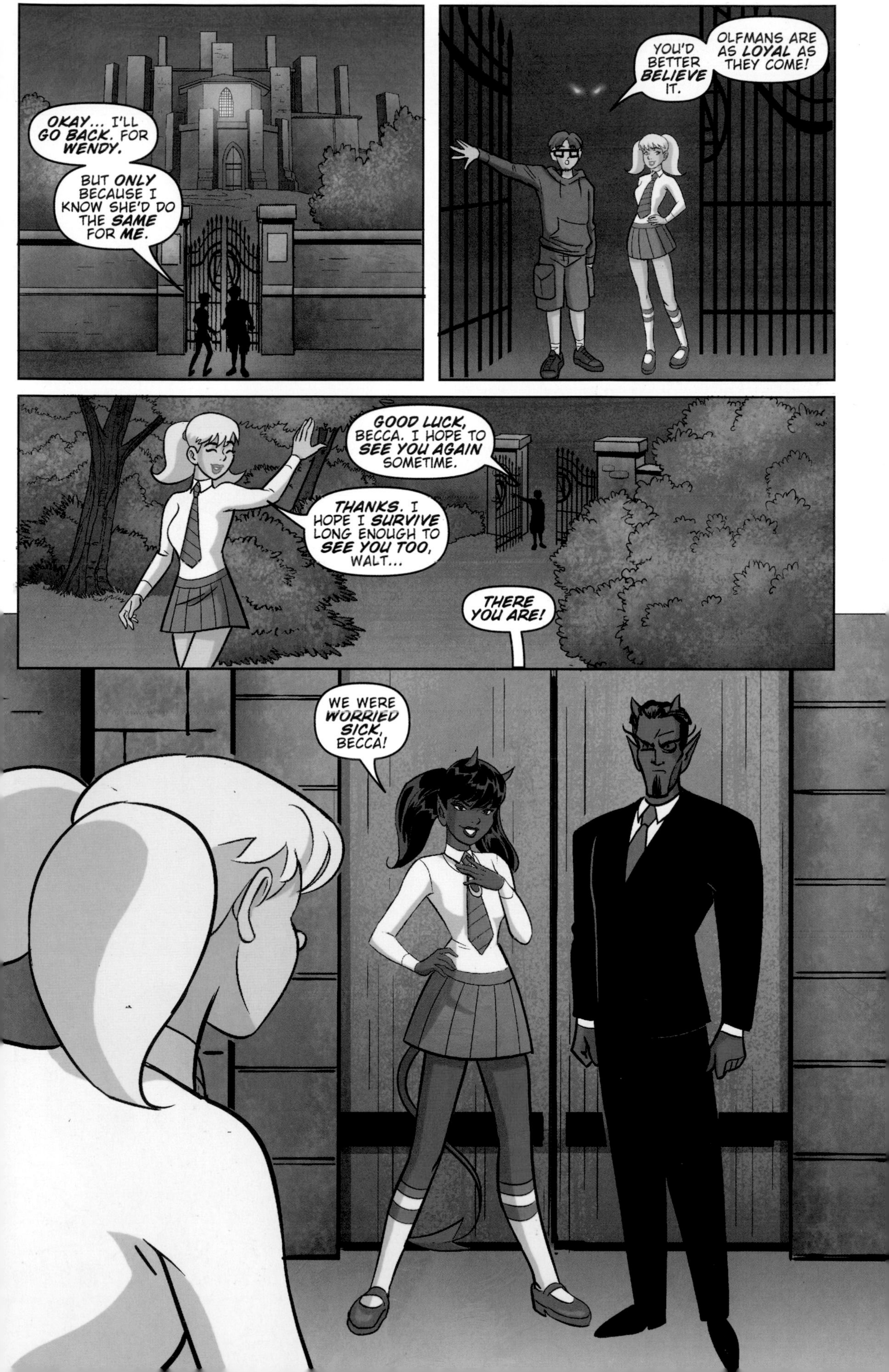
OKAY... I'LL GO BACK. FOR WENDY.
BUT ONLY BECAUSE I KNOW SHE'D DO THE SAME FOR ME.
YOU'D BETTER BELIEVE IT.
OLFMANS ARE AS LOYAL AS THEY COME!
GOOD LUCK, BECCA. I HOPE TO SEE YOU AGAIN SOMETIME.
THANKS. I HOPE I SURVIVE LONG ENOUGH TO SEE YOU TOO, WALT...
THERE YOU ARE!
WE WERE WORRIED SICK, BECCA!

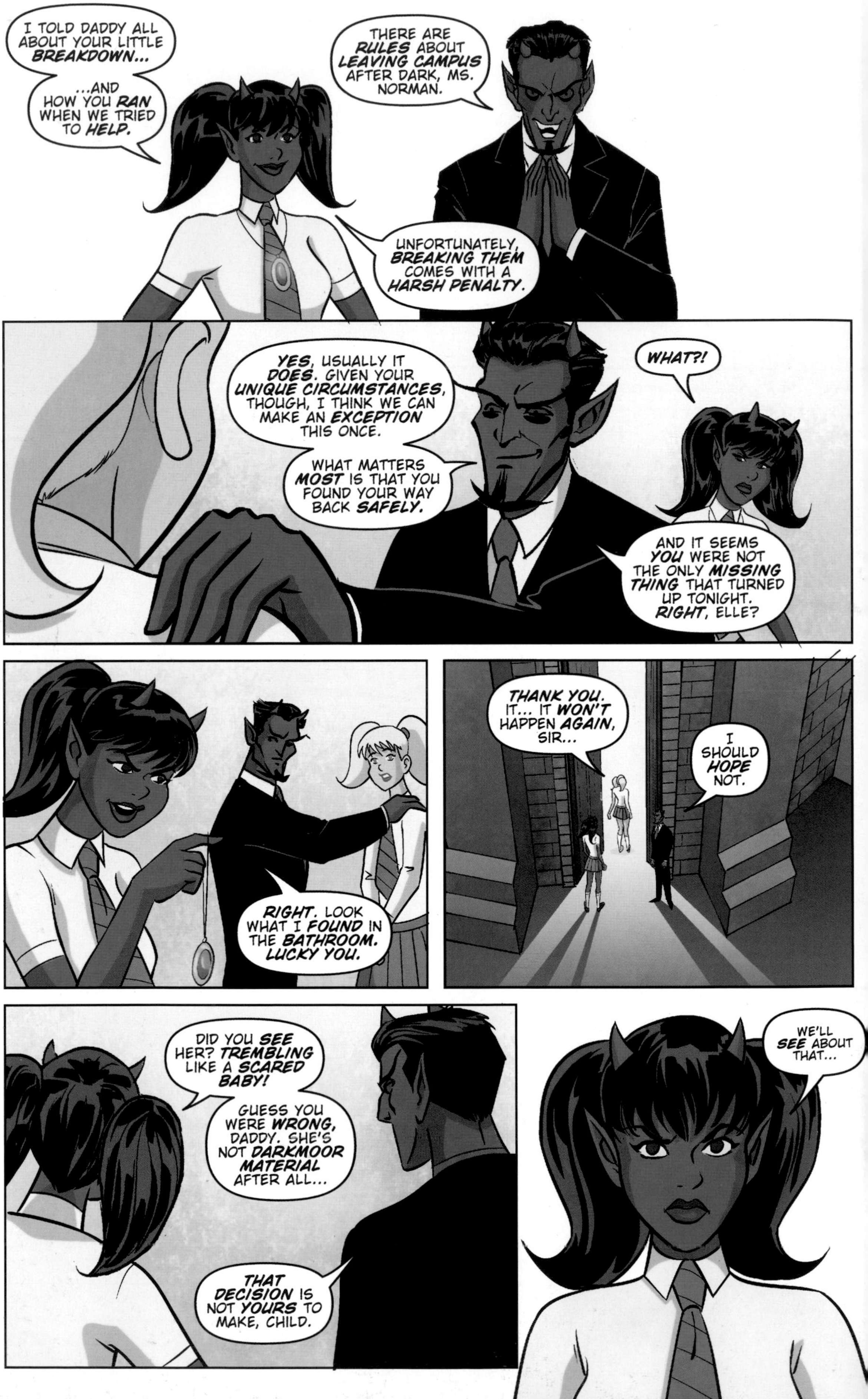
I TOLD DADDY ALL ABOUT YOUR LITTLE BREAKDOWN...
...AND HOW YOU RAN WHEN WE TRIED TO HELP.
THERE ARE RULES ABOUT LEAVING CAMPUS AFTER DARK, MS. NORMAN.
UNFORTUNATELY, BREAKING THEM COMES WITH A HARSH PENALTY.
YES, USUALLY IT DOES. GIVEN YOUR UNIQUE CIRCUMSTANCES, THOUGH, I THINK WE CAN MAKE AN EXCEPTION THIS ONCE.
WHAT?!
WHAT MATTERS MOST IS THAT YOU FOUND YOUR WAY BACK SAFELY.
AND IT SEEMS YOU WERE NOT THE ONLY MISSING THING THAT TURNED UP TONIGHT. RIGHT, ELLE?
RIGHT. LOOK WHAT I FOUND IN THE BATHROOM. LUCKY YOU.
THANK YOU. IT... IT WON'T HAPPEN AGAIN, SIR...
I SHOULD HOPE NOT.
DID YOU SEE HER? TREMBLING LIKE A SCARED BABY!
GUESS YOU WERE WRONG, DADDY. SHE'S NOT DARKMOOR MATERIAL AFTER ALL...
THAT DECISION IS NOT YOURS TO MAKE, CHILD.
WE'LL SEE ABOUT THAT...

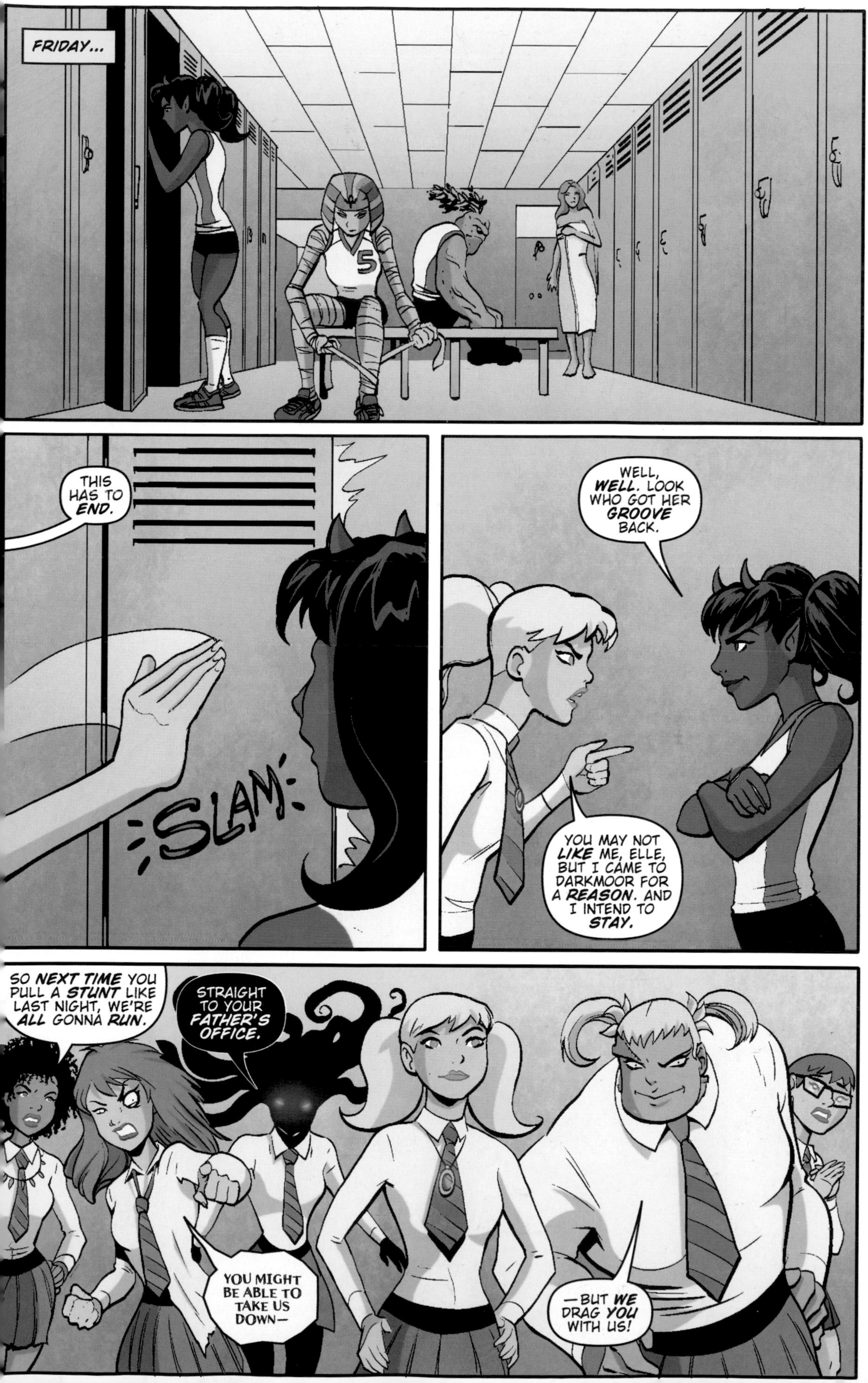
FRIDAY...
THIS HAS TO END.
SLAM
WELL, WELL. LOOK WHO GOT HER GROOVE BACK.
YOU MAY NOT LIKE ME, ELLE, BUT I CAME TO DARKMOOR FOR A REASON. AND I INTEND TO STAY.
SO NEXT TIME YOU PULL A STUNT LIKE LAST NIGHT, WE'RE ALL GONNA RUN.
STRAIGHT TO YOUR FATHER'S OFFICE.
YOU MIGHT BE ABLE TO TAKE US DOWN—
—BUT WE DRAG YOU WITH US!

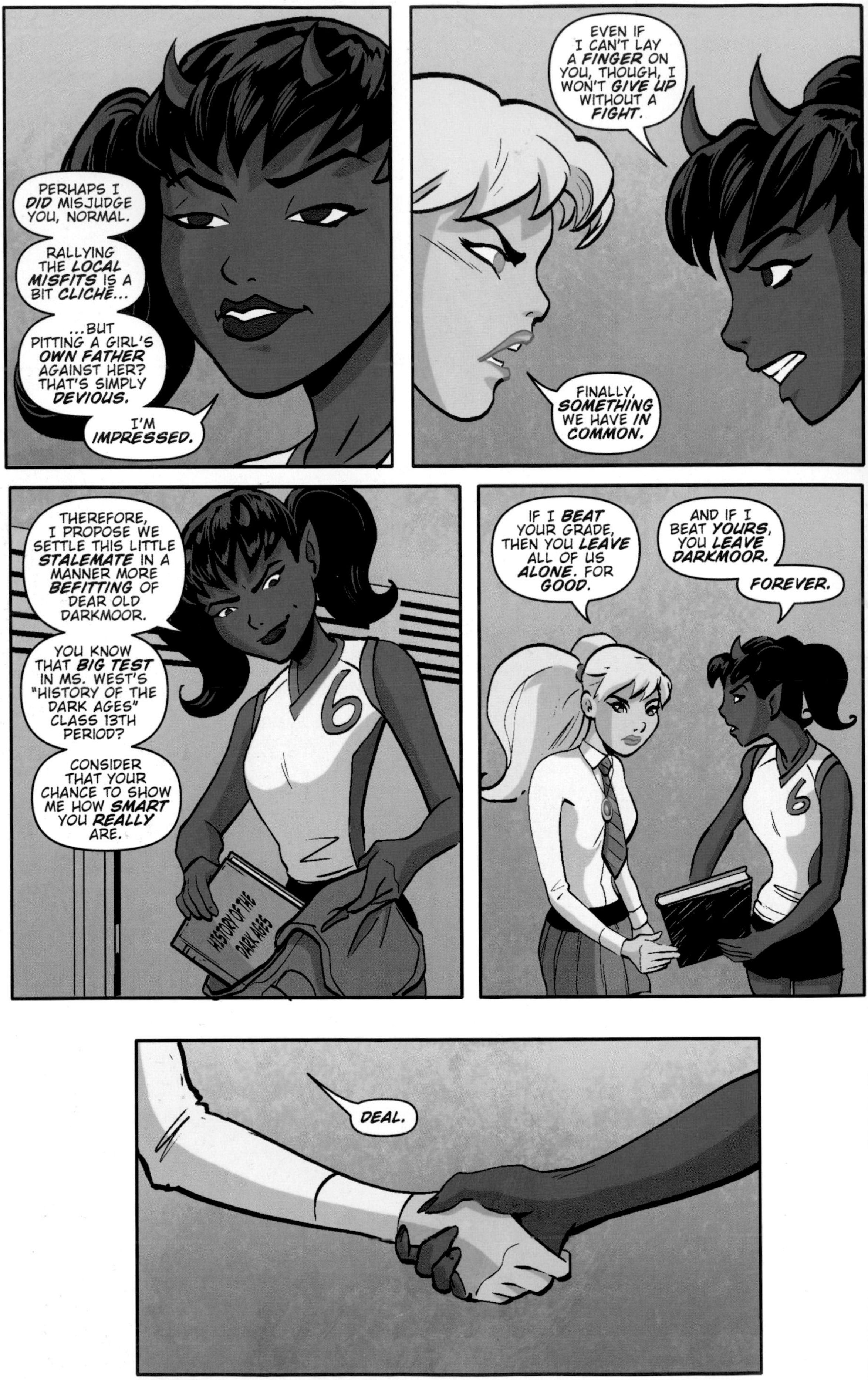
PERHAPS I DID MISJUDGE YOU, NORMAL.
RALLYING THE LOCAL MISFITS IS A BIT CLICHÉ...
...BUT PITTING A GIRL'S OWN FATHER AGAINST HER? THAT'S SIMPLY DEVIOUS.
I'M IMPRESSED.
EVEN IF I CAN'T LAY A FINGER ON YOU, THOUGH, I WON'T GIVE UP WITHOUT A FIGHT.
FINALLY, SOMETHING WE HAVE IN COMMON.
THEREFORE, I PROPOSE WE SETTLE THIS LITTLE STALEMATE IN A MANNER MORE BEFITTING OF DEAR OLD DARKMOOR.
YOU KNOW THAT BIG TEST IN MS. WEST'S "HISTORY OF THE DARK AGES" CLASS 13TH PERIOD?
CONSIDER THAT YOUR CHANCE TO SHOW ME HOW SMART YOU REALLY ARE.
HISTORY OF THE DARK AGES
IF I BEAT YOUR GRADE, THEN YOU LEAVE ALL OF US ALONE. FOR GOOD.
AND IF I BEAT YOURS, YOU LEAVE DARKMOOR.
FOREVER.
DEAL.

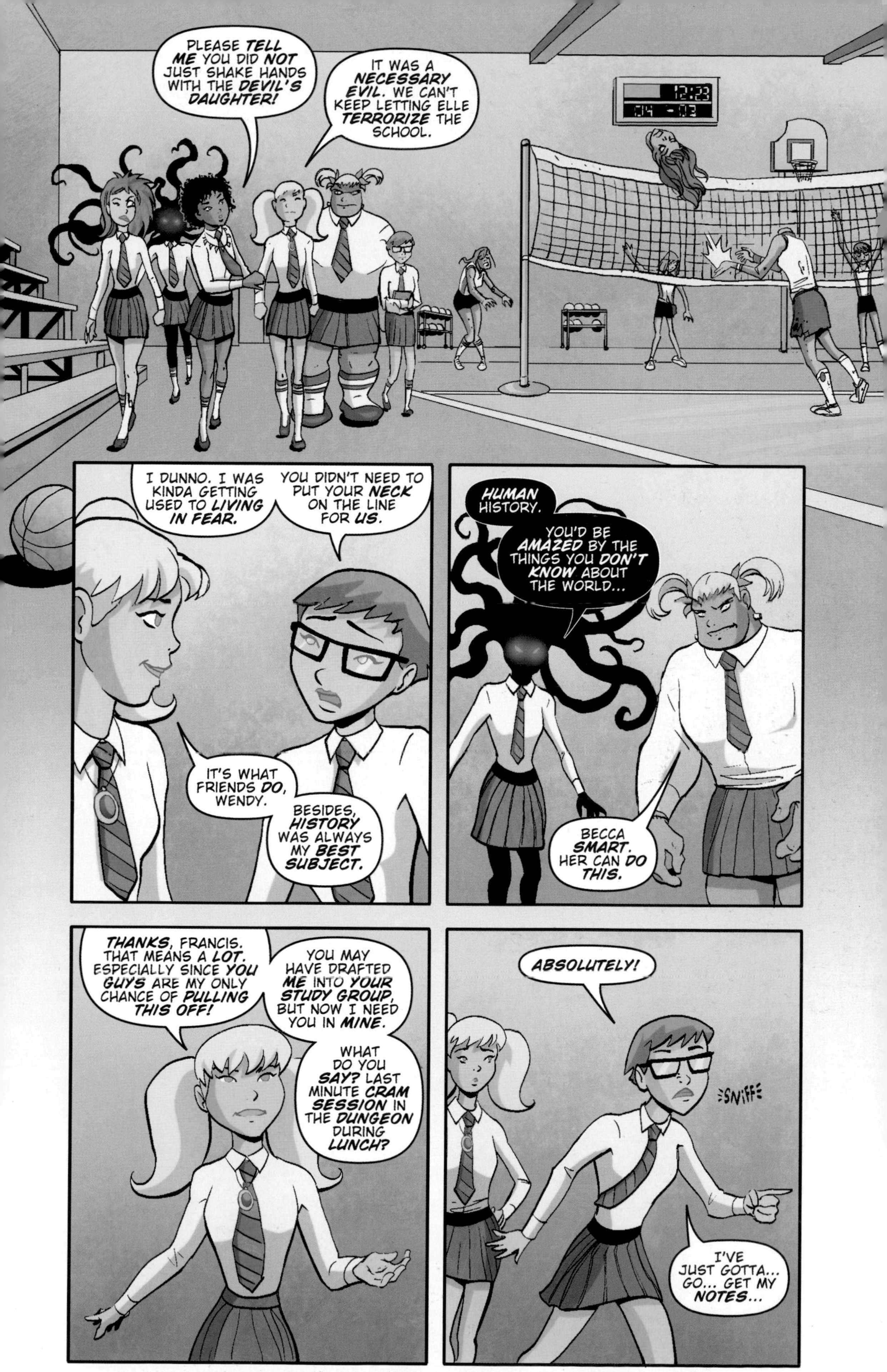

PLEASE TELL ME YOU DID NOT JUST SHAKE HANDS WITH THE DEVIL'S DAUGHTER!
IT WAS A NECESSARY EVIL. WE CAN'T KEEP LETTING ELLE TERRORIZE THE SCHOOL.
I DUNNO. I WAS KINDA GETTING USED TO LIVING IN FEAR.
YOU DIDN'T NEED TO PUT YOUR NECK ON THE LINE FOR US.
IT'S WHAT FRIENDS DO, WENDY.
BESIDES, HISTORY WAS ALWAYS MY BEST SUBJECT.
HUMAN HISTORY.
YOU'D BE AMAZED BY THE THINGS YOU DON'T KNOW ABOUT THE WORLD...
BECCA SMART. HER CAN DO THIS.
THANKS, FRANCIS. THAT MEANS A LOT. ESPECIALLY SINCE YOU GUYS ARE MY ONLY CHANCE OF PULLING THIS OFF!
YOU MAY HAVE DRAFTED ME INTO YOUR STUDY GROUP, BUT NOW I NEED YOU IN MINE.
WHAT DO YOU SAY? LAST MINUTE CRAM SESSION IN THE DUNGEON DURING LUNCH?
ABSOLUTELY!
SNIFF
I'VE JUST GOTTA... GO... GET MY NOTES...

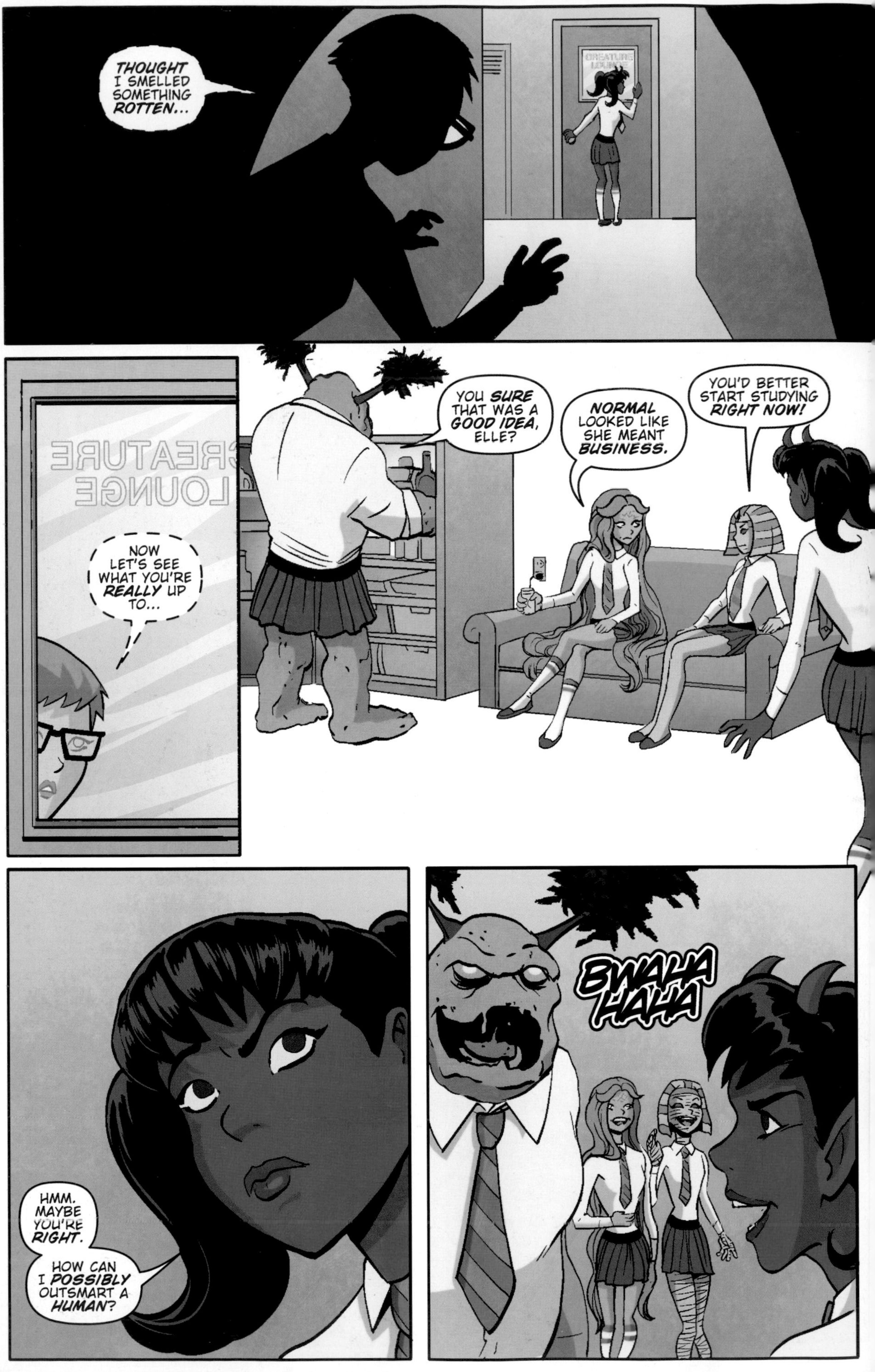
THOUGHT I SMELLED SOMETHING ROTTEN...
CREATURE LOUNGE
NOW LET'S SEE WHAT YOU'RE REALLY UP TO...
YOU SURE THAT WAS A GOOD IDEA, ELLE?
NORMAL LOOKED LIKE SHE MEANT BUSINESS.
YOU'D BETTER START STUDYING RIGHT NOW!
HMM. MAYBE YOU'RE RIGHT.
HOW CAN I POSSIBLY OUTSMART A HUMAN?
BWAHA HAHA

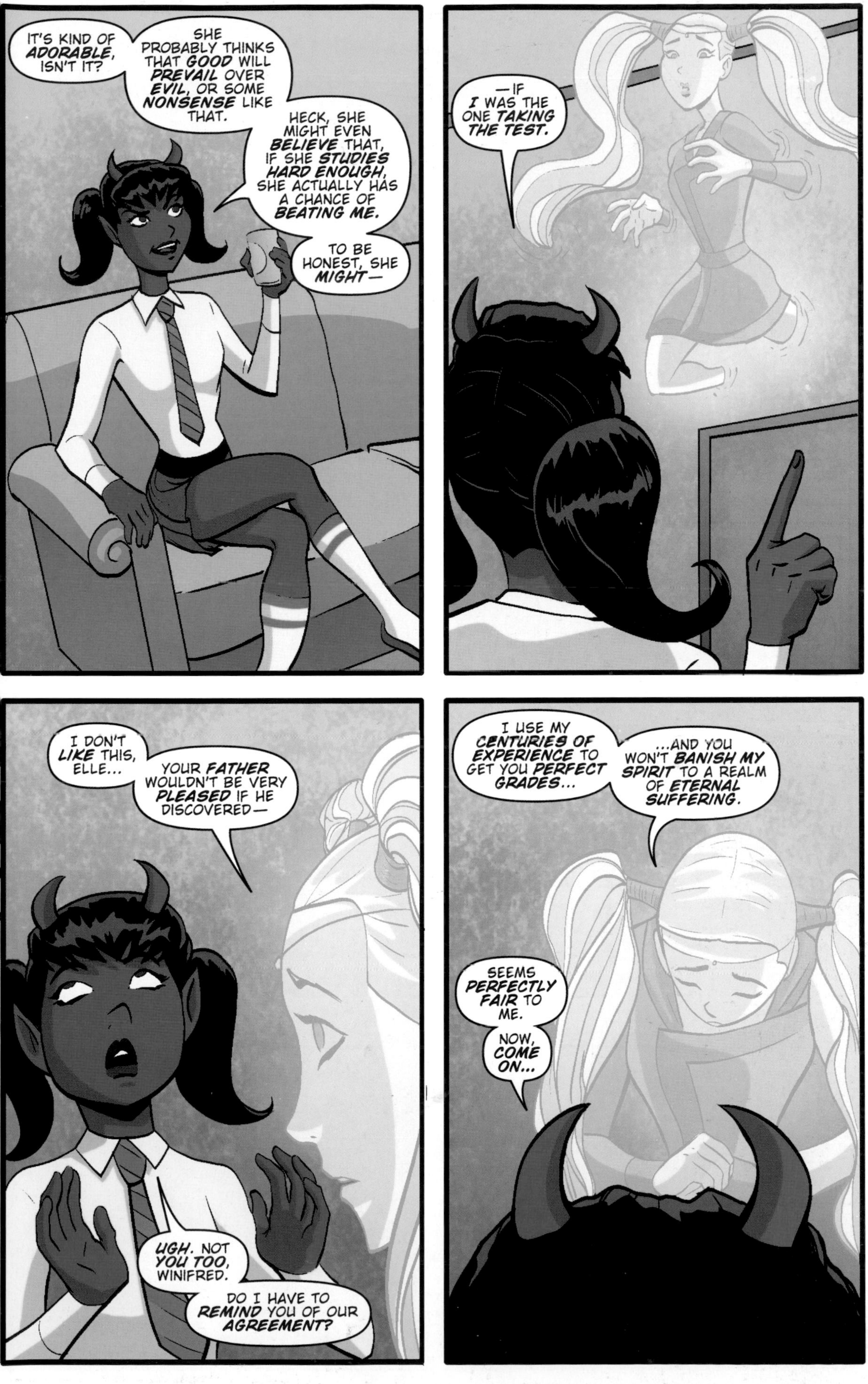
IT'S KIND OF ADORABLE, ISN'T IT?
SHE PROBABLY THINKS THAT GOOD WILL PREVAIL OVER EVIL, OR SOME NONSENSE LIKE THAT.
HECK, SHE MIGHT EVEN BELIEVE THAT, IF SHE STUDIES HARD ENOUGH, SHE ACTUALLY HAS A CHANCE OF BEATING ME.
TO BE HONEST, SHE MIGHT—
—IF I WAS THE ONE TAKING THE TEST.
I DON'T LIKE THIS, ELLE...
YOUR FATHER WOULDN'T BE VERY PLEASED IF HE DISCOVERED—
UGH. NOT YOU TOO, WINIFRED.
DO I HAVE TO REMIND YOU OF OUR AGREEMENT?
I USE MY CENTURIES OF EXPERIENCE TO GET YOU PERFECT GRADES...
...AND YOU WON'T BANISH MY SPIRIT TO A REALM OF ETERNAL SUFFERING.
SEEMS PERFECTLY FAIR TO ME.
NOW, COME ON...

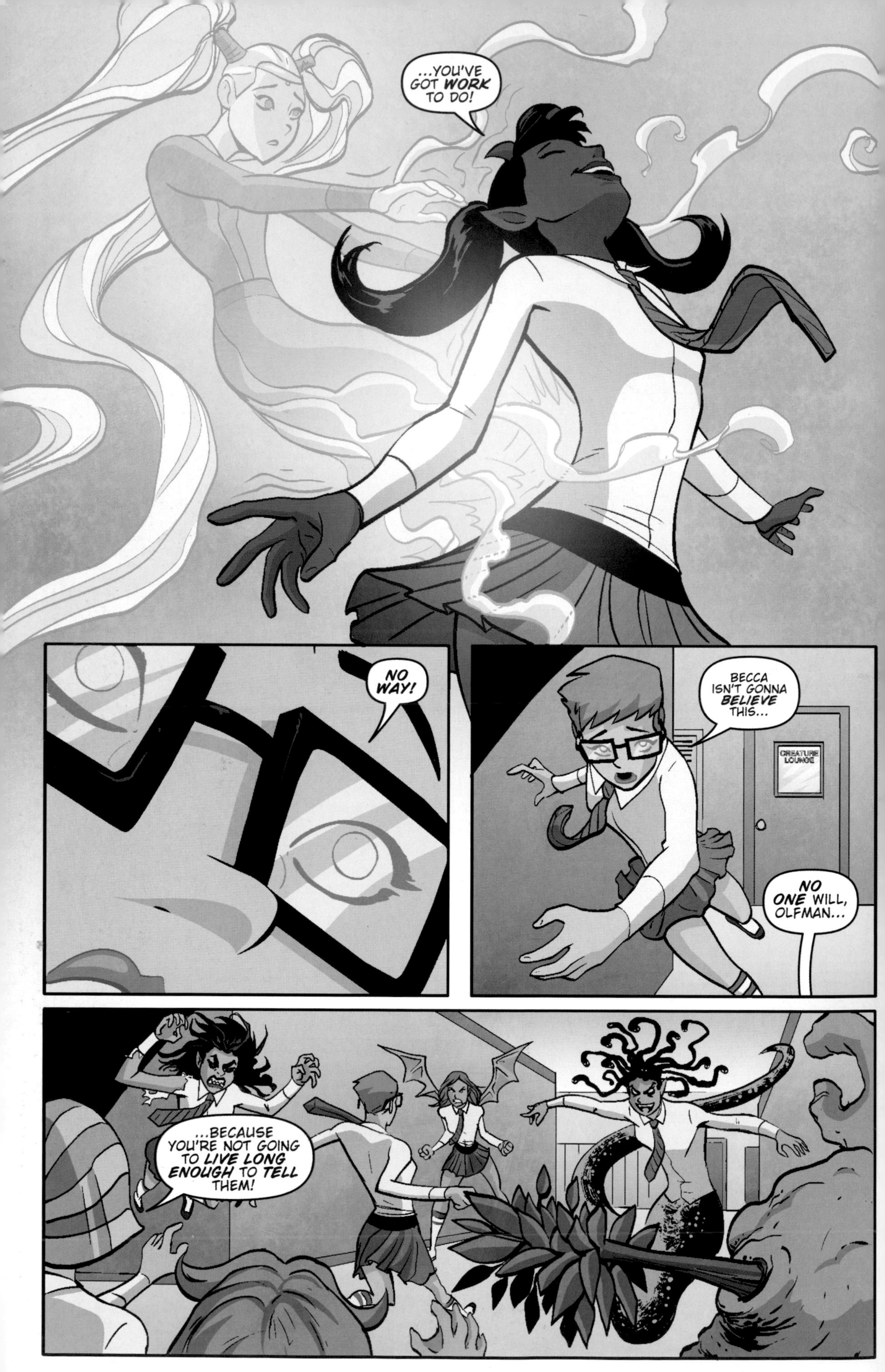
...YOU'VE GOT WORK TO DO!
NO WAY!
BECCA ISN'T GONNA BELIEVE THIS...
CREATURE LOUNGE
NO ONE WILL, OLFMAN...
...BECAUSE YOU'RE NOT GOING TO LIVE LONG ENOUGH TO TELL THEM!

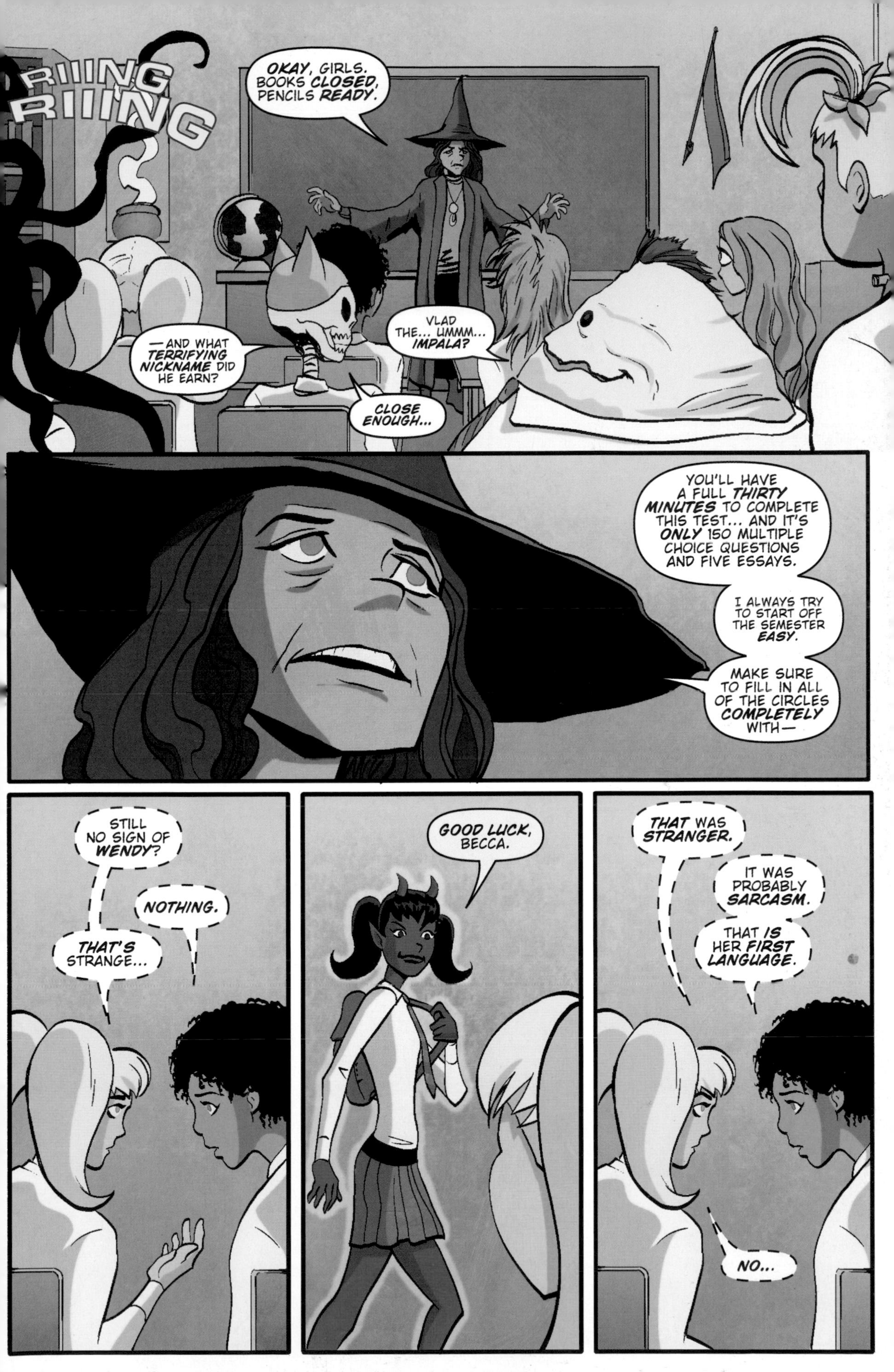
RIIING RIIING
OKAY, GIRLS. BOOKS CLOSED, PENCILS READY.
—AND WHAT TERRIFYING NICKNAME DID HE EARN?
VLAD THE... UMMM... IMPALA?
CLOSE ENOUGH...
YOU'LL HAVE A FULL THIRTY MINUTES TO COMPLETE THIS TEST... AND IT'S ONLY 150 MULTIPLE CHOICE QUESTIONS AND FIVE ESSAYS.
I ALWAYS TRY TO START OFF THE SEMESTER EASY.
MAKE SURE TO FILL IN ALL OF THE CIRCLES COMPLETELY WITH—
STILL NO SIGN OF WENDY?
NOTHING.
THAT'S STRANGE...
GOOD LUCK, BECCA.
THAT WAS STRANGER.
IT WAS PROBABLY SARCASM.
THAT IS HER FIRST LANGUAGE.
NO...

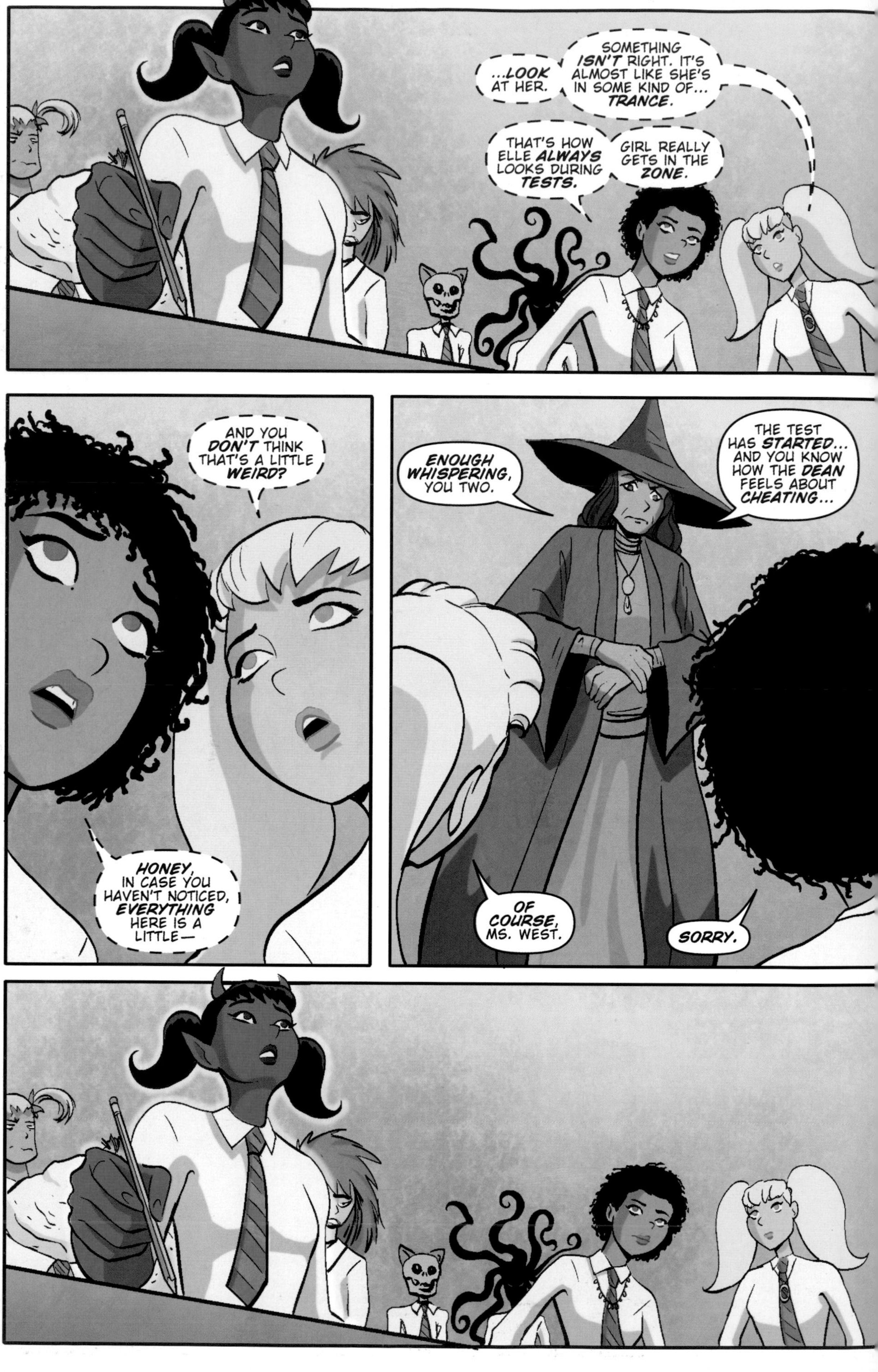
...LOOK AT HER.
SOMETHING ISN'T RIGHT. IT'S ALMOST LIKE SHE'S IN SOME KIND OF... TRANCE.
THAT'S HOW ELLE ALWAYS LOOKS DURING TESTS.
GIRL REALLY GETS IN THE ZONE.
AND YOU DON'T THINK THAT'S A LITTLE WEIRD?
HONEY, IN CASE YOU HAVEN'T NOTICED, EVERYTHING HERE IS A LITTLE—
ENOUGH WHISPERING, YOU TWO.
THE TEST HAS STARTED... AND YOU KNOW HOW THE DEAN FEELS ABOUT CHEATING...
OF COURSE, MS. WEST.
SORRY.

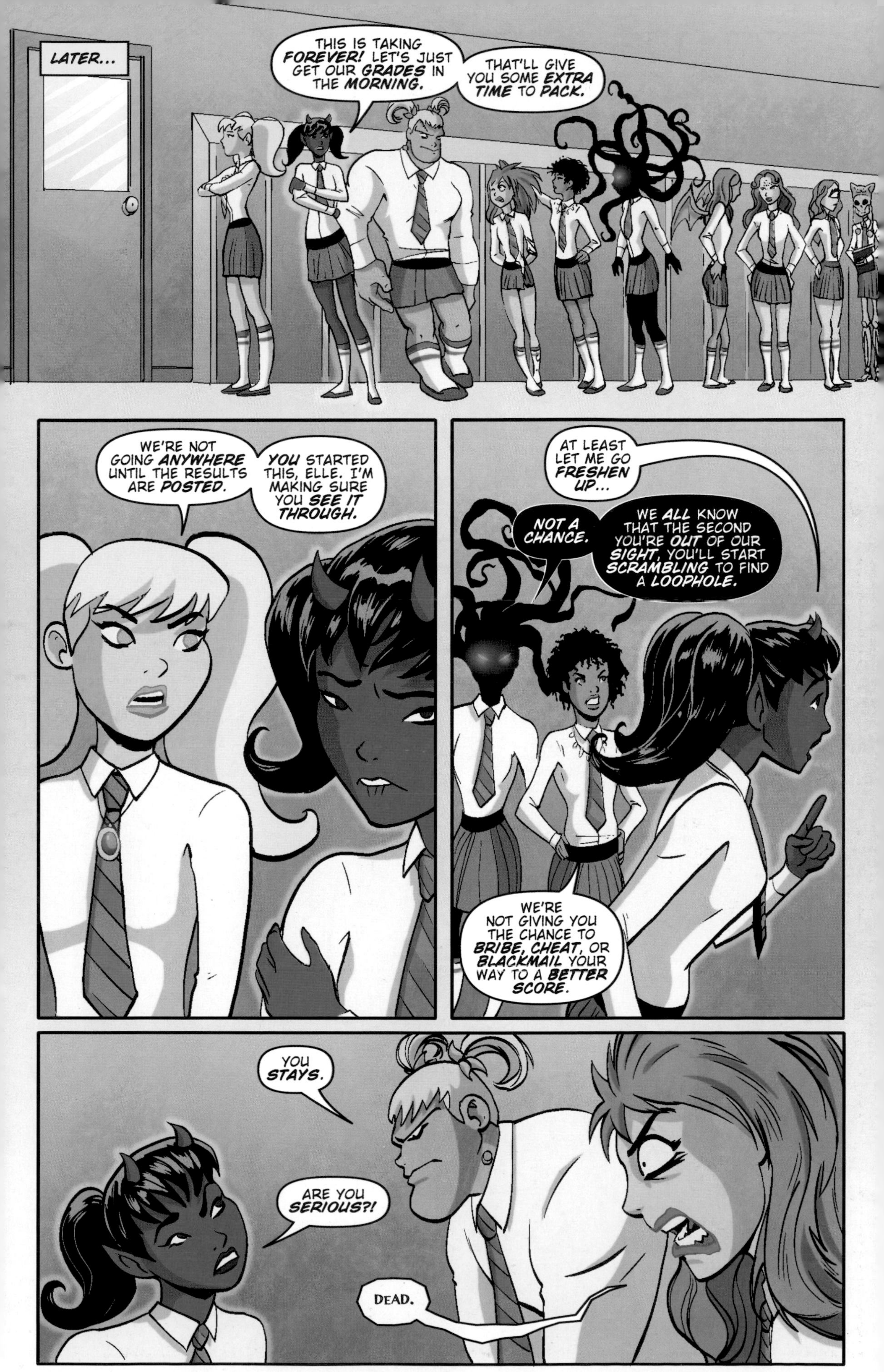
LATER...
THIS IS TAKING FOREVER! LET'S JUST GET OUR GRADES IN THE MORNING.
THAT'LL GIVE YOU SOME EXTRA TIME TO PACK.
WE'RE NOT GOING ANYWHERE UNTIL THE RESULTS ARE POSTED.
YOU STARTED THIS, ELLE. I'M MAKING SURE YOU SEE IT THROUGH.
AT LEAST LET ME GO FRESHEN UP...
NOT A CHANCE.
WE ALL KNOW THAT THE SECOND YOU'RE OUT OF OUR SIGHT, YOU'LL START SCRAMBLING TO FIND A LOOPHOLE.
WE'RE NOT GIVING YOU THE CHANCE TO BRIBE, CHEAT, OR BLACKMAIL YOUR WAY TO A BETTER SCORE.
YOU STAYS.
ARE YOU SERIOUS?!
DEAD.

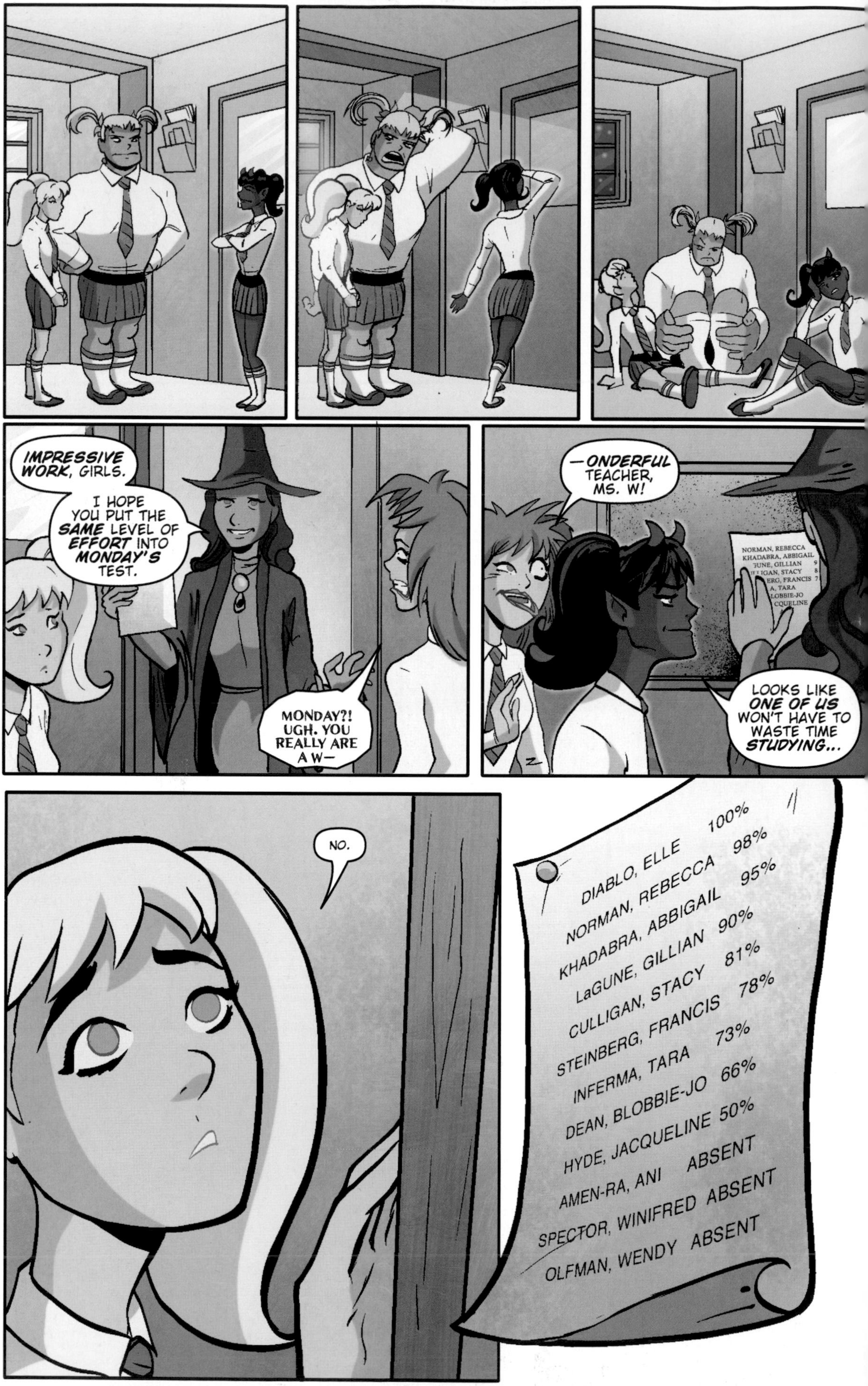
IMPRESSIVE WORK, GIRLS.
I HOPE YOU PUT THE SAME LEVEL OF EFFORT INTO MONDAY'S TEST.
MONDAY?! UGH. YOU REALLY ARE A W—
—ONDERFUL TEACHER, MS. W!
LOOKS LIKE ONE OF US WON'T HAVE TO WASTE TIME STUDYING...
NO.
DIABLO, ELLE 100%
NORMAN, REBECCA 98%
KHADABRA, ABBIGAIL 95%
LaGUNE, GILLIAN 90%
CULLIGAN, STACY 81%
STEINBERG, FRANCIS 78%
INFERMA, TARA 73%
DEAN, BLOBBIE-JO 66%
HYDE, JACQUELINE 50%
AMEN-RA, ANI ABSENT
SPECTOR, WINIFRED ABSENT
OLFMAN, WENDY ABSENT

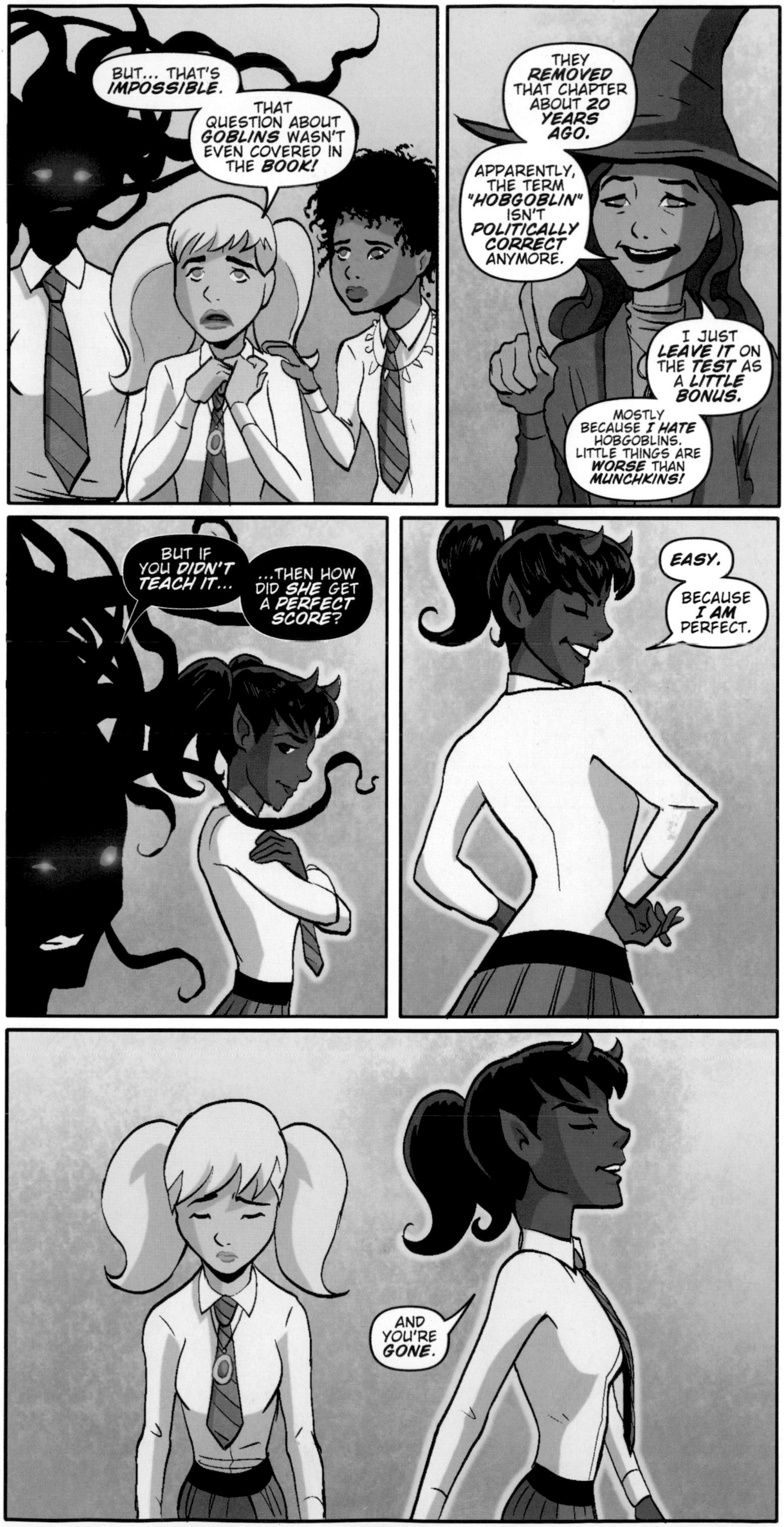
BUT... THAT'S IMPOSSIBLE.
THAT QUESTION ABOUT GOBLINS WASN'T EVEN COVERED IN THE BOOK!
THEY REMOVED THAT CHAPTER ABOUT 20 YEARS AGO.
APPARENTLY, THE TERM "HOBGOBLIN" ISN'T POLITICALLY CORRECT ANYMORE.
I JUST LEAVE IT ON THE TEST AS A LITTLE BONUS.
MOSTLY BECAUSE I HATE HOBGOBLINS. LITTLE THINGS ARE WORSE THAN MUNCHKINS!
BUT IF YOU DIDN'T TEACH IT...
...THEN HOW DID SHE GET A PERFECT SCORE?
EASY.
BECAUSE I AM PERFECT.
AND YOU'RE GONE.

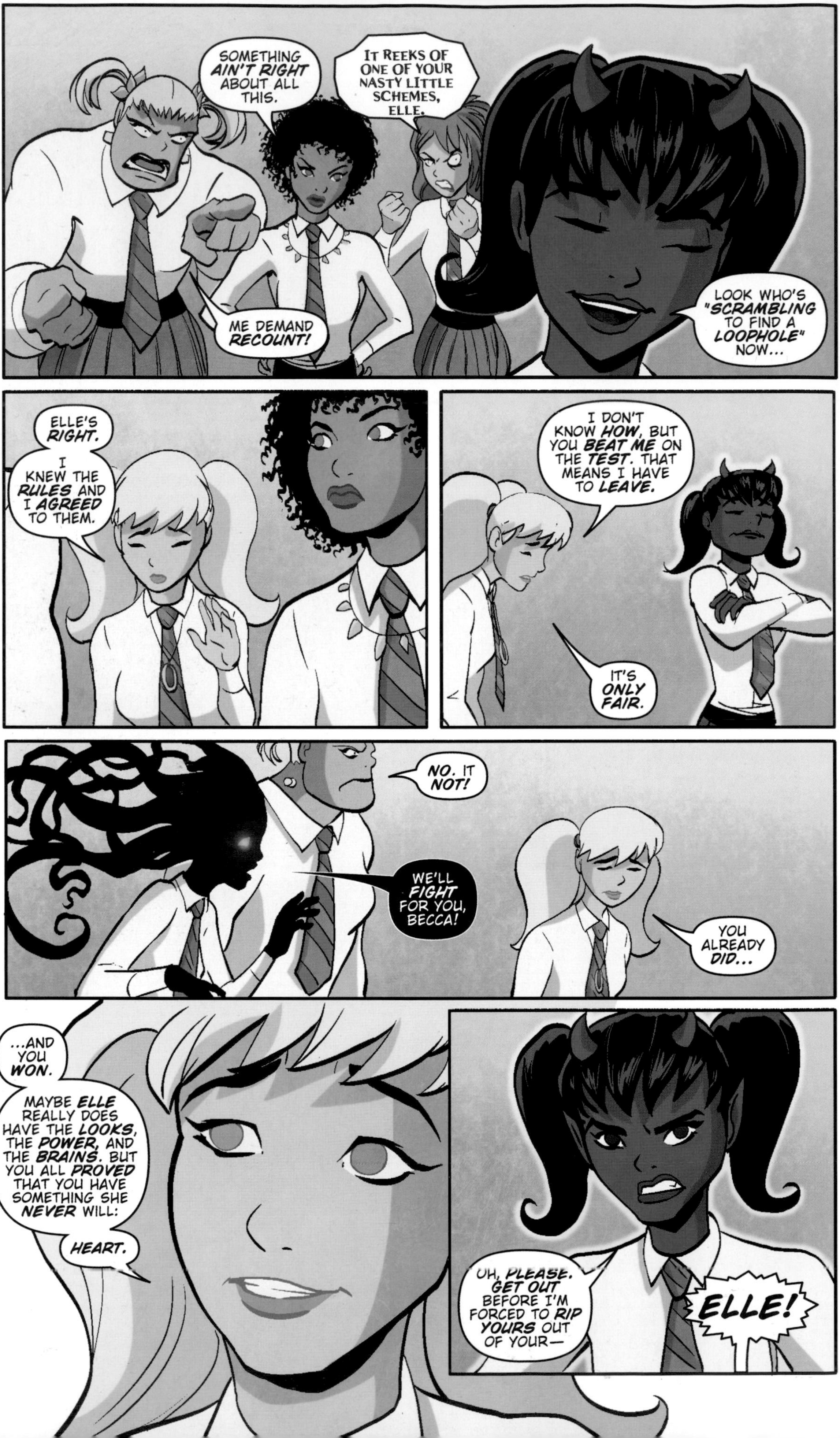
SOMETHING AIN'T RIGHT ABOUT ALL THIS.
IT REEKS OF ONE OF YOUR NASTY LITTLE SCHEMES, ELLE.
ME DEMAND RECOUNT!
LOOK WHO'S "SCRAMBLING TO FIND A LOOPHOLE" NOW...
ELLE'S RIGHT.
I KNEW THE RULES AND I AGREED TO THEM.
I DON'T KNOW HOW, BUT YOU BEAT ME ON THE TEST. THAT MEANS I HAVE TO LEAVE.
IT'S ONLY FAIR.
NO. IT NOT!
WE'LL FIGHT FOR YOU, BECCA!
YOU ALREADY DID...
...AND YOU WON.
MAYBE ELLE REALLY DOES HAVE THE LOOKS, THE POWER, AND THE BRAINS. BUT YOU ALL PROVED THAT YOU HAVE SOMETHING SHE NEVER WILL:
HEART.
OH, PLEASE. GET OUT BEFORE I'M FORCED TO RIP YOURS OUT OF YOUR—
ELLE!

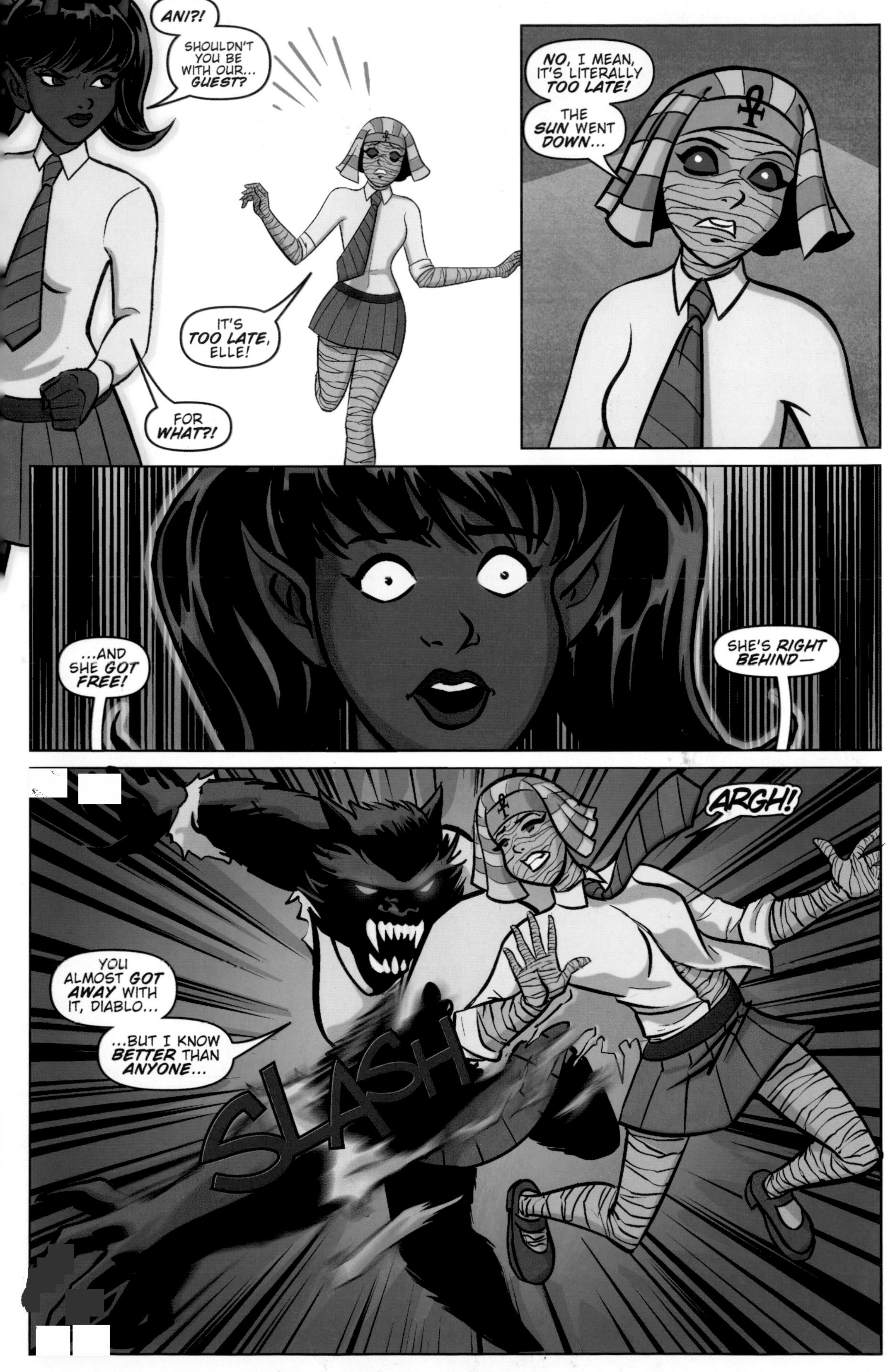
ANI?!
SHOULDN'T YOU BE WITH OUR... GUEST?
IT'S TOO LATE, ELLE!
FOR WHAT?!
NO, I MEAN, IT'S LITERALLY TOO LATE!
THE SUN WENT DOWN...
...AND SHE GOT FREE!
SHE'S RIGHT BEHIND—
ARGH!
YOU ALMOST GOT AWAY WITH IT, DIABLO...
...BUT I KNOW BETTER THAN ANYONE...
SLASH

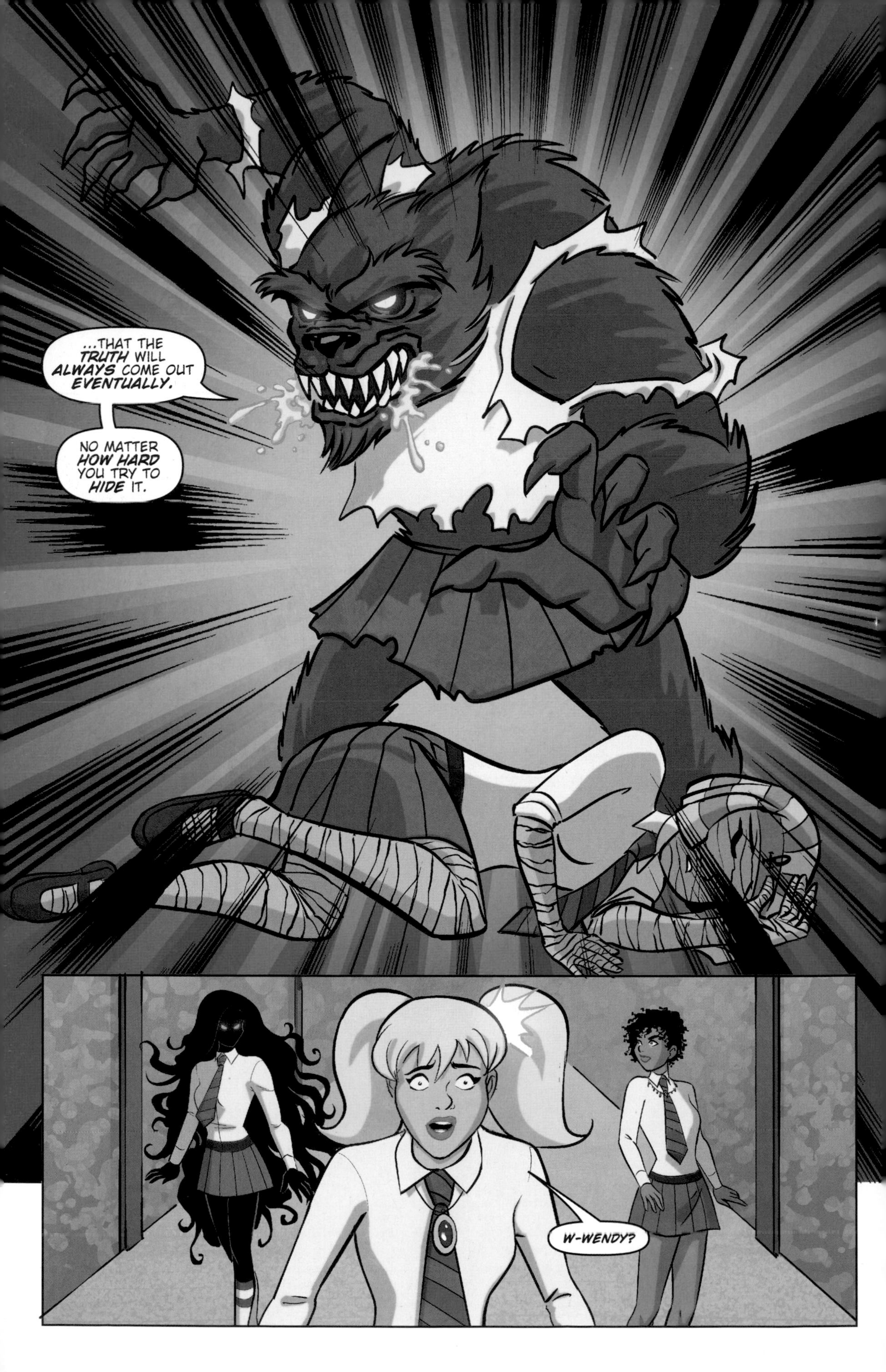
...THAT THE TRUTH WILL ALWAYS COME OUT EVENTUALLY.
NO MATTER HOW HARD YOU TRY TO HIDE IT.
W-WENDY?

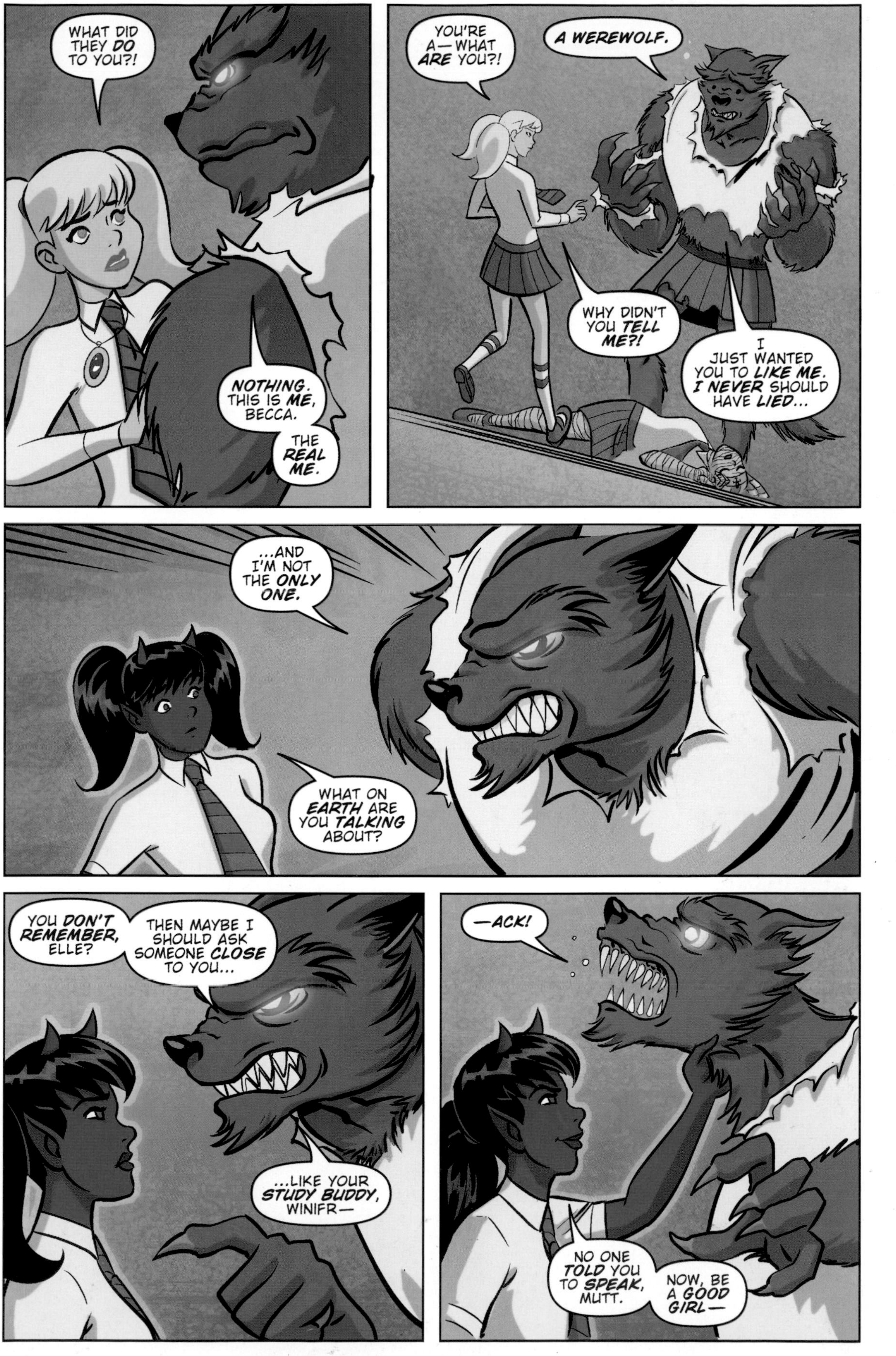
WHAT DID THEY DO TO YOU?!
NOTHING. THIS IS ME, BECCA.
THE REAL ME.
YOU'RE A—WHAT ARE YOU?!
A WEREWOLF.
WHY DIDN'T YOU TELL ME?!
I JUST WANTED YOU TO LIKE ME. I NEVER SHOULD HAVE LIED...
...AND I'M NOT THE ONLY ONE.
WHAT ON EARTH ARE YOU TALKING ABOUT?
YOU DON'T REMEMBER, ELLE?
THEN MAYBE I SHOULD ASK SOMEONE CLOSE TO YOU...
...LIKE YOUR STUDY BUDDY, WINIFR—
—ACK!
NO ONE TOLD YOU TO SPEAK, MUTT.
NOW, BE A GOOD GIRL—

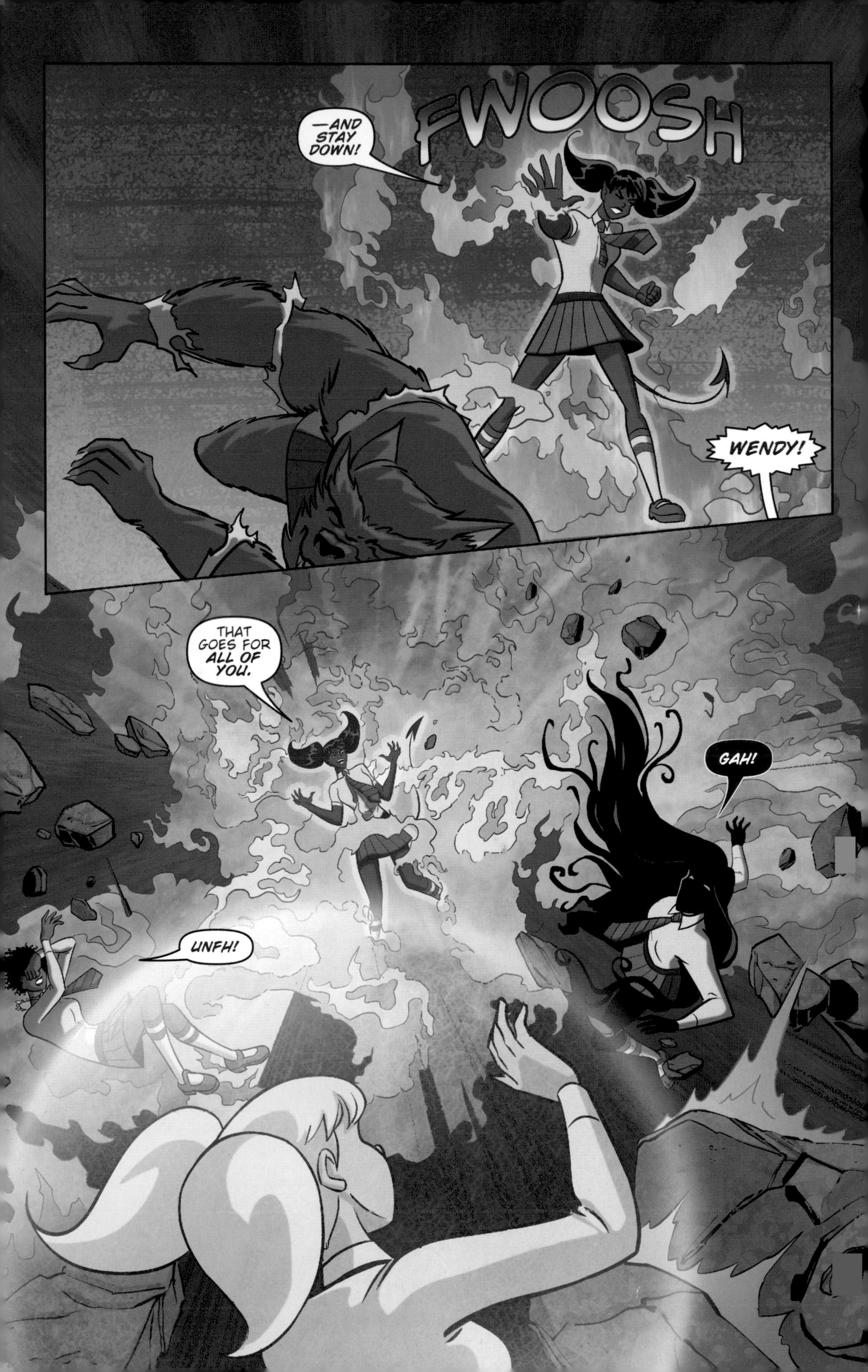
FWOOSH
—AND STAY DOWN!
WENDY!
THAT GOES FOR ALL OF YOU.
GAH!
UNFH!

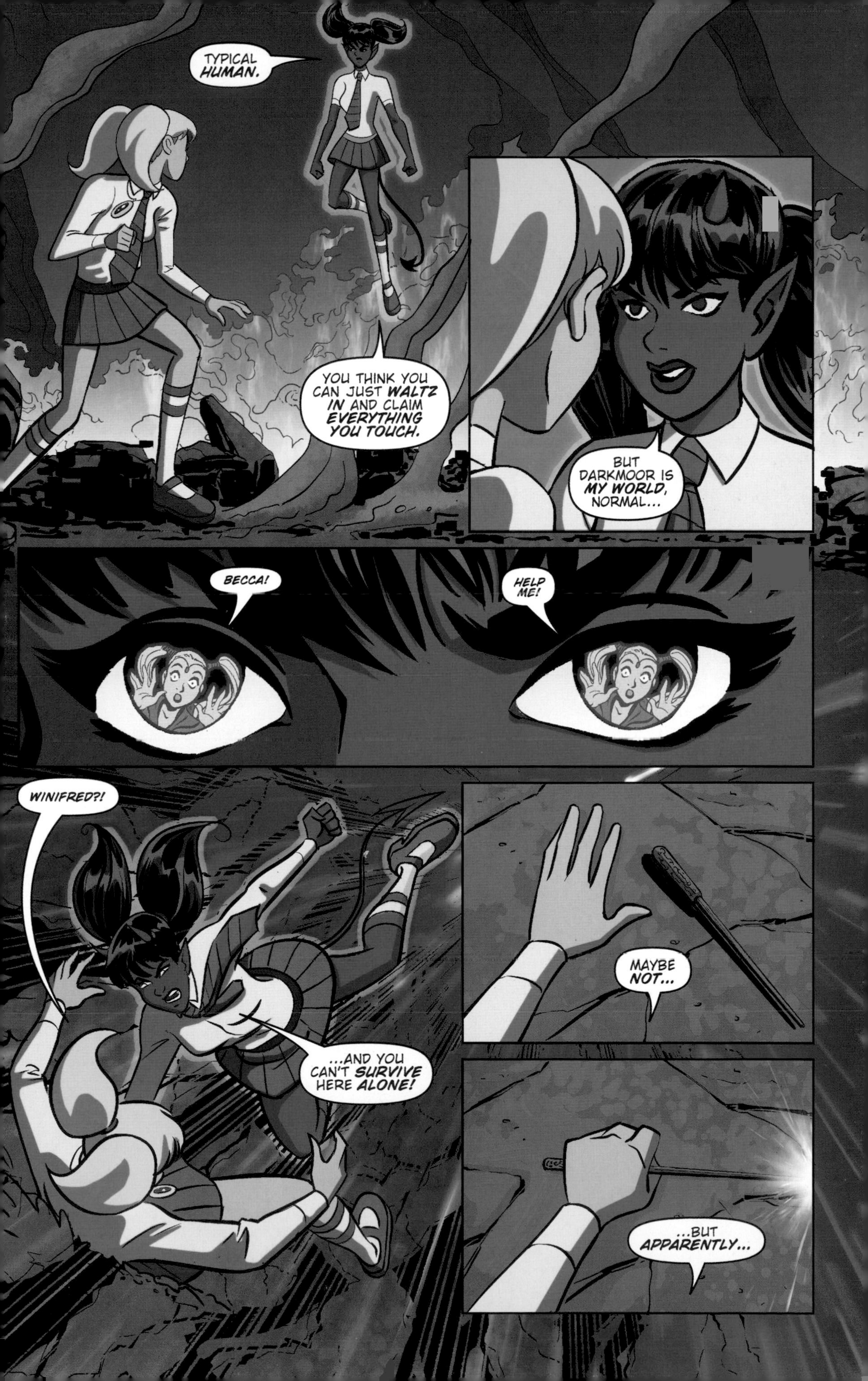
TYPICAL HUMAN.
YOU THINK YOU CAN JUST WALTZ IN AND CLAIM EVERYTHING YOU TOUCH.
BUT DARKMOOR IS MY WORLD, NORMAL...
BECCA!
HELP ME!
WINIFRED?!
...AND YOU CAN'T SURVIVE HERE ALONE!
MAYBE NOT...
...BUT APPARENTLY...

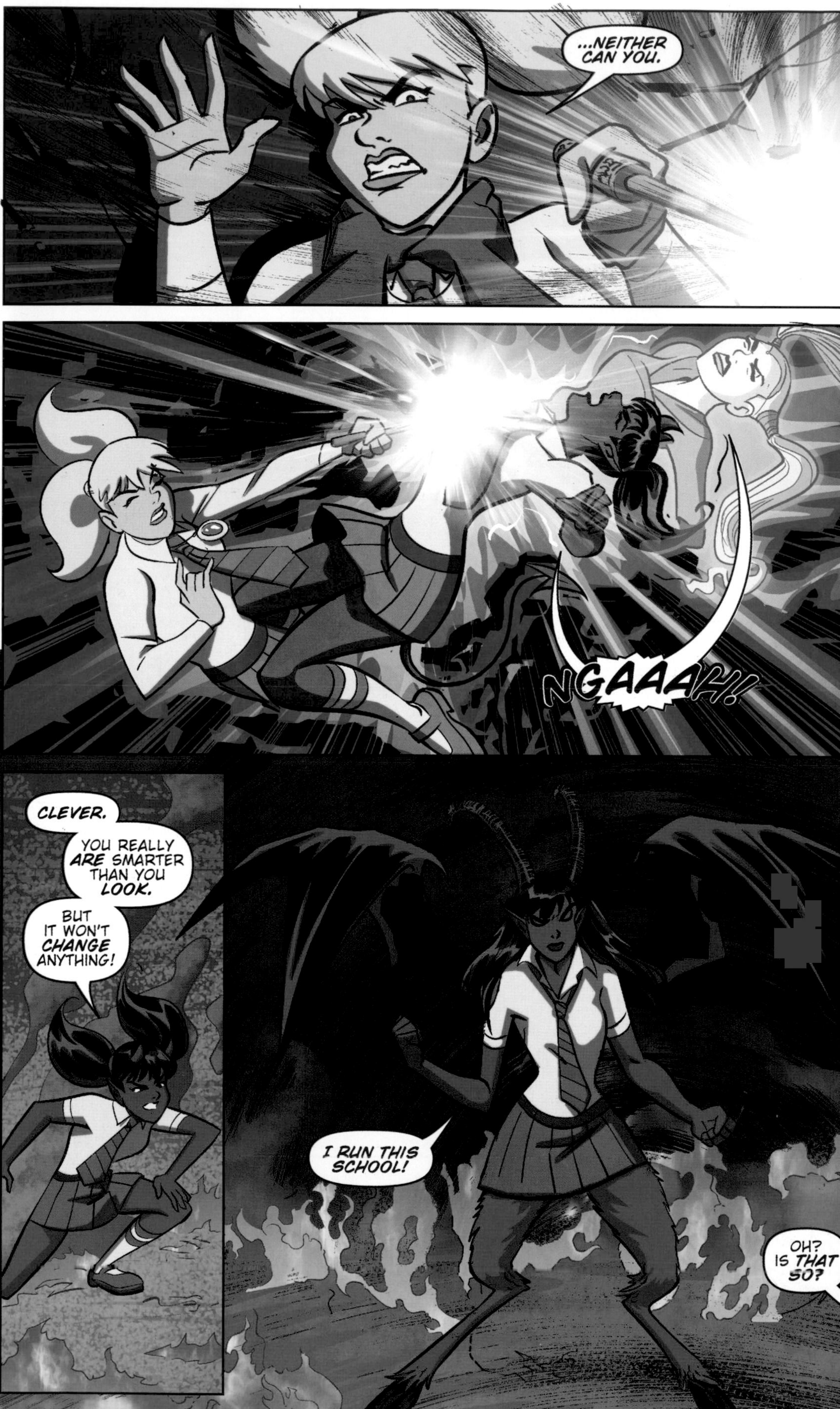
...NEITHER CAN YOU.
NGAAAH!
CLEVER.
YOU REALLY ARE SMARTER THAN YOU LOOK.
BUT IT WON'T CHANGE ANYTHING!
I RUN THIS SCHOOL!
OH? IS THAT SO?

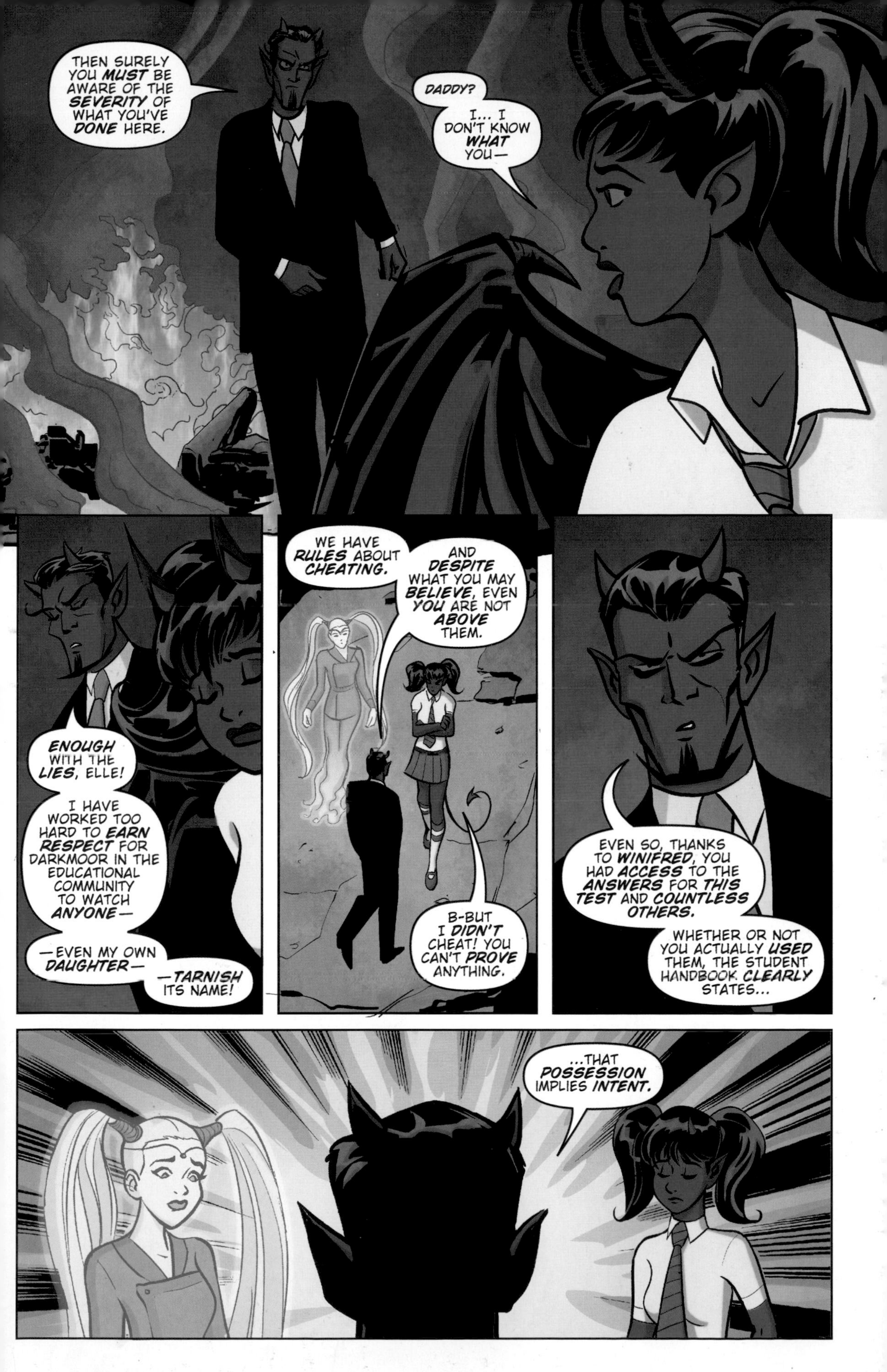
THEN SURELY YOU MUST BE AWARE OF THE SEVERITY OF WHAT YOU'VE DONE HERE.
DADDY?
I... I DON'T KNOW WHAT YOU—
ENOUGH WITH THE LIES, ELLE!
I HAVE WORKED TOO HARD TO EARN RESPECT FOR DARKMOOR IN THE EDUCATIONAL COMMUNITY TO WATCH ANYONE—
—EVEN MY OWN DAUGHTER—
—TARNISH ITS NAME!
WE HAVE RULES ABOUT CHEATING.
AND DESPITE WHAT YOU MAY BELIEVE, EVEN YOU ARE NOT ABOVE THEM.
B-BUT I DIDN'T CHEAT! YOU CAN'T PROVE ANYTHING.
EVEN SO, THANKS TO WINIFRED, YOU HAD ACCESS TO THE ANSWERS FOR THIS TEST AND COUNTLESS OTHERS.
WHETHER OR NOT YOU ACTUALLY USED THEM, THE STUDENT HANDBOOK CLEARLY STATES...
...THAT POSSESSION IMPLIES INTENT.

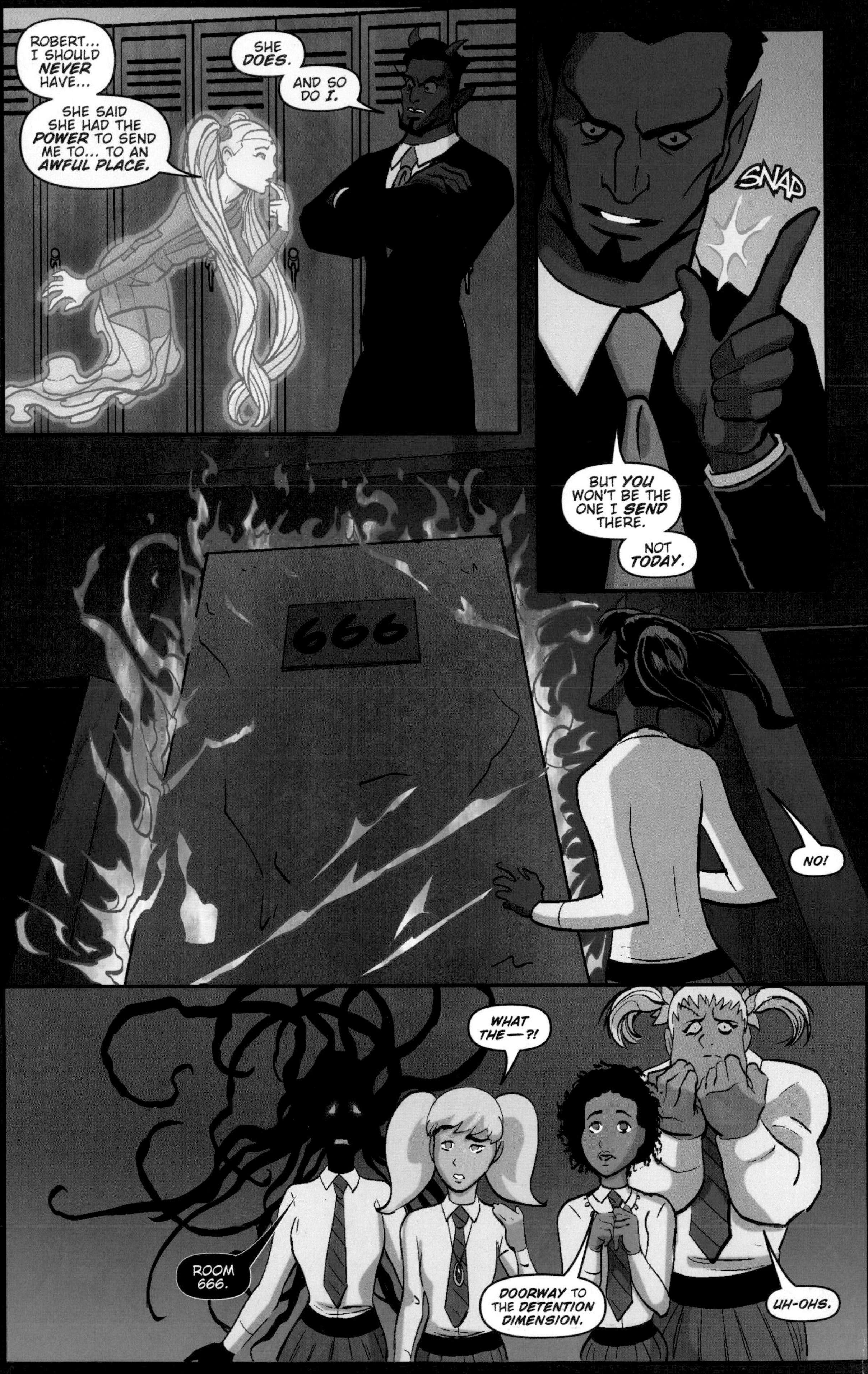
ROBERT... I SHOULD NEVER HAVE...
SHE SAID SHE HAD THE POWER TO SEND ME TO... TO AN AWFUL PLACE.
SHE DOES.
AND SO DO I.
SNAP
BUT YOU WON'T BE THE ONE I SEND THERE.
NOT TODAY.
666
NO!
WHAT THE—?!
ROOM 666.
DOORWAY TO THE DETENTION DIMENSION.
UH-OHS.

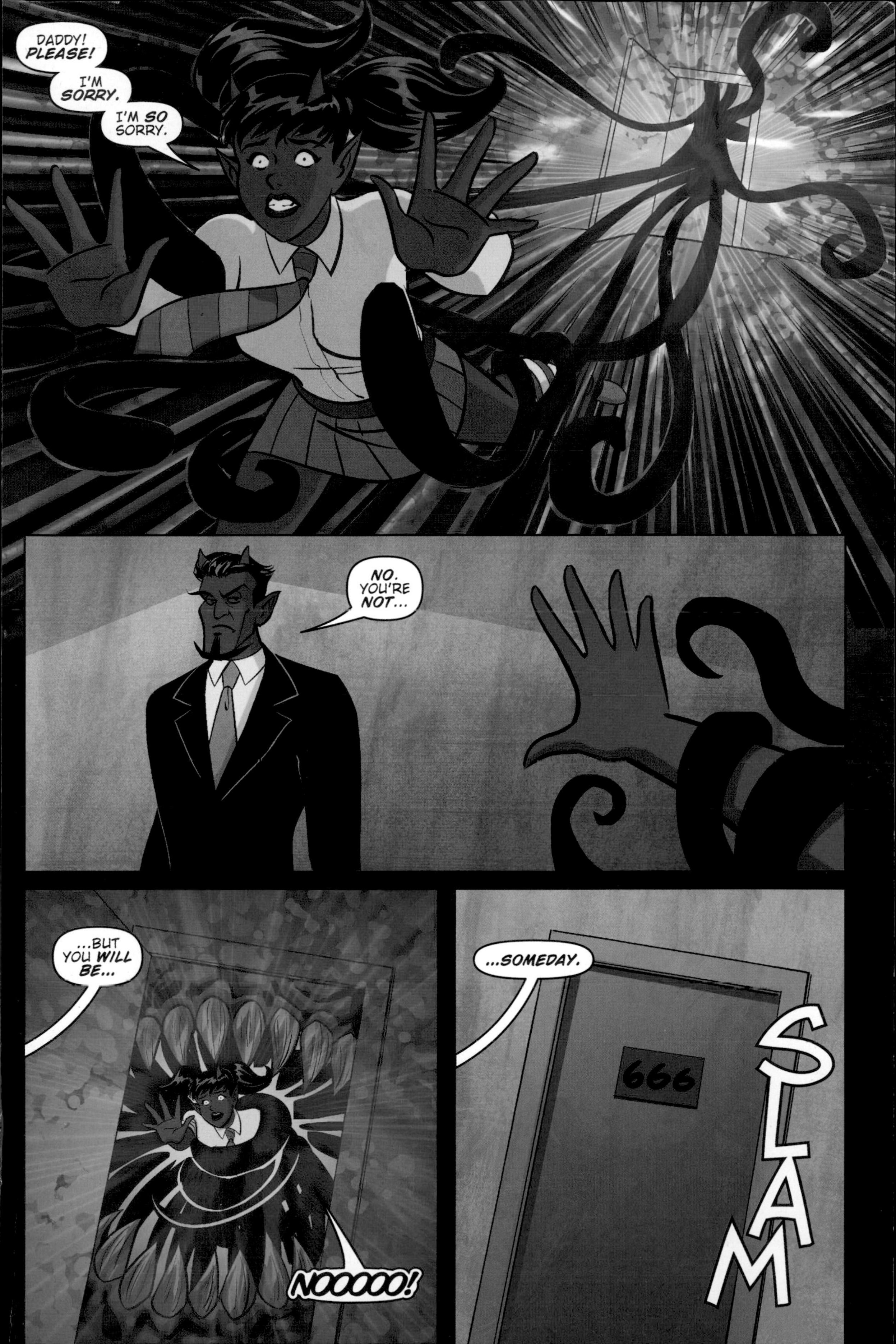
DADDY! PLEASE!
I'M SORRY.
I'M SO SORRY.
NO. YOU'RE NOT...
...BUT YOU WILL BE...
NOOOOO!
...SOMEDAY.
666
SLAM

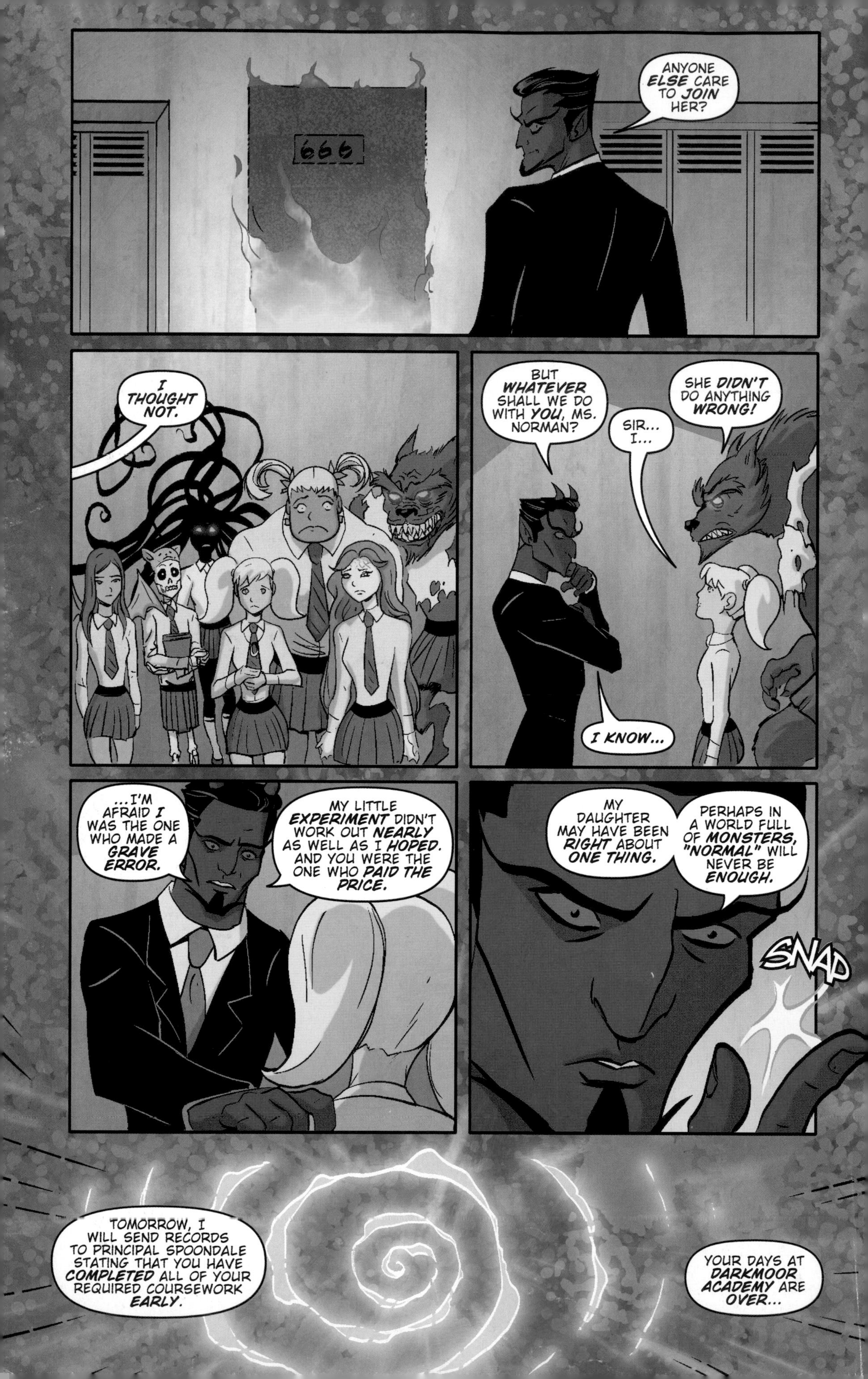
ANYONE ELSE CARE TO JOIN HER?
I THOUGHT NOT.
BUT WHATEVER SHALL WE DO WITH YOU, MS. NORMAN?
SIR... I...
SHE DIDN'T DO ANYTHING WRONG!
I KNOW...
...I'M AFRAID I WAS THE ONE WHO MADE A GRAVE ERROR.
MY LITTLE EXPERIMENT DIDN'T WORK OUT NEARLY AS WELL AS I HOPED. AND YOU WERE THE ONE WHO PAID THE PRICE.
MY DAUGHTER MAY HAVE BEEN RIGHT ABOUT ONE THING.
PERHAPS IN A WORLD FULL OF MONSTERS, "NORMAL" WILL NEVER BE ENOUGH.
SNAP
TOMORROW, I WILL SEND RECORDS TO PRINCIPAL SPOONDALE STATING THAT YOU HAVE COMPLETED ALL OF YOUR REQUIRED COURSEWORK EARLY.
YOUR DAYS AT DARKMOOR ACADEMY ARE OVER...

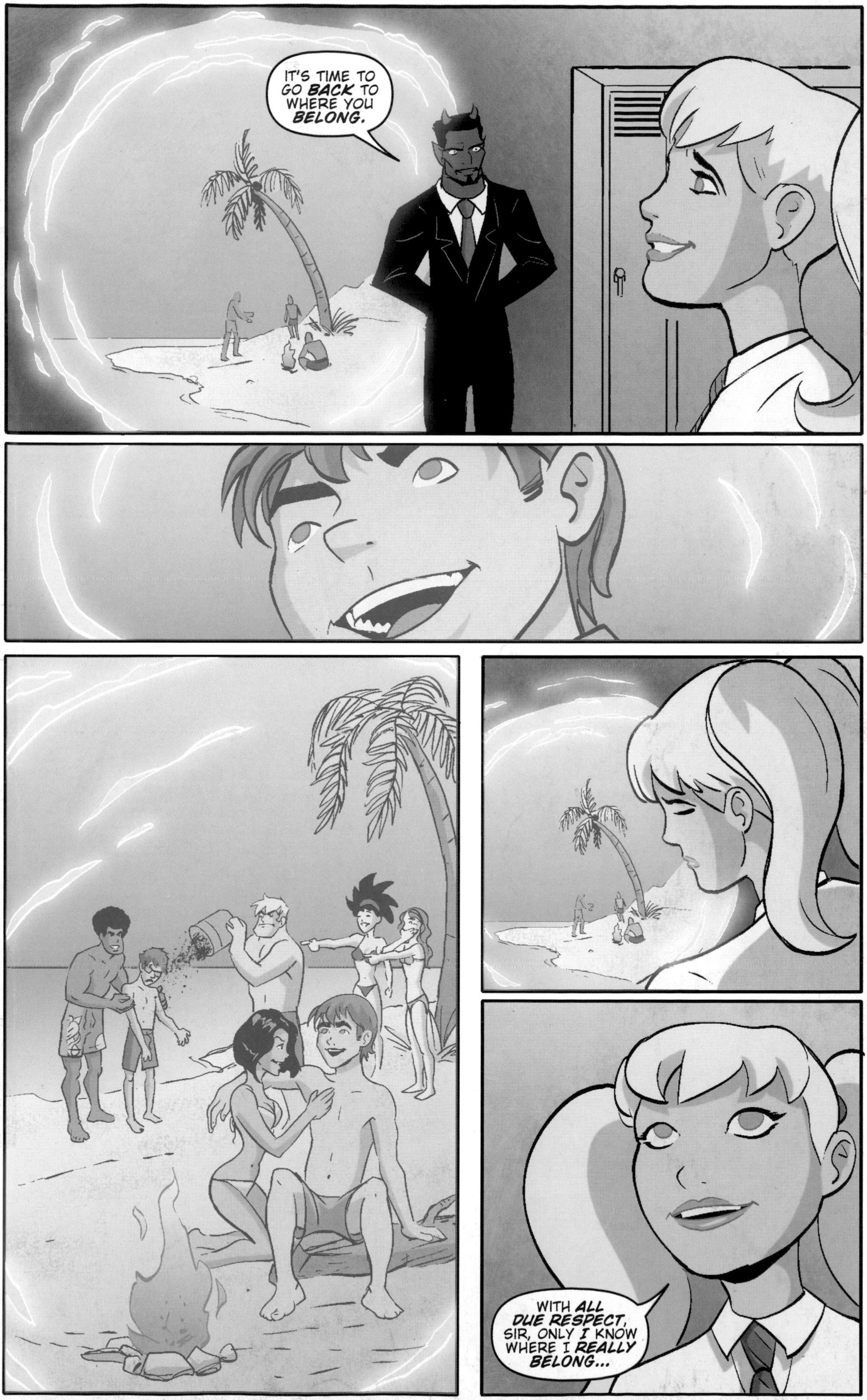
IT'S TIME TO GO BACK TO WHERE YOU BELONG.
WITH ALL DUE RESPECT, SIR, ONLY I KNOW WHERE I REALLY BELONG...

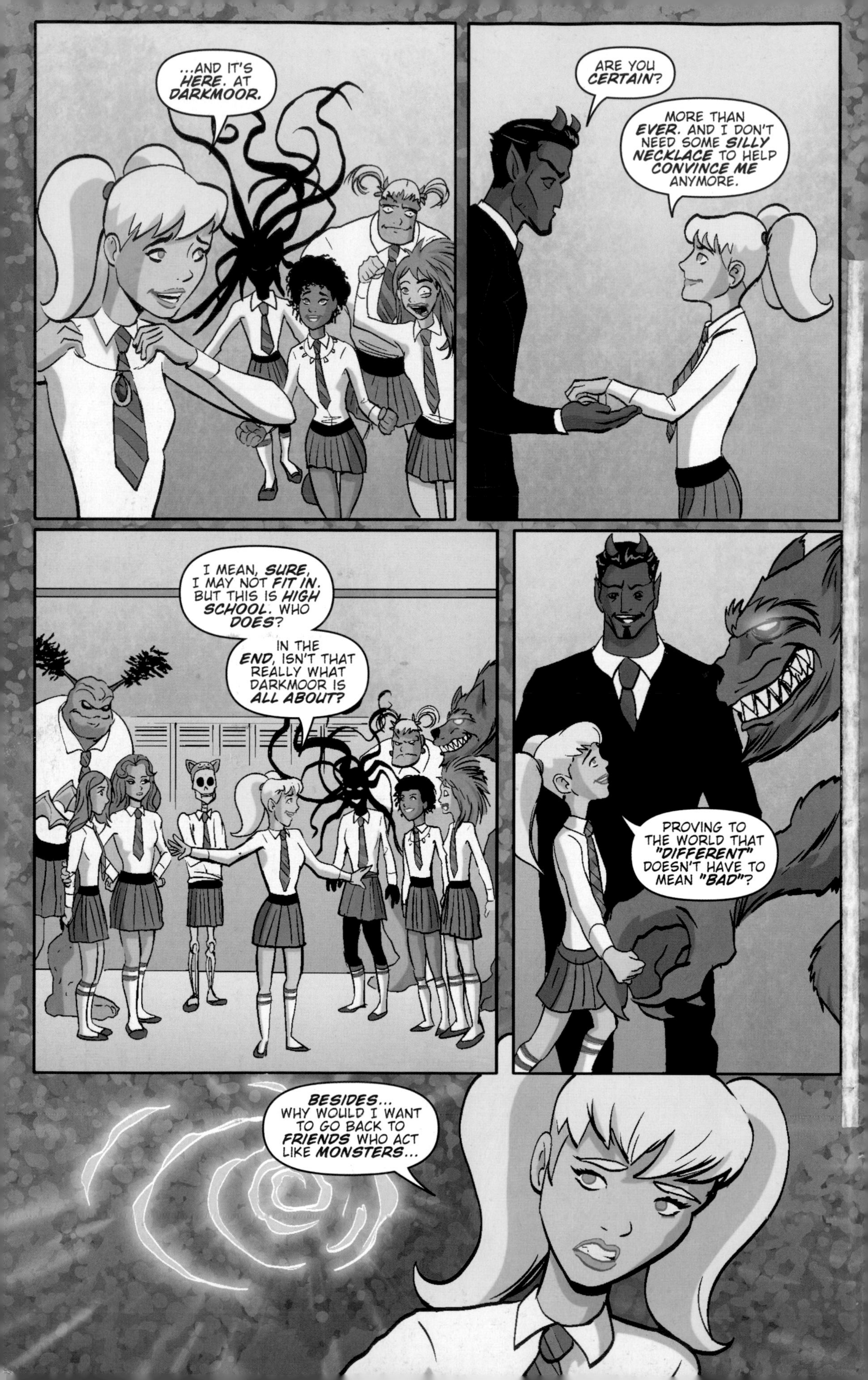
...AND IT'S HERE. AT DARKMOOR.
ARE YOU CERTAIN?
MORE THAN EVER. AND I DON'T NEED SOME SILLY NECKLACE TO HELP CONVINCE ME ANYMORE.
I MEAN, SURE, I MAY NOT FIT IN. BUT THIS IS HIGH SCHOOL. WHO DOES?
IN THE END, ISN'T THAT REALLY WHAT DARKMOOR IS ALL ABOUT?
PROVING TO THE WORLD THAT "DIFFERENT" DOESN'T HAVE TO MEAN "BAD"?
BESIDES... WHY WOULD I WANT TO GO BACK TO FRIENDS WHO ACT LIKE MONSTERS...

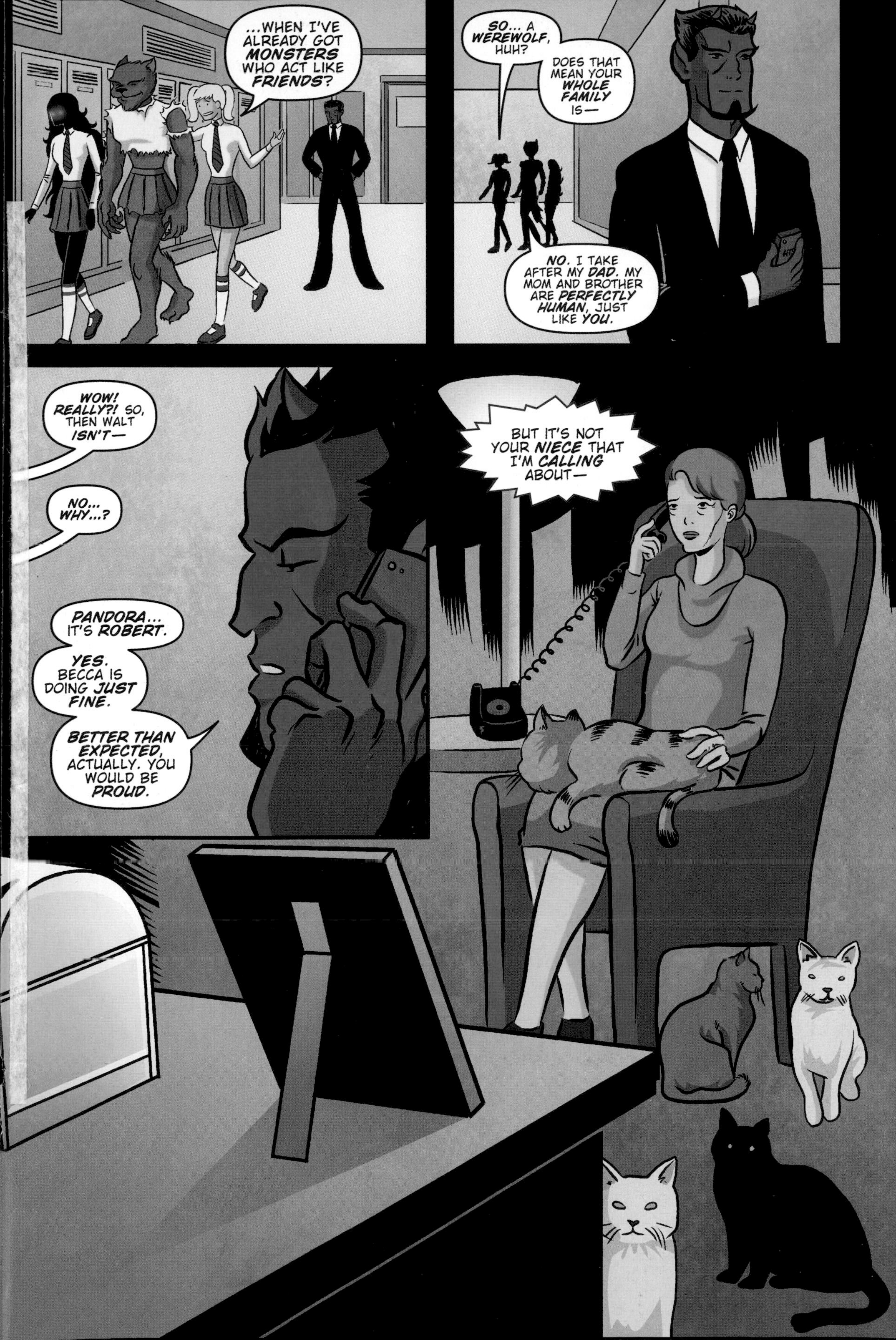
...WHEN I'VE ALREADY GOT MONSTERS WHO ACT LIKE FRIENDS?
SO... A WEREWOLF, HUH?
DOES THAT MEAN YOUR WHOLE FAMILY IS—
NO. I TAKE AFTER MY DAD. MY MOM AND BROTHER ARE PERFECTLY HUMAN, JUST LIKE YOU.
WOW! REALLY?! SO, THEN WALT ISN'T—
NO... WHY...?
PANDORA... IT'S ROBERT.
YES. BECCA IS DOING JUST FINE.
BETTER THAN EXPECTED, ACTUALLY. YOU WOULD BE PROUD.
BUT IT'S NOT YOUR NIECE THAT I'M CALLING ABOUT—

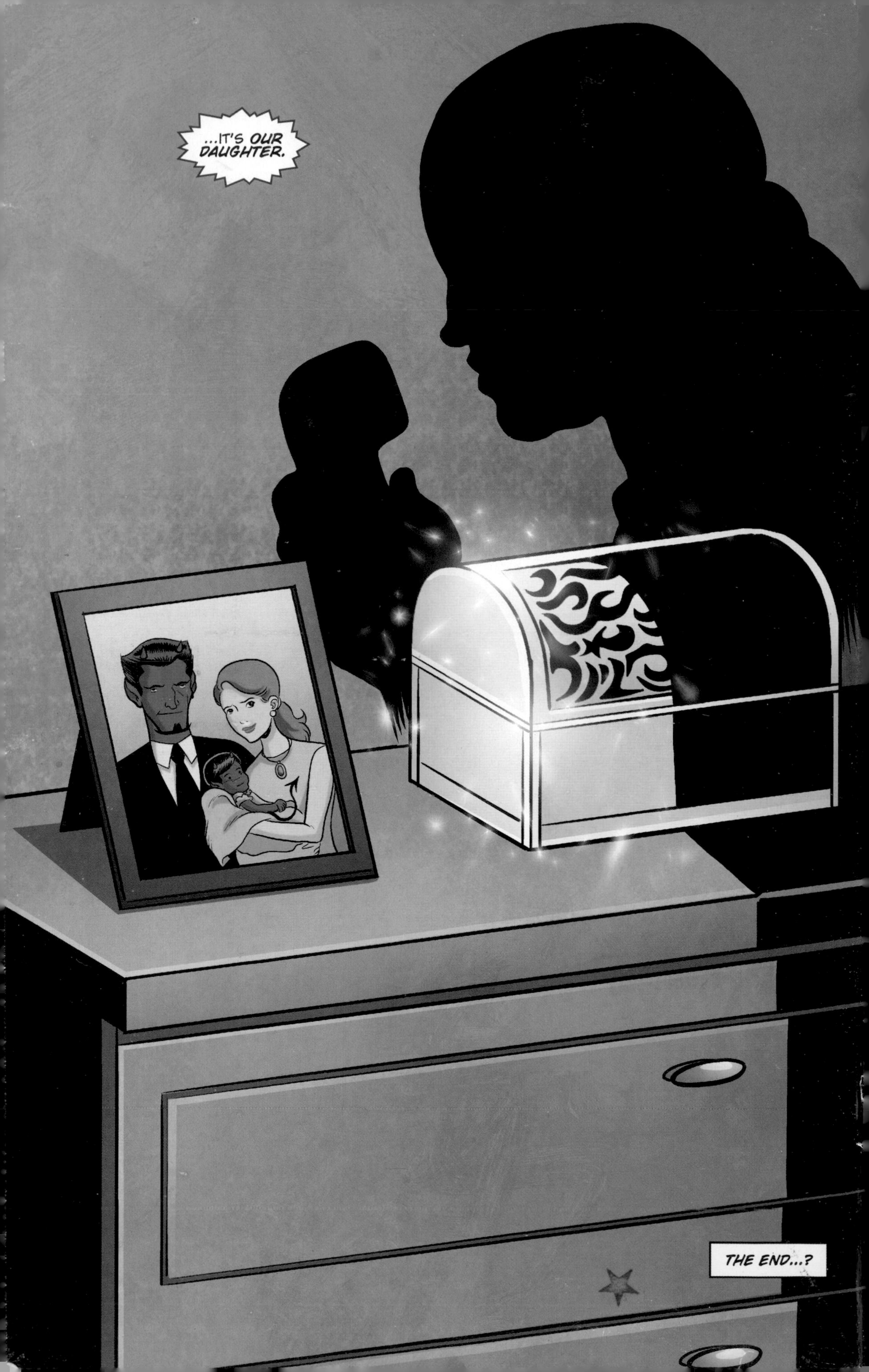
...IT'S OUR DAUGHTER.
THE END...?